TITOISM

PATTERN FOR
INTERNATIONAL COMMUNISM

TITOISM

PATTERN FOR

INTERNATIONAL COMMUNISM

Charles P. McVicker

ST MARTIN'S PRESS · NEW YORK

MACMILLAN & CO LTD · LONDON

PRINTED IN THE UNITED STATES OF AMERICA
BY THE COLONIAL PRESS INC., CLINTON, MASS.

Note: The following abbreviations are used instead of full titles in the footnotes:

NYL—New Yugoslav Law, a quarterly journal published in English in Belgrade by the Union of Jurists' Associations of Yugoslavia.

QAS—Questions Actuelles du Socialisme, a bimonthly journal published in Paris by L'Agence Yougoslave d'Information.

RIA—Review of International Affairs, a twice-monthly magazine published in English in Belgrade by the Federation of Yugoslav Journalists.

SL—Službeni List, the Official Gazette of the People's Republic of Yugoslavia, published in Serbo-Croat in Belgrade.

YR—Yugoslav Review, a monthly magazine published in English in New York by the Yugoslav Information Center.

Preface

This book is the result of research done in connection with a dissertation accepted by the Politics Department of Princeton University in candidacy for the degree of Doctor of Philosophy. It was the intention of the dissertation, just as it is the intention of this book, to present an analysis of the development of the political and social system of Yugoslavia since the time the Titoists were forced to seek their own salvation. I like to think that my personal biases insofar as this research has been concerned are essentially those of the average scholar who knows no doubts as to the superiority of constitutional democracy as a political system. The examination of the ends and means of Titoism has only served to reinforce this conviction.

I gratefully acknowledge my debt to friends and acquaintances both here and abroad who have assisted me with the research and with the final publication. My sincere gratitude is due to Professor William B. Ebenstein of Princeton, whose boundless interest with respect to new and challenging political ideas has been a constant inspiration to me. I am also indebted to Professors Cyril Black and Marver Bernstein of Princeton for their helpful criticism and assistance. I am likewise beholden to Mr. Ian MacKenzie of St Martin's Press who has given vast amounts of his time and talent in assisting me to prepare this book for publication. Several students at Yale University have lent valuable assistance with respect to the preparation of the final manuscript; among these John Bradley deserves my special thanks. And, finally, my thanks to Olga Alexievna Holenkoff for her initial interest.

Yale University
May 1957

CONTENTS

CHAPTER I

Introduction

The political and social system which Tito is presently attempting to work out in his country is important not only to approximately seventeen million Yugoslavs forced to serve as its guinea pigs but to the remainder of the world as well. This is so, precisely because the system represents the first positive and sustained effort of a practicing Marxist to temper the crass fundamentals of Marx, Lenin, and Stalin with mercy, with some consideration for the living individual. Tito no longer demands that his countrymen sacrifice themselves entirely for the supposedly better life they are to bring to future generations. Forced to seek wider popular support for his rule, he has learned to cater to some of the basic needs and aspirations of the individual Yugoslav. In so doing, he has abandoned the Soviet Marxist school in which Marx's own astonishing ignorance of the individual had effortlessly fused with the age-old Russian tradition of stressing the community above the individual. The Titoists have discovered that in socialist Yugoslavia the individual is the most important component of the community. Here they are attempting a synthesis of the vital fundamental of Western liberal thought with the fallacious Marxist axiom that all human relationships spring entirely from materialist causes.

The Titoist system is yet in its infant stages. There is still an inexcusable discrepancy between the liberality of its essential theory and the totalitarianism of its actual practice. Nevertheless, it is the author's opinion that Tito and his advisers have tacitly admitted the overriding inconsistency of Marxism: the belief that man lives by bread alone. Even to the limited extent to which it has now progressed, the

Titoists' political and social system is a much more humane variety of Marxism than the world has yet known. Its advantages have impressed some of the post-Stalinist leaders of the Soviet Union. In a tactical effort to dominate the Yugoslav "heresy" they brought themselves to accept it as a valid socialist system in May 1955. The obvious ease with which the Polish and Hungarian Communists took to the Titoist pattern in October and November 1956 could leave no further doubt as to its potency within the Communist world.

Even if Tito and his system were to be destroyed tomorrow, the path he has pioneered will not readily disappear. Tito's experiment has been an attempt to force a futuristic system upon a backward society. As such his successes and failures contain profitable illustrations for forward-looking men of all political inclinations. To be forewarned is to be forearmed.

In June 1948, Stalin had set out to exterminate Tito by ordering Yugoslavia's expulsion from the Cominform. That Tito was able to survive the blow and eventually to wrest some of the initiative in international communism from the Kremlin is probably due to the peculiarities of the international situation. Yugoslavia's strategic location between East and West, combined with Tito's unchallenged control over both his Party and his army, made it impossible for either the East or the West to unseat him without endangering world peace. The Western powers, materially interested in Tito's survival, were not in a position to insist that he relinquish his determination to lead his people toward socialization as the first step in the ultimate transition to communism. Ironically, the Western powers willingly paid some of the financial costs of his socialist experiments. Since 1948, Tito has had an abnormally free hand in directing his country's internal development as he alone saw fit. The result has been the political theory and practice now commonly referred to as Titoism.

The visit of Khrushchev and Bulganin to Belgrade in May 1955 symbolized the end of an important era of Titoist development—the end of the period of "splendid isolation" and the beginning of a new and more standard phase wherein a small nation attempts to obtain the maximum benefit from playing two powerful rivals off against each other. The rearming of the West after the outbreak of the Korean War combined with Tito's growing strength at home made it less and less likely that he could be replaced by a Soviet puppet. Gradually gifts and credits from the West to pay the costs of his domestic experiments were somewhat more grudgingly given. Finally, Stalin's death and the sudden peace tactic of the new Soviet leadership threatened to disturb the East-West tension which had maintained the power vacuum in which the Titoists enjoyed such a free hand in forcing their theories upon the unwilling majority of the people they ruled.

The Yugoslav Marxists could never hope to have the sincere understanding or affection of either the Soviet or the Western bloc. The former would never completely forget that the Yugoslav Communists were the only members of the flock who successfully denied Moscow's omnipotence. The latter looks upon all forms of Marxism as the work of the Antichrist. Therefore, the conciliatory offers from post-Stalinist Moscow permitted the Titoists a graceful as well as a practical means of adding their weight to the maintenance of the bipolar world *status quo*. This would give them more time to improve domestic conditions, to broaden the popular foundations of their rule, and thereby to reduce their dependence upon continued East-West tension. Better still, they might now strengthen their position by convincing the Soviet Union or China of the advantages of their more liberal approach to Marxism and in so doing obtain the outside support needed to counteract the dangers of undue pressure from the West.

There is no doubt that the home of the October Revolution has always retained at least a strong hold on the ideological loyalty of the Titoists, as confirmed Marxists. Then, too, they are Slavs with the customary Pan-Slavic proclivities. On the other hand, they are aware that the success they have had in formulating their own more liberal brand of socialism represents one of the most serious theoretical and practical challenges the Soviet system has yet had to face. Apparently the Titoists consider themselves sufficiently strong to be able to maintain their independence in the face of any Soviet move to unseat them or to force them to return to satellite status. Undoubtedly they count upon the Western powers to make certain that they are neither crushed nor enslaved in the process of *rapprochement* with the Soviet Union. The approval by the Bolshevik party at its Twentieth Congress (February 1956) of the Titoist pattern of development as a permissible variant of socialism strengthened the Titoists' confidence in their ability to maintain their separate identity. Prior to the nationalist, anti-Communist uprisings in Hungary in November 1956, the Titoist leaders must have felt a glowing pride in the obvious influence their system was exerting abroad. However, the counter-revolution in Hungary must have given the Yugoslav leaders many sleepless nights. They most certainly do not intend their system to produce or even to encourage liberalization to the extent where it will be able to threaten the Communists' monolithic control.

The shift in Titoist Yugoslavia's international policy will have its effect upon internal policy. In the less normal period in which the importance of Titoist Yugoslavia's survival to one great group of powers made the Westerners exercise the utmost care to respect her every sensibility, the development of internal policy had little connection with foreign policy. Tito had but to threaten to leap off the precipice to frighten the Western powers into granting the major portion of his requests for uncompromising assistance. But in the more standard small-power tactic of playing one suitor off against the other, Tito's threats to throw himself into the arms of one or the other of the rivals might entail a fate

worse than death. To re-enter the Soviet bloc with the status
of satellite would require him to give up his profitable independence. To submit totally to the Western powers would
mean the end of his socialist revolution. Henceforth Yugoslav
internal policy will have to be somewhat more closely attuned to foreign policy, especially since the Titoist economy
seems chronically insolvent and requires constant assistance
from abroad. Nevertheless, the Titoists certainly feel that
the roots of their new system are firmly enough established
to assure its international independence.

In the earliest years of their isolation from both the East
and the West the Titoists staunchly insisted that their system
represented nothing new theoretically. Rather, they insisted
that it was merely restoring what had been lost through
Stalin's deviation from the true Marxist path. With the passing of time, however, they were forced to abandon this
position. The extreme vagueness of Marxist orthodoxy, combined with the growing need to define and to defend their
position in order to maintain their self-respect amongst other
Communists and to keep from being absorbed by the non-
Communist world, required them to provide a suitable theoretical rationale. Unfortunately, although the Yugoslav Marxists now claim that Titoism is a new and distinct ideology,
they have yet to produce a truly comprehensive explanation
and analysis of it. Most of their theoretical explanations and
rationalizations have been delivered piecemeal when and as
required. To date, the best single official statement of the
theory of Titoism is the address entitled "Socialist Democracy in Yugoslav Practice"[1] delivered in Oslo in September
1954 by Edvard Kardel, who is second only to Tito in the
Yugoslav hierarchy and generally considered the Yugoslav
Marxists' leading theoretical spokesman.

"Social democracy" is the name given by the Titoists to the
political and social system which they intend to serve in
Yugoslavia during the period of transition from capitalism to
socialism. They carefully point out that their social democ-

[1] The text of this address appears in *Borba* (Belgrade), Jan. 1, 1955, p. 1.

racy is not a panacea for all the ailments of every transitional society. Rather, it is the method most closely attuned to Yugoslav requirements. While the Titoists admit that highly industrialized countries may achieve socialism by the evolutionary process, they also insist that revolution is the only possible means by which an underdeveloped, relatively poor country such as Yugoslavia can achieve socialism. Poorer countries have little or no chance today to establish for themselves a viable capitalist system. Without the basic owner-worker relationships of capitalism, it is not possible for a society to proceed to socialism by orthodox Marxist revolutionary or evolutionary methods. Only by a Leninist-type revolution can the poor country skip the capitalist stage and begin its socialization.

In effect the Titoists claim that their social democracy is Marxism-Leninism as applied to their own environment. Implicitly they insist that its essential theoretical tenets are the most practical means by which all revolutionary Marxist-Leninist systems can avoid succumbing to Stalinism, a reprehensible revision of Marx leading only to state capitalism. The Titoists suggest that methods of social democracy may differ from country to country, but the essential principles underlying the system must always prevail. Here it is important to stress that the Titoists, especially when compared with the Stalinists, have not relapsed into dogma to camouflage their system's weaknesses and shortcomings. Like Lenin when he first came to power in Russia, the Titoists are actually political pragmatists. In spite of its high-sounding claims to a purely "scientific" rationale, Marxism is only a very abstract and far from proved political and social theory. Except for Leninist and Stalinist practice, the Titoists have little or no practical precedent to serve as their guide. The power and natural wealth of Russia permitted the Bolsheviks to lapse into dogma. Yugoslavia's much smaller potential does not permit Tito the same escape. He therefore must attempt to find the "proper" Marxist path to socialism by the process of trial and error. Since their expulsion from the Cominform, the Titoists, except at the very highest levels of Marxist "scientific" generalization, have constantly been sniffing the wind for new inspiration.

By 1957, Titoist social democracy has divested itself of all but the most elementary of Marxist-Leninist dogma. The Titoists have found it convenient to look upon Marx, Engels, and Lenin as no more than ordinary mortals who could not possibly have anticipated every ramification of dialectical materialism at each given stage of its development. Therefore, wherever practical, the Titoists use Marx, Engels, and Lenin as the source of their theoretical and practical policies, but wherever Marxist-Leninist principles are impractical they are openly and unhesitatingly bypassed. Or, where it is not practical to link specific policy with Marxist or Leninist dictum but at the same time it is unsafe to ignore the inconsistency completely, policy is justified on the grounds that it is contributing to the eventual creation of a Marxist-Leninist society. In such instances the implied reasoning is that the concept of the ends justifying the means is a Marxist-Leninist principle.

As a political system, Titoist social democracy is pragmatism influenced by the Marxist-Leninist heredity of its draftsmen who are making a conscious effort to warp that doctrine to fit what they see as its Yugoslav environment. The essentially pragmatic character of social democracy is perhaps one reason why the Titoists have so far failed to provide a clear and succinct theoretical definition of their system in Marxist dialectical terms. Practicality as its primary justification can hardly be expected to serve as an ideology. Nevertheless, the Titoists tacitly present their system as a proper Marxist dialectical synthesis growing out of the struggle between a thesis and its antithesis. The thesis is one of an underdeveloped, predominantly agrarian, nationalistic society. This thesis is contradicted by the antithesis of the totally centralized, autocratic, and bureaucratic system required during the earliest period of the revolution to create the proper material relationships for socialization.

Call the results what one may—Yugoslav social democracy, Marxism-Leninism-Stalinism-Titoism, or just plain Titoism —the ideology developed by the Titoists since 1948 has come to represent a new theory of socialism and of democracy. And that theory has in turn demanded a new assortment of political and administrative policies designed to implement it.

The emphasis of this study is more upon the development of Titoist ideology and domestic policy than upon detailed analysis of how each policy actually works in practice. It would be well to keep in mind, however, that Marxists generally hold that there is an indissoluble connection between theory and practice. In fact, one outstanding expert on Marxism maintains that this union of theory and practice is one of the most important elements in Marxist thought. [2] While the interested foreigner is permitted much greater freedom of action in Yugoslavia today than heretofore, it is still not possible for him to make a complete or unhampered investigation of the actual practice of even the basic programs in ideology and policy.

This study traces the evolution of the ideology and domestic policy of Titoism as a political development. As Communists the Titoists are bound to respect the Marxist axiom that all causes of political phenomena are economic. However, despite the fact that economics are at all times minutely concerned with politics and vice versa, in the development of Titoism politics have been more important than economics. As an English expert in East European affairs has aptly pointed out, politics as such are not a triviality to be dismissed with contempt; in a Communist state they are every aspect of private and public life, present every moment of the day and night. [3] In dealing with Titoist economic policies, the emphasis must be upon their

[2] R. N. Carew Hunt, *The Theory and Practice of Communism* (New and rev. ed.; New York: 1952), p. 33.

[3] Hugh Seton-Watson, *The East European Revolution* (2d ed.; London: 1952), p. viii.

political substance and background rather than upon their purely economic content.

It is important to note that the dates of issue of the laws, decrees, and regulations used to trace the development of Titoism very often have little to do with the exact time at which a certain policy was instigated. The Titoists' system is mainly one of trial and error, conceived by a group of men whose previous experience left them ill-prepared to rule by law. In their search for a viable system which would permit them to achieve socialism and to maintain their independence as well, it was not only their political philosophy which had to submit to painful appraisal and readjustment. Their own personal attitudes and aptitudes had to be adjusted as well. In the earliest years of reform the new policies were carried out primarily by the will of the comparatively small group of men who exercise total power in Yugoslavia. Many of these new policies were (and still are) tried out before appropriate legislation or regulations were issued. Thus, many of the laws, decrees, and regulations were often little more than an attempt to codify the *status quo*. Frequently, laws and regulations were found, after issuance, to be impractical and therefore were not implemented but still were not removed from the statute books. Furthermore, laws and regulations were often partially adjusted without making the required amendments to published statutes.

Titoist social democracy has attempted to substitute a reformed judicial system for the arbitrary police surveillance methods practiced during the Stalinist period of Yugoslav development. As the Yugoslav leaders gained confidence and experience, they sought to draft effective legislation and regulations which would permit more and more responsibility for administrative supervision to be shifted from the centralized bureaucracy to the law courts. Thus, many of the purely subjective and personal aspects of Titoist administrative practice now appear to have been withdrawn behind the system's legal façade. But the Titoist system remains one of minority rule. The leaders make the laws and in the final analysis make certain that they are executed. It is, of course, to their advantage to draft laws and regulations which anticipate as many as possible of the problems which arise through implementation. Nevertheless, even though the details of legislation and regulations offer the best means available through which to trace the development of Titoism, these legal details are frequently deceptive in that they all too often have more theoretical than practical meaning. Hence, it is more important for the observer to grasp the spirit of the laws and regulations than their purely legal expression.

It must also be stressed here that the observer who wants as complete and unbiased a picture as possible of the development of Titoism would do well to avoid the habit of comparing contemporary Yugoslavia with the United States or with the more advanced European countries. Tito's Yugoslavia should only be compared with Yugoslavia as it existed prior to World War II.

PART I

EXPULSION FROM THE COMINFORM—
THE GOLDEN OPPORTUNITY

CHAPTER II

From Liberation from the Enemy to Liberation from Dogma, 1945-49

FROM LIBERATION THROUGH CONVERSION

Tito's Partisan army captured Belgrade on October 20, 1944. The Red Army divisions which had given the Partisans support in the operation immediately withdrew into Hungary in pursuit of the Nazis. Tito lost no time proving to the Kremlin that this mark of confidence had been well placed. He had fought and won his war and he saw little reason to procrastinate in what he considered to be his destiny: to bring Soviet communism to Yugoslavia with as little delay as possible. There was no one in Yugoslavia of sufficient stature or organizational strength to challenge his authority. At first he made slight concessions to wartime agreements involving Anglo-American demands; he included members of prewar Yugoslav parties in his government and parliament. But one by one he cast aside these pretenses as unworthy annoyances. Even before a Constituent Assembly had been elected, he ordered a sweeping agrarian reform. He then provided himself with a parliament and a government entirely of his own choosing. A law establishing agricultural collectivization was followed by a law nationalizing business and industry. By the beginning of 1947, the Yugoslav economy was sufficiently centralized to permit him to announce the first Five Year Plan for industrialization. Truly Tito was the Horatio Alger of communism. He had risen within a remarkably short time from comparative anonymity to the role of the Kremlin's most outstanding pupil.

Early in the spring of 1944, the British Foreign Office began a search for a suitable person to make peace between the Royal Yugoslav government in London and Tito. The choice fell upon Dr. Ivan Subašić, a Croatian Peasant party leader who had the support of important Yugoslav-American groups. On June 1, in the face of relentless pressure from the British Government, young King Peter reluctantly named Dr. Subašić his Prime Minister and sent him off to confer with Tito. The two men met on the Adriatic island of Vis on June 16 and reached an uneasy agreement which prepared the way for the final Tito-Subašić accord signed in Belgrade in December 1944. They agreed to establish a regency to act in the King's behalf until the future of the monarchy had been determined by popular plebiscite; the political assembly formed by the Partisans during the war was to be enlarged to include members of the last prewar parliament who had not been compromised by collaboration with the enemy; acts of the new legislative body were to be ratified by a duly elected Constituent Assembly.

The Tito-Subašić agreement was approved by the Big Three at Yalta on February 11, 1945. On March 6, a provisional government was formed in Belgrade which gave Tito a new legal respectability. It was headed by Tito and composed of his Communist cohorts and five representatives of the country's democratic elements: Dr. Subašić and Dr. Juraj Šutej for the Croat Peasant party; Dr. Milan Grol for the Serbian Democratic party; Sava Kosanović for the Democratic Independent party; and Dr. Drago Marušić for the Slovene Liberals. The last two men* had been political supporters of Tito during the war, and are still connected in one way or another with his government.

The three "bourgeois" members soon found they had no standing within the new government and no influence in the affairs of state. They were looked upon as little more than unsolicited encumbrances resulting from the Kremlin's lingering desire to placate the Western allies. But whatever

* Mr. Kosanović died in November, 1956.

inconvenience their presence may have caused Tito, it was to be of short duration. In August, Dr. Grol resigned in protest from the government, and the following October a short official announcement informed the public that Dr. Subašić and Dr. Šutej had likewise quit their official posts. Thus, the last conceivable check on Tito's internal control was removed. As a result of careful wartime organization, both the Yugoslav Communist party and the Yugoslav Army willingly if not joyously looked to Tito as their unchallenged leader. The state administrative apparatus had been reorganized so that it was safely within his control. The police and other internal security forces had also been radically reorganized to meet his specifications; the Communist-baiting gendarmerie of the old regime had been liquidated and replaced by Tito's own Militia and State Security Administration. The reins of power were firmly and entirely in Tito's hands.

Without waiting for the election of a Constituent Assembly, Tito set out to alter the basic characteristics of the Yugoslav state. On August 23, 1945, the temporary parliament passed his Law on Agrarian Reform[1] which liquidated all big estates and limited peasant holdings of arable land to from twenty to thirty-five hectares.[2] It also liquidated without compensation estates belonging to banks, enterprises, land corporations, and other corporate bodies. Churches and monasteries considered to be historically significant were allowed to keep arbitrarily fixed amounts of their land.

Elections for the Constituent Assembly were held on November 11, 1945. The results were a foregone conclusion. The polling places were patrolled by vigorous Communist supporters, both civilian and military. Only hand-picked candidates for the "People's Front" were allowed to stand for election. About forty representatives of the prewar

---

[1] For the text of this law and of subsequent amendments, see *SL* Nos. 64 (1945), 24 (1946), and 105 (1948). A résumé of texts is given in *NYL*, I:2-3 (1950), pp. 47-49.

[2] One hectare equals 2.471 acres.

political parties agreed to play a part in this farce and were duly elected. However, these forty "opposition" members were soon forced to conform or to resign; most of those who refused to do either were eventually imprisoned as enemies of the people.

Provided now with a "legal" government and parliament completely free from serious opposition, Tito set out in earnest to remake Yugoslavia in the Soviet Union's image. At its first meeting on November 29, 1945, the new Constituent Assembly declared the dissolution of the Karageorgević monarchy and the establishment of the Federal People's Republic of Yugoslavia. On January 31, 1946, a new constitution was formally adopted. It was the first and, for a while, the closest imitation of the Soviet Union's Stalinist Constitution of 1936. It established a similar political system, assumed the same economic doctrine, and embraced similar ideological objectives.

In the summer of 1946, the Law on Co-operatives[3] was enacted. It provided for collective planning and farming in agricultural areas, established state tractor stations and other centers for heavy farm equipment, and designated the co-operatives as the primary channels of distribution of industrial products in the village. The Soviet *kolkhoz*-type collective farm was to serve as the Yugoslav model. In the application of their agricultural collectivization law, however, the Titoists did not follow standard Stalinist tactics. For many reasons these were not practical in Yugoslavia. Right up to the time of their expulsion from the Cominform in June 1948, the Titoists exercised relative caution in their attempts to collectivize their peasants.

A comprehensive Nationalization Law was passed in December 1946.[4] In many respects it was merely a formalization of the *status quo*. Nationalization had already been

---

[3] This law will be discussed at greater length in Chapter VI.
[4] For text of this law, see *SL* No. 98 (1946). For résumé of text as amended by the law of April 29, 1948, see *NYL, op. cit.*, pp. 55-57.

carried out either without legal sanction or under the cover
of a law passed in November 1944[5] which provided for the
confiscation of property belonging to the enemy, to collaborators, or to absentee owners. More detailed legislation
was required to deal with foreign-owned property which
had been nationalized. It had been a fairly simple matter
for the Titoists to nationalize whatever they chose; many a
loyal Yugoslav was convicted of collaboration merely because the state desired to seize his assets. According to
Borba, the official newspaper of the Yugoslav Communist
party, immediately after the close of the war in 1945, 55
per cent of private industry had been nationalized as a
result of the confiscation of property belonging to absentees
or collaborators, 27 per cent had been taken by the state
under forced sequestration, and only 18 per cent was still in
private hands.[6] Theoretically, private ownership was permitted in the few branches of commerce and industry not
listed in the 1946 nationalization law, but the existence of
private businesses depended entirely upon the tolerance
of the government. This gap was soon filled in, however,
by a supplementary nationalization law,[7] passed in April
1948, which ordered the nationalization of all private enterprises above the level of artisans and small shopkeepers.
The general definition of property subject to nationalization
was now to be all private holdings "having general importance in the economy, health, and cultural activities of the
country." By the end of 1948, all industry regardless of its
nature and size had become state property.

The 1946 nationalization law cleared the way for the Five
Year Plan for Industrial Development proclaimed on April
28, 1947.[8] The plan had been politically, organizationally,

[5] For text of this law, see *SL* No. 2 (1945). For résumé of text as
amended in July 1946, see *NYL, op. cit.,* pp. 46-47.
[6] Quoted in Josef Korbel, *Tito's Communism* (Denver: 1951), p. 193.
[7] For text of this law, see *SL* No. 35 (1948).
[8] For text of the Five Year Plan law, see *SL* No. 36 (1947). For a
résumé of text, see *NYL, op. cit.,* pp. 59-67.

and technically prepared for many months before it was published. In the spring of 1946, Boris Kidrić, then the Prime Minister of the constituent Republic of Slovenia, left for Moscow with a staff of economic and technical experts to study the Soviet Union's economic system. In June, he was appointed Minister of Industry in the federal government and chairman of the Federal Economic Council. At the same time, the Law on the State Economic Plan was enacted and new institutions formed and entrusted with the task of drawing up a single working plan for the entire economy. After approximately one year's work, the completed Five Year Plan was announced. This was another "first" for Yugoslavia. Her plan preceded similar plans in the other satellite countries by nearly two years.

Thus, by mid-1947, Tito appeared to be firmly established and might justifiably have expected high praise from the Kremlin. None of the other fledglings had done half so well. Most of them were still feeling their way behind the masks of governments which included many representatives of non-Communist parties. No other state in the Russian sphere had so readily and consistently challenged the governments and public opinion of the West. Surely Tito was *secundus inter pares* in the Communist world. At the foundation meeting of the Cominform in Warsaw in September 1947, the top Yugoslav delegates (Kardelj and Djilas) made little effort to disguise their feelings of superiority. Unlike the representatives from the other people's democracies, neither Kardelj nor Djilas showed themselves unduly grateful to the Red Army for its help in liberating the Balkans. In fact, Kardelj in his report to the gathering did not once mention that his country owed its liberation to the Soviet Union. To the casual observer at the time, the leading position of the Yugoslav Communists within the Soviet bloc would seem to have been confirmed by the selection of Belgrade as the site of the headquarters of the newly established Cominform.

CRIME AND PUNISHMENT

Natural as it may have been to assume that Moscow must be vastly proud of Tito and his accomplishments, the truth was that neither the Russian nor the Yugoslav leaders were overly pleased with the others' behavior. The Yugoslav delegates had gone to the Warsaw conference with a profound irritation over certain aspects of Soviet policy toward Yugoslavia. The arrogance and subversive activities of Red Army officers and other "experts" sent by the Kremlin to train Yugoslav Communists for military, government, and Party service were a source of constant irritation to the Partisans flushed with their wartime successes and intensely loyal to Tito. Furthermore, Stalin was not at all pleased with Tito's intention to industrialize Yugoslavia. The Kremlin preferred to keep Yugoslavia as a supplier of raw materials, as an adjunct to Soviet industries. The Russians used every conceivable economic ruse to frustrate the development of Tito's Five Year Plan. It is now evident that Stalin created the Cominform at least partially in anticipation of future difficulties with Tito. Belgrade was probably chosen as its headquarters with the thought in mind that the international Communist luminaries there assembled would be able to help quiet the membership of the Yugoslav party, should it become necessary to get rid of Tito.

The evidence is incomplete, but a reasonable surmise of the events which led to the expulsion of the Yugoslavs from the Cominform on June 28, 1948, can be constructed from the parts of the Moscow-Belgrade correspondence published by the Yugoslavs immediately following the break[9] and from the "Titoist" trials held in other satellite countries in the years which immediately followed. Yugoslav spokesmen have from time to time chosen to shed some further light

[9] The complete texts of this published correspondence are contained in *The Soviet-Yugoslav Dispute* (London: Royal Institute of International Affairs, 1948).

on those specific aspects of the disagreement which they
have felt called upon to dispute publicly.

The cause of the break has been variously traced to ideological, political, economic, nationalistic, and even psychological conflict. However, there is little doubt that the break
resulted primarily from the fact that Stalin considered Tito's
strength and independence dangerous as well as personally
offensive. Other explanations seem secondary. The entire
struggle was between the aging Communist god and a
younger minor deity whose star the senior authority had in-
advertently allowed to rise too high. But Tito, in the role of
minor deity, would unquestionably have tried the patience
of even a far more longsuffering superior.

The seeds of the conflict were sown almost from the beginning. To undermine Tito's firm grasp at home, Moscow
sent large groups of political, economic, military, and cultural "experts" to Belgrade to help him set up housekeeping.
The largest such mission was a group of Red Army officers
sent to instruct the Yugoslav Army. Scattered throughout
the country with different Yugoslav Army units, these
Russians were in an ideal position to carry out incidental
assignments as Soviet intelligence agents. Ironically, they
received their wages from the Yugoslav Government, and
at rates considerably higher than those paid to Yugoslav
officers of like rank. According to Aleš Bebler, a Titoist
official, the troubles with the Soviet Union started because
these Russian officers began to behave as if they were the
masters of the Yugoslav Army. The conflict started, he con-
fided in November 1948, when local quarrels were brought
to Tito who in most instances took the side of the Yugoslav officers.[10]

Tito was somewhat concerned about his army when he
returned from a visit to Moscow in June 1946.[11] He was
disturbed by the Kremlin's attempts to keep him from

[10] Korbel, *op. cit.*, p. 301.

[11] See Hamilton Fish Armstrong, *Tito and Goliath* (London: 1951), p. 62,
and Adam B. Ulam, *Titoism and the Cominform* (Harvard, 1952), p. 82.

building his own armaments industry, and by the Soviet offer to supply the Yugoslav Army with modern equipment. He did not want his army to lose its character as a guerrilla force and to become in effect an auxiliary of the Red Army, a part of a vaste horde of anonymous foot soldiers, as the Soviet high command seemed to have in mind. Questions of the nature, role, and command of the new Yugoslav Army undoubtedly became a prime reason for Tito's growing restlessness and for his eventual decision to stand up to the Kremlin.

While Russian military experts were attempting to subvert Yugoslav Army officers, other experts were trying to recruit supporters and spies within the government and the Party. As in the case of the army, these efforts met with surprisingly little success. In almost every instance the agents of the Soviet Union found themselves frustrated by the solidarity of the Yugoslav Communist party and by the reluctance of the Yugoslavs to subordinate the interests of their own country to those of the U.S.S.R. without a valid ideological excuse.

The constant effort made by the Soviet Union to sabotage Yugoslav plans for rapid industrialization was another major source of irritation to the Titoists. It is true that the Yugoslav Five Year Plan was in many respects irrational and ridiculously ambitious. Nevertheless, the Titoists often seemed more concerned with their purely Marxist conviction that industrialization was the necessary prerequisite for socialization than with the practical aspects of their plan's implementation. The Russians, on the other hand, were more devoted to practicality. The only Yugoslav Five Year Plan acceptable to them was one which would serve merely as a chapter in the Soviet Plan. Their practicality did not even make allowances for Yugoslav national pride or for the fact that Yugoslavia's closer geographical and historical association with the West had given the ordinary Yugoslav a much greater respect for individualism than had ever existed among the Russians. Stalin's desire was simply that Yugoslavia expend her energies upon increasing her capacity to furnish raw materials to Soviet and satellite industries. That Yugoslavia had thereby changed her status from a country exploited by capitalists to one exploited by socialists should, in Stalin's opinion, be sufficient practical and ideological compensation to the Yugoslav Communists.

The techniques employed by the Soviet Union in its trade dealings with Yugoslavia were all carefully calculated to hamper the latter's industrialization. Loans and other specific agreements made to implement industrialization plans were honored more in the breach than in the execution. Raw materials from Yugoslavia were shipped in huge quantities to Soviet and satellite industries, and, in return, instead of the promised machinery for Yugoslav industry, repayments arrived in the form of finished products. Tales of how the Soviet Union employs the trade factor to keep her satellites under control are legion and need no further elaboration here. It is sufficient to say that all of the methods were brought fully to bear in the Kremlin's determination to inhibit the development of Yugoslavia's Five Year Plan.

The failure of Soviet spokesmen to give proper credit to the Partisans for their part in liberating Yugoslavia was an important secondary cause of the friction which came to characterize relations between Belgrade and Moscow. The Yugoslav Communists were justifiably proud of their unique record among local Communist movements to liberate the Balkans, and there was little doubt that the Russians found the Partisans' successes somewhat galling, especially since the Yugoslavs were not inclined to be overly modest concerning their wartime achievements. The patronizing attitude of the Red Army officers stationed in Yugoslavia served as a daily source of irritation to all Partisans. Russian pettiness in this respect worked to Tito's advantage when the showdown came in June 1948. He found little difficulty in manipulating Partisan resentment into a rallying point in his campaign to withstand the Kremlin's efforts to destroy him and his regime.

Shortly after the formation of the Cominform in September 1947, the Yugoslav-Soviet conflict entered its decisive phase. By January 1948 the Kremlin was consulting certain members of the Central Committees of Communist parties in other satellite countries about the need to curb Tito's excessive independence.[12] The opening gun of the final assault was undoubtedly the item on the last page of *Pravda* of January 28, 1948, announcing that the Soviet Government did not support the idea of federation in the Balkans.

The eventual creation of a federation of Yugoslavia, Bulgaria, and Albania had been the principal motif of Tito's foreign policy since 1944.[13] High-ranking representatives of the Yugoslav and Bulgarian Communist parties had consulted frequently on the matter. They had even traveled jointly to Moscow seeking from the Kremlin itself a working arrangement for federation. Exploratory talks between the Yugoslavs and Bulgarians continued right up to the end of 1947. The treaty of alliance between Yugoslavia and Bulgaria, signed at Bled in August 1947, was generally considered the first formal step toward federation. The January 28th article in *Pravda* obviously meant to signify the complete and irretrievable collapse of the entire venture. It is interesting to note, however, that any serious *rapprochement* between Belgrade and Moscow will unquestionably once again bring the matter of federation into the realm of possibility. Tito still cherishes the idea of a South Slav and Albanian union.

Late in February 1948, Vice-Premier Kardelj led a singularly unsuccessful mission to Moscow to persuade the Soviet authorities to speed up trade with Yugoslavia and to start the flow of Soviet industrial equipment needed for the progress of the Yugoslav Five Year Plan. If after the dismal failure of this mission, there was still some doubt in Belgrade as to Stalin's intention to bring about a showdown,

---

[12] See Armstrong, *op. cit.*, p. 66.
[13] For a concise historical analysis of Tito's efforts to bring about a Yugoslav-Bulgarian-Albanian federation, see Ulam, *op. cit.*, pp. 86-95.

the Yugoslav leaders did not have long to wait for clarifica-
tion. On March 18, Tito received formal notification of the
Soviet decision to withdraw all military advisers and in-
structors on the ground that they were "surrounded by
hostility," and the next day the Soviet Chargé d'Affaires
in Belgrade informed Tito that all civilian missions would
also be withdrawn because of the "lack of hospitality and
lack of confidence" shown toward them.[14] On March 20,
Tito wrote an abject letter to Molotov asking for an explanation.[15] Thus began the now famous correspondence
between Tito and Stalin and Molotov which reached its
climax in the June 28th Cominform resolution expelling
the Yugoslav party from the organization and, in effect,
calling for Tito's demise.

Because Stalin hardly dared openly accuse Tito of the
grievous sin of having imitated him much too closely for
the former's own satisfaction, the crux of the accusations
made against the Yugoslav regime were trumped-up
charges of deviation from Marxism-Leninism. Many of
these are outstanding simply because of their *do as I say
and not as I do* quality. For example, the Yugoslav party
was accused of having developed into a system of military
despotism controlled from above by a small power clique
which had replaced the Marxist-Leninist principle of democratic centralism with commands from above to be obeyed
without question or discussion. Furthermore, the Kremlin
felt called upon to observe that criticism and auto-criticism
in the Yugoslav party had thereby been made impossible.
The tendency of Titoists to claim that their revolution could
proceed in accordance with special Yugoslav conditions was
hailed as the most ridiculous sort of opportunism.

One criticism of faulty ideology followed another, many
of them actually chastising Tito for being a closer observer
of Marxist-Leninist-Stalinist history than of Marxist-Lenin-

[14] *The Soviet-Yugoslav Dispute, op. cit.,* pp. 9 and 10, respectively.
[15] See *ibid.,* pp. 9-11.

ist-Stalinist doctrine. The striking feature of the Soviet letters is that they contain no evidence that the Soviet leaders felt that the Yugoslav authorities had taken action particularly hostile to the Soviet Union or friendly to the "Western imperialists"; it seemed always to be a matter of petty discourtesies. The point which Stalin appeared to be trying to impress upon Tito and his associates was that, since they were unwilling to have their government, Party, and army come under the direct supervision of the Kremlin, they had forfeited their right to exist.

OUT OF THE NIGHT

Immediately following his expulsion from the Cominform, Tito took steps to consolidate his position at home. He published pertinent portions of the fatal correspondence with Moscow. At first he behaved in public as though a gross misunderstanding existed between the Yugoslavs and the Cominform and that as soon as the Kremlin became aware of the unfairness of the Cominform's action all would be well again. Then, as the Soviets themselves attempted to ruin him by propaganda barrages, economic blockade, and troop movements on his frontiers, Tito began to appeal to the West which answered with lifesaving aid and assistance. As the Titoists emerged from the wilderness they began to grasp the full meaning of their new position. They saw that their continued existence was important to the Western powers and that they could therefore deal with the West without endangering their drive for socialization. It now began to dawn upon them that their expulsion from the Communist camp was actually a heaven-sent liberation from bondage. Gradually but firmly they seized the initiative, and by the end of 1949 they were preparing to take the first steps in the creation of a new political and social system which by 1956 threatened to ruin the existing Communist world.

Tito may have winced on June 28, 1948, but his control did not falter for an instant. Except for two men[16] in the higher echelons and one or two lesser leaders in the provinces, all of whom were soon isolated, the Party remained unswervingly loyal. There was never any question of the loyalty of the army and the police, even though three or four top-ranking army officers had been successfully recruited by Soviet agents (with one exception these were either arrested or killed while trying to flee the country; the one who did escape soon faded into oblivion). Thus, the day after the Cominform's decree of excommunication, the Titoist regime, somewhat shaken perhaps but not at all cowed, was open for business as usual. Almost immediately the clientele from the East became conspicuous by its absence, while new customers from the West hung back until the situation became sufficiently clarified.

In the very beginning the Kremlin chose to hide behind the Cominform façade in directing its campaign against Tito. It was only a matter of one or two days before Tito's former satellite colleagues began to blast him with their propaganda machines. One of the very first shots was fired by Albania, Tito's own satellite. In his turn, Tito felt constrained to restrict his defense to protesting against the behavior of the satellites. In spite of the fact that it was obvious to the world that the Kremlin was responsible for the Cominform's action against him, Tito preferred to take the public stand that if Stalin only knew what injustice was being heaped upon Yugoslavia he would come to the rescue.

About a month before the break, the convocation of the first Yugoslav Communist Party Congress to be held since 1928 had been announced. Unquestionably, the decision

---

[16] Andrija Hebrang and Sreten Žujović, whose preference for Moscow was apparently known in advance to the Titoists, for the former was transferred from a major to a minor post in the federal administration in January 1948, and both were arrested in May 1948. It is possible that the demotion of Hebrang added to Stalin's irritation with Tito and his regime and hastened the final break.

to hold this meeting had received its inspiration from the pointed references made to the illegal secrecy of the Yugoslav party in the fatal correspondence from Moscow. It was true that the Yugoslav Communist party had remained a highly secret organization, carrying out all of its programs through the People's Front. Between liberation and expulsion from the Cominform not one Party decision had been published officially, and until the opening of the Party Congress on July 21, 1948, it would not have been possible to name with any degree of certainty the officials of the Party or even its Secretary-General.

At the Congress, Tito delivered a lengthy speech[17] in which he traced the history of the development of the CPY, and in the final section discussed some of the accusations which had been made by the Kremlin against his leadership. He avoided any direct attack upon either the Soviet Union or the satellites. He ended the speech by emphasizing that: ". . . we shall work with all our might to mend the relations between our Party and the CPSU(B). We hope that the comrades, leaders of the CPSU(B), will give us an opportunity to show them here, on the spot, everything that is inaccurate in the [Cominform] Resolution. We consider that it is possible to arrive at the truth only in such a case and in such a way." [18] This statement was greeted with a standing ovation accompanied by cries of "Stalin-Tito!"

For some time thereafter the Titoists, while continuously refuting each new propaganda blast from the East, preferred to act as though disputes among Communist parties did not necessarily involve governments. At the Danube Conference in Belgrade, in August 1948, the Yugoslav delegation lent its full support to Soviet moves which resulted in placing large sections of the Danube firmly under Soviet control. At the United Nations' General Assembly

[17] *Political Report of the Central Committee of the Communist Party of Yugoslavia: Report Delivered at the V Congress of the CPY* (Belgrade: 1948).

[18] *Ibid.*, p. 136.

meeting in Paris later that year, Kardelj—though pointedly
ignored by Soviet bloc delegates—still attacked "Western
imperialists" as vehemently as ever. Maintaining constantly
that they were faithful Marxists, the Titoists continued to
support the Soviet bloc in attacking the North Atlantic Pact
and in branding the Marshall Plan as a threat to the independence of European countries. Nor was there a letup in
the attacks on the West by the Yugoslav press. In January
1949, the Yugoslav Government applied for admission to
the newly formed Council for Mutual Economic Assistance,
the Russians' Marshall Plan for the East. The application
was nothing more than a gesture of ideological preference
since the Yugoslavs must have known it would be turned
down with the greatest of indignation.

Undaunted, the Titoists continued to maintain as common
a foreign policy front as possible with the Russian bloc.
Louis Adamic, a Yugoslav-American who was in Yugoslavia during the first half of 1949 gathering material for
a book, has quoted from a series of interviews and informal
meetings with Tito, Kardelj, Pijade, Ranković, Djilas, Kidrić,
and other top Titoists, which poignantly illustrate the vain
hopes which still existed within the leadership that something would somehow happen to permit a reconciliation
with Moscow.[19] Adamic writes that, in Tito and Kardelj the
hope-against-hope sentiment lasted until the end of June.[20]
This was the month that Vyshinsky, at the Council of Foreign Ministers' meeting in Paris, announced that the Soviet
Union no longer supported Tito's claims to Austrian Carin-
thia. Vyshinsky's announcement jarred Tito and his colleagues loose from all conscious and subconscious hopes
for reconciliation. The Titoists retaliated by closing their
frontier against the Greek Communist rebels. Yugoslavia
had discontinued its active role in the Greek War soon after
the break with the Cominform, but until now it had taken

[19] See Louis Adamic, *The Eagle and the Roots* (New York: 1952), pp. 76,
130, and 250.
[20] *Ibid.*, p. 260.

no formal step to assist the Western powers to bring the Greek crisis to a close.

At the end of 1948, Moscow had announced the curtailment of the Soviet Union's trade with Yugoslavia by seven-eighths. This was but a formal confirmation of the situation as it already existed. The Soviet Union and the satellites had since the time of the break been slowing down their exports to Yugoslavia under one pretext or another. By the beginning of 1949, all trade between Yugoslavia and the Soviet bloc had reached a virtual standstill. At least 50 per cent of Yugoslavia's export trade had hitherto been carried out with the Soviet bloc. Almost all of the investment arrangements connected with the Yugoslav Five Year Plan had been made exclusively with the Soviet Union, Czechoslovakia, Hungary, and Poland. Therefore, the Cominform blockade seemed to spell disaster.

In December 1948, Tito informed his parliament of the Cominform's campaign to strangle Yugoslavia economically. He took the opportunity to warn the Kremlin that if the blockade were not lifted he would be compelled to seek markets for Yugoslav raw materials exclusively in the West. These remarks signaled the beginning of a new period of trade with the West. And as the denunciations and vituperation from the East increased and the economic blockade tightened, the Yugoslav leaders were released from their set strategy of trying to remain as "neutral" as possible between East and West. Their fears of being contaminated by too close relations with the capitalist West began to diminish in the face of the knowledge that even though the Western powers might not like Yugoslavia's communism they could not afford to see Tito replaced by a Soviet puppet. As their confidence in the possibility of doing business with the West without making important political or ideological concessions grew, the Titoists began to intensify their search for lifesaving trade and loans from the West. Thus, when, on September 29, 1949, the Soviet Union announced the abrogation of its twenty-year Treaty of Friendship, Assistance, and Co-operation with Yugoslavia (the satellites immediately followed suit), Yugoslavia's trade and credit relations with the Western powers were already firmly established.

Until the beginning of 1949, most of the vehemence and contempt in the Cominform's verbal attacks had stressed the "bourgeois" nationalist and ideological deviationist tactics of Tito and his clique. Tito gave wide and continuing publicity to all such attacks, for here the Cominform was unwittingly presenting him to his own people not as the puppet they had heretofore considered him but as the flesh and blood defender of Yugoslavia's national independence. Even those Yugoslavs who sincerely hated Tito began to hope for his survival, if only because his demise would undoubtedly mean a return to the blind fury of a master whom they already knew and hated more. Early in 1949 the Kremlin and satellite propaganda machines lowered the content of their attacks to the realm of vulgar name-calling. The Titoists now became "Fascists," "Western imperialists," "enemies of socialism," etc. These epithets also served Tito in good stead at home; they helped him to dislodge pro-Soviet sympathies in all but the most stubborn of Party affiliates.

In his need to justify increasing trade relations with the West to the Party rank and file, Tito was forced to lift the veil of secrecy which had always covered inter-Communist trade relations. Until the break with the Cominform, the Yugoslav public had heard nothing but grateful praise for all that the Soviet Union was supposedly contributing to the reconstruction and development of the country. A series of articles begun in *Borba* in March 1949 revealed for the first time the shabby facts and figures of the ruthless exploitation actually carried out by the Soviets in their economic dealings with Yugoslavia. One of the principal results of this shift in tactics, which brought the Soviet Union into the forefront of the Yugoslav attack, was that Stalin himself, until now exempt from all criticism, was held up for public admonishment. His portraits and busts were soon removed from all public places.

In the summer of 1949, political pressure from the Soviet bloc was intensified. The Russians woke to the fact that their propaganda offensives were two-edged swords. They failed to bring Tito to his knees; in fact, they were actually serving to increase his popularity at home. Units of the Red Army were deployed on Yugoslavia's eastern frontier. An exchange of formal diplomatic notes began between the Kremlin and the satellite capitals and Belgrade which contained abusive language the like of which had seldom if ever before been heard in diplomatic parlance. Tito answered all threats with defiance. He let it be known that he would defend Yugoslavia if it were attacked. In November, the Cominform met for the first time since it had expelled Yugoslavia. It resolved that the Yugoslav Communist party was in the hands of murderers and spies and called upon all loyal Communists everywhere to work for a return of Yugoslavia to the true path of salvation. But this exhortation fell upon deaf ears in Yugoslavia. Tito replied that he would not be intimidated. By now he and his supporters had discovered the initiative, and Stalinism was branded as bureaucratic and un-Marxian. Stalinism, the Titoists now pointed out, was the highest and most reprehensible form of capitalism in which the state became the "private" owner of the means of production and exploited the workers in an even more systematic fashion than that practiced in bourgeois capitalist countries.

In their propaganda war against their former allies, the Titoists had taken some time before they began to develop an ideological rationalization of their own. Socialism had been so exclusively identified in their minds with Soviet theory and practice that they had great difficulty in reappraising their new situation. In the beginning they argued purely from a Marxist-Leninist-Stalinist vantage point. Eventually, however, with the Soviet Union itself being brought more and more into the range of their attack, and as

Tito's top "public opinion" and theoretical experts dealt with the day-to-day verbal battle, a new and distinctive ideological basis upon which to rest the Titoist case began to emerge.

The ideological justification for Titoism was presented in its first palatable form in the autumn of 1949. In the beginning it was primarily a denial of the Marxist-Leninist validity of Stalinist foreign policy. It contained little of an explicitly new and positive nature. It was not until November 1949 that the first public criticism was heard which ignored the effects of Stalinist "revision" of Marxism-Leninism as reflected in Soviet foreign policy and concentrated upon explaining the internal lines of authority in the Soviet Union itself. This critical comment showed how the Bolshevik revolution had been strangled to death by the hold which the Soviet Politburo had gradually taken on all facets of Russian life.[21] This criticism was the forerunner of the positive Titoist policy of decentralization. From the desire to decentralize grew the policies of workers' self-management and citizens' self-government which are today the central pillars of Titoism. And from the desire to give these two policies real meaning in practice has sprung the important discovery by the Titoist improvisers of the fact that the individual and not the community is the vital factor of all social life.

[21] See Makso Bače, "On Criticism and Auto-Criticism in the U.S.S.R.," *Komunist*, No. 6 (Belgrade: Nov. 1949), and reprinted in *QAS*, No. 5-6 (July-Sept. 1951), pp. 61-143.

CHAPTER III

Nineteen Fifty—
The Year of Change

Soviet moves to intimidate Yugoslavia were intensified during 1950. Red Army divisions maneuvered menacingly on her eastern frontiers, trenches were dug, mobilization measures were rumored or announced in Hungary, Rumania, and Bulgaria. The number of border incidents grew. Trade with the Eastern countries ceased entirely and economic pressure was tightened by depriving Yugoslavia of the international use of the Danube. Yugoslav diplomats and minorities in the Cominform countries were now subjected to treatment even worse than that customarily reserved for non-Communists, and Yugoslav ambassadors were eventually withdrawn—the mission in Albania was closed down entirely. Making a virtue out of necessity, the Titoists began to defend the rights of small nations, and as a result established friendly relations with Greece and Austria, and eventually with Italy.

Respect for the Western powers grew proportionately during 1950. Necessity forced the Titoists to seek increasing aid and assistance from countries still regarded as capitalist in every uncomplimentary Marxist sense of the word. The Western powers, aware that it was important to their own well-being to keep Tito from succumbing to Soviet pressure, granted aid in increasing quantities. The United States led the pack. The Titoists were extremely sensitive as to their status as Communists and therefore gave wide publicity to the fact that Western aid and assistance was being granted without requests for either material or ideological concessions. By October, Tito was openly praising the United States for its policy toward Yugoslavia.[1]

Aid from the West made it possible for the Yugoslav Communists to withstand not only the pressure from the Soviet bloc but also the ruinous internal disruption caused by their own economic incompetence, their over-ambitious industrialization program, and their ill-advised agricultural collectivization policy. Their difficulties were compounded by the devastating drought of the summer of 1950.

In many ways this drought was a turning point in Titoist development. The threat of starvation forced Tito to ask the United States for aid in the form of food. The fact that the American Government's response was immediate and without qualification did much to dispel whatever animosity and uncertainty remained in the Titoist leaders' attitude toward the West. Just prior to the close of the food agreement negotiations, Tito was reminded by the American Ambassador at Belgrade[2] that, while his government's executive branch had agreed to send food to Yugoslavia, it would be well for Tito to keep in mind that the cost of food would eventually have to be authorized by the legislative branch and that Congress had been openly critical of the lack of civil and religious liberties in Yugoslavia. Tito replied that he was well aware of the attitude of the United States Congress in this respect. It was from this time forward that steps were taken to relax some of the oppressive restrictions imposed by the Titoist government upon the large majority of its subjects.

[1] Speaking in Zagreb on October 29, 1950, Tito praised the United States for the assistance it was giving to Yugoslavia and pointed out particularly that no conditions were attached to this aid. He also for the first time recognized the fact that the United States had been by far the largest contributor to the United National Relief and Rehabilitation Assistance aid which had come to Yugoslavia right after the war—pointing out that the United States had contributed $430,000,000 and that absolutely no conditions whatsoever had been made by Washington in making this contribution. See *New York Times,* Oct. 30, 1950, p. 1.

[2] The American Ambassador at the time was George V. Allen.

Large quantities of food were dispatched from the United States to Yugoslavia during the winter of 1950-51. In a formal agreement the Titoists pledged themselves to give full publicity at home to the food assistance program and to permit the distribution of the food to be observed by a staff of Americans sent to Yugoslavia expressly for the purpose. This agreement was carried out to the satisfaction of both governments.[3] American observers roamed through the country at random accompanied by Yugoslav interpreters—most of whom were, of course, either members of the Yugoslav Communist party or at least sympathetic to it. Here was an invaluable opportunity for young Yugoslav Communists to see for themselves that much of the anti-American propaganda upon which they had been raised since the war was conspicuously false.

At the end of 1950, it was suddenly discovered that stocks of certain vital industrial raw materials were almost depleted. Outside help was required immediately if numerous factories were not to close. The United States, Great Britain, and France responded to appeals for grants-in-aid of raw materials to keep factories open. This set the pattern for the subsequent yearly tripartite agreements by which these three powers have underwritten and still underwrite Yugoslavia's continuing foreign trade deficits.

Thus, the year 1950 witnessed both the flowering of the Titoists' confidence in their ability to deal with the West without jeopardizing their independence and the beginnings of a serious reformulation of internal policy as well. By the end of 1949 the Yugoslav leaders had rationalized the power conflict between their own nationalist-type communism and that of Stalin in terms of a new ideological position that they claimed was Marxist-Leninist but anti-Stalinist. That Stalinism was bureaucratic and un-Marxian became the battle cry of the Titoists. The political, social, and economic reforms

---

[3] The author was American Consul in Zagreb at the time, and as such served as one of the directors of this program.

they have since worked out have made basic theoretical and practical changes in the Yugoslav system of government. These changes are of primary importance both to Titoism and to world communism as well since they have all been instigated in the name of Marxism-Leninism. They have given the country a new democratic constitution, a new theory of the role of the state, a new attitude toward the role of the Communist party, a new conception of the importance of the individual, and a new approach toward the concept of public and private ownership of property. In effect the Titoists put Stalinism on the defensive as a political creed.

The Yugoslavs' principal themes of anti-Stalinist criticism were plainly stated by the beginning of 1950. These were succinctly summed up by Milovan Djilas in a campaign speech delivered just before the March 1950 elections for the federal parliament. The indictment was long, but much of it is of particular interest when compared with some of the reforms attempted six years later by Khrushchev within his own Party and government. Among other things, Djilas accused the Stalinist leaders of vulgar, historical falsifications and idolatries similar to those in absolute monarchies; of permitting differences in pay scales which are greater than those in bourgeois bureaucracies; of causing the ideological promotion of Great Russian nationalism and subordinating the role, culture, and history of other peoples; of following a policy of dividing the world into spheres of influence with the capitalist powers; of monopolizing the interpretation of Marxist ideology and of the tactics of the international working class movement; of introducing lying and slandering methods into the working class movement; of neglecting the study of Marx, Engels, and Lenin, and especially of their precepts concerning the laws of the transition period and of the Communist society; of tendencies toward the actual liquidation of socialist democracy and transforming it into a mere form; of rendering the struggle of opinions impossible and putting a brake on the initiative of the masses; and of revising the philosophical foundations of Marxism.[4] In other words, Stalinism was a horrendous deviation from Marxism-Leninism and must be condemned and combated as such.

Djilas claimed that the new Yugoslav socialism disowned all of these Stalinist heresies and would henceforth strive to bring about the true Marxist state in Yugoslavia by constantly broadening the participation of the masses in the "dictatorship of the proletariat." This was to be achieved by democratizing the state from within through an unending struggle against not only the reactionary segments of the population but also against the natural inclination toward increasing bureaucracy inherited from the Stalinist system. The masses must be drawn into the administration of the state and the economy, they must be encouraged in every way possible to develop individual initiative. In brief, Yugoslavia was to avoid the evils of Stalinism by decentralizing its own bureaucracy.

But to broaden mass participation in Yugoslavia's new social democracy would not be a simple matter. While Tito's popularity at home had undoubtedly increased as a result of his break with the Cominform and his *rapprochement* with the West, his people knew that he remained a confirmed Communist with not the slightest intention of lessening his determination to lead Yugoslavia through socialism en route to communism. The Titoists themselves knew that the revolutionary period in their country was far from completed; since bourgeois reactionary tendencies still had to be carefully policed, it would not be a simple matter to dispense with intimidation as a major factor in their type of administration. To peddle Marxism-Leninism without intimidation had shown meager results elsewhere in the world, and in this respect Yugoslavia would unquestionably prove no exception. Furthermore, the Titoist leaders' difficulties at this stage were complicated by the fact that they themselves had little or no understanding of any other method of ruling than

[4] Milovan Djilas, *On New Roads of Socialism* (Belgrade: 1950), pp. 11-12.

that learned from Stalin. Nevertheless, since Stalin and his methods had been openly condemned, they had to find new techniques with which to rule. Eventually they decided to try to replace intimidation with persuasion. The experiments with this new tactic were begun in 1950 and continue to this day.

The tactic has turned out to be less visionary than it might at first have seemed. As it has developed in practice, the policy has become a synthesis, to borrow a Marxist abstraction, which makes intimidation a part of persuasion if and when persuasion alone should fail. Or, to state this axiom in more "reactionary" terms, the policy has developed into none other than that of the "carrot and the stick." While persuasion has most certainly not succeeded in converting the large majority of Yugoslavs to a recognition of the all-encompassing "truths" of Marxism-Leninism, it has resulted in several worthwhile improvements. The ordinary Yugoslav now has the opportunity to make up his mind during a particular "persuasion" period as to whether or not it is worth his while to hold out and be intimidated. An even more important result of the policy is that it has mellowed the intimidators. Most of these now realize that there are advantages to the old adage that you can catch more flies with sugar than with vinegar. Consequently, there is more personal freedom in Yugoslavia today than there has been at any time since Tito came to power. Many non-Yugoslav visitors, such as Harry Schwartz of the *New York Times*, feel that this atmosphere of relative freedom is perhaps the most important difference between Yugoslav and Russian communism. As Schwartz has observed, while it is true that many people look around and lower their voices when they wish to criticize the regime, even a newcomer to Yugoslavia can soon hear much criticism and can see for himself that opponents of Tito are living normally even in his capital city of Belgrade.[5] This new degree of freedom in turn permits

[5] Harry Schwartz, "Yugoslavia's Communism—and Russia's," *New York Times*, May 29, 1955, Sect. IV, pp. 11 ff.

the Titoists a much better opportunity to judge the real results of specific policies, more and more of which are inspired by the honest desire to make their system work as painlessly as possible.

The first concrete administrative experiment with persuasion rather than intimidation was the new electoral law enacted in January 1950 to become effective for use in the parliamentary elections of the following March.[6] The hopes raised by some of the liberal provisions of the new law were short-lived, however, and the 1950 elections were as totalitarian in conduct as any previous election under Tito's supervision. The attempt to use the carrot-and-the-stick tactic in the 1950 elections had turned out to be premature. The next electoral reform law (of 1953) and its application showed that as time progressed the Yugoslav leaders had become much more adept at wielding both the carrot and the stick.[7]

One of the most encouraging signs that the Titoist leaders honestly and earnestly desired to substitute persuasion for intimidation was the announcement in the autumn of 1950 that a new criminal code was to be drafted. The code in existence at the time was the usual model of its Soviet prototype, having little or no real connection with judicial practice. The police in Yugoslavia were a code unto themselves. They made arrests in secret, detained suspects at will, and meted out punishments under an administrative procedure which left no method of appeal for the victims. The new criminal code was intended as the initial step in the general reform of the entire legal system. It was promulgated in 1951, and since that year there has been a steady and encouraging reformulation of the concept of "social legality" in Yugoslavia.

The shift in the role of the Communist party from intimidation to persuasion was begun in 1950, even though a comprehensive public explanation of the Party's role and

---

[6] For the text of this law see *SL*, Jan. 25, 1950. For a résumé see *NYL*, I:1 (1950), pp. 28-35.

[7] See Chapter VII.

responsibilities under the new tactic was not forthcoming until the Sixth Party Congress in November 1952. In October 1950, Tito decreed the abolition of many of the special privileges in food, housing, and other services hitherto available to Party and government officials, army officers, and miscellaneous members of the ruling clique. The decree was undoubtedly inspired by the fact that the summer's drought presented many sections of the country with the prospect of starvation, and Tito must have realized how unpopular special privileges for the "advanced guard of the proletariat" would have been with the masses if allowed to continue. This decree constituted a distinctly revolutionary act in the history of Communist states. To take steps which tended to reduce the tremendous differences between the rulers and the ruled was a decided swing away from the practice of Stalin toward the more equalitarian practices of the early Lenin. Whatever the real cause of the move, the decree acted to curb the privileges of Party members. It served as a first step in the new policy of having the Party assume the role of persuasive leadership of the masses rather than one of arrogant intimidation. So far as could be observed, the decree was rigidly respected at the time. However, in the years which followed many of the privileges have been reinstated, but only for a much smaller group within the higher echelons of the Party hierarchy.[8]

1950 also saw the Yugoslav Communists trying to withdraw some of the unnecessarily antagonistic measures they had taken against the peasants. In the end, however, a drought forced them to postpone these conciliatory intentions. At the close of 1948, as if inspired by Cominform criticism of their agrarian policies and tactics, the Titoists had begun an all-out campaign to force the private peasants to form collective farms. In the years preceding the break with the Cominform, the Party had used only comparatively mild measures of

[8] See Djilas' references to the "closed world" of his fellow Party officials who "had automobiles, travel in sleeping cars, buy their food and clothing at the special stores, spend its holidays in special villas and summer resorts." (From the translation of *Nova Misao* article [*Life*, April 12, 1954, p. 90].)

persuasion to emphasize the importance of voluntary action on the part of private peasants. Now, by 1949, a full-fledged intimidation campaign was being carried out. Mass propaganda was directed at the medium and poor peasants as well as at the rich. All who resisted received impossibly heavy assessments either in income taxes or in quantities of produce to be handed over to the state under its produce-collection policy. Despite the bankruptcies and broken heads which resulted from the drive, the large majority of private peasants held out against the government. As a result of the sullen defiance built up within the peasantry, there was a disastrous decline in agricultural production, and the drought of 1950 presaged virtual ruin.

It was imperative that the regime should take steps to rectify the rapidly deteriorating agricultural situation. Tito, in his campaign speeches for the March 1950 elections, promised that forcible collection of produce would be made more equitable and that local functionaries who in the past may have acted unfairly in applying the policy would be punished. However, by the middle of the summer, the leniency which Tito promised had been forgotten. The ruinous drought forced the government to continue to extract exorbitant amounts of produce from the private peasants. Nevertheless, during 1950 the pace of the collectivization campaign slackened. By mid-1951 it had come to a complete standstill, and during that same year most of the forcible collection of farm produce was stopped.

In the autumn of 1950, the Titoist government made several concessions to the religious feelings of its people. It returned certain important properties to the Serbian Orthodox and Lutheran churches. In September, Tito paid an official call upon the Serbian Orthodox Patriarch who had just been chosen head of his church after a long struggle in the Synod between anti-Communist bishops and those who wanted to make peace with the regime. In November 1950, as a concession to the strong anti-Titoist reaction amongst American Catholics, Tito publicly restated an informal offer

he had made in 1949 to free Archbishop Stepinac, Yugoslavia's leading Catholic prelate who was sentenced to prison
in 1946 as an enemy of the people, if the Archbishop would
leave the country or retire to a monastery.[9] Stepinac refused.
Only complete admission of his innocence or orders from
the Pope would persuade him voluntarily to leave his prison
cell. At the end of 1951, Tito compromised between his own
conscience and Catholic world opinion and released Stepinac
from prison, but confined him to his native village of Krašić
near Zagreb. During 1950 and the years that followed, other
priests whose sentences might have been questionable were
released from prison. Eventually this attitude of leniency
was extended to other categories of political prisoners.

By 1950, the clearly visualized objective of the Titoist
leaders was to divest their system of its Stalinist-type bureaucracy which they now saw as leading inevitably to the
most drastic form of capitalism, namely "state capitalism."
It is natural that the Yugoslav Marxists, whose accepted
creed insists that the cause of all behavior is materialistic,
should begin their internal reforms within the economic
sector of Yugoslav life. And it is equally inevitable that, of all
the internal reforms initiated in 1950, those taken in the
economic field were the most effective in leading the Titoists
out of the Stalinist mire into which they had fallen since
their accession to power.

The earliest steps to correct Yugoslav over-bureaucratization were taken at the end of 1949 and the beginning of 1950.
They consisted mainly in the indiscriminate transfer of some
economic-administrative functions from the federal government to the governments of the six constituent republics,
and wherever practical from the republics to the people's
committees (the village, town, city, and district organs of
government). But the simple shift of these functions from
one level to another in the totalitarian hierarchy was not

---

[9] See *New York Times,* Nov. 13, 1950, p. 1. Tito had made the informal
offer during an interview in 1949 with Cyrus L. Sulzberger of the *New York
Times.*

really effective in decreasing bureaucracy. It was only after the inexperienced Yugoslav leaders themselves had had time to become adept in the new type of leadership required of them that the general overhaul of their administration began to show some orderly progress. This stage did not reach its culmination until January 1953 when a new Constitution was adopted. At that time a complementary series of measures for reorganization were carried out under the heading of "administrative decentralization."

Nevertheless, the most important single decentralization measure was taken in 1950. To the Titoists it was a step of revolutionary importance as fundamental as the actual conquest of power during the war. In the final analysis, the Basic Law Concerning the Management of State Economic Enterprises and Higher Associations by the Working Collectives passed in June of 1950 became the keystone of the new ideological and political structure the Titoists have since built in Yugoslavia. Usually referred to as the Workers' Council Law, this act legally turned the management and control of all economic organizations over to the workers of each individual enterprise. In the words of one Yugoslav Communist, "with the adoption of this law Yugoslavia, having severed its political connections with the Soviet Union in 1948 . . . now also severed its ideological connections with Stalin's theories on socialism, and set out upon a new path of socialist development." [10]

The Titoists justifiably claim that their Workers' Council Law is of universal importance. This claim has particular meaning when it is noted that no other government—after Lenin's initial attempts with the Russian workers' soviets failed—has indicated its willingness to turn the so-called means of production over to the producers in so categorical and legal a fashion. On the other hand, the application of the law has come to serve the Yugoslav leaders as proof of something not quite so revolutionary: namely, that, like so many

[10] Leon Geršković, "The Tasks of the New Federal Assembly," *YR*, II (Dec. 1953), p. 7.

well-meaning Marxist innovations, the spirit of the Workers'
Council Law is frequently much too utopian for the conditions in which it is expected to function. Far from the least
important result of the law is the fact that through its attempted application the Yugoslav leaders have been forced
to recognize some of the everyday realities of human nature
and especially of human limitations, realities which Marxists
seem congenitally prone to ignore.

The Workers' Council Law and its application will be discussed in greater detail in Chapter V. Workers' self-management of a constantly expanding variety has become both
the mainspring and the fervent and primary hope of Titoist
theory. As a policy, workers' self-management was invented
to serve as an antidote to the Stalinist type of over-bureaucratization then dominating Titoist practice. The year 1950
witnessed the injection of the initial dose of workers' self-
management by the appearance of the Workers' Council Law.
This single fact is sufficient to distinguish 1950 as the real
year of change in the Titoists' attempt to live alone and to
prosper in a politically predatory world. The law has served
to decrease the over-bureaucratization which then existed,
and from it have stemmed the extensive political and administrative decentralization reforms required to give workers' self-management the maximum practical meaning.

PART II

FEDERATION, AN EARLY FORM
OF DECENTRALIZATION

CHAPTER IV

Intranational Dissension Checked

There are at least nineteen groups in Yugoslavia having distinctly separate ethnical, racial, historical, or religious personalities.[1] The existence of so many groups with acute national feelings demands the presence of a strong central control. Between the two World Wars the Karageorgevic monarchy tried to maintain peace among the factions by attempting to Serbianize all non-Serb Yugoslav groups and by ignoring or mistreating most non-Yugoslav minorities. As a result, when the state was threatened from the outside it disintegrated with unseemly alacrity. Profiting from the disastrous experience of the monarchy, Tito decentralized his state. By making Yugoslavia a federation and by insisting upon racial and religious equality, he has brought not only internal unity but greater efficiency to centralized government.

[1] According to the preliminary results of the 1953 census as presented in Table 3-5 of *Statistički Godišnjak FRNJ 1955* (Belgrade: July 1955), p. 54, the number of individuals in each ethnic group was as follows:

(In thousands) Total population:
16,927

Serbs	7,064	Slovaks	83
Croats	3,970	Germans	80
Slovenes	1,492	Gypsies	62
Macedonians	897	Rumanians	62
Montenegrins	476	Bulgarians	57
*Unspecified		Vlachs	37
Yugoslavs	992	Czechs	34
Albanians	752	Italians	33
Hungarians	507	Ruthenians	30
Turks	254	Russians	13
		All others	34

* Most of these are Moslems of either Serb or Croat origin who have religious rather than racial preferences. See footnote No. 5.

The adoption of the federative principle even before the liberation war was won represents Tito's earliest use of decentralization as a technique to attain the unity and harmony of purpose vital to his continued control of the country. Unlike the economic, political, and social decentralization reforms to be discussed in the chapters which follow, decentralization through the federative principle has only indirect bearing upon fundamental Titoist social or political theory. It was a purely pragmatic step which had to succeed if the Titoists were to be free to force socialism upon Yugoslavia. Unless they first suppressed the ruinous racial and religious dissensions within their country, they would have been required to concentrate their energy upon protecting themselves against plots and counterplots engineered by scheming nationality groups. The federative principle and the series of formal and informal equalization policies accompanying it have managed to push racial and religious differences below the surface. Especially when compared with the disastrous Greater Serbia policy practiced by his predecessors, the federative principle represents one of Tito's most successful reforms. It is a reform effected prior to the period in which Titoism took shape as a separate political philosophy. Nevertheless, it is so fundamental to the success of Tito's post-Cominform reforms that no exposition of Titoism as a separate political philosophy is complete without an explanation of how Tito has dealt with the problem of intranational dissensions.

THE FEDERATIVE PRINCIPLE

The Serbian, Croatian, Slovene, Macedonian, and Montenegrin national groups which were amalgamated to form the first Yugoslav state immediately following World War I had each been forged through a long and tortuous history. Originally they were tribes of the South- or Yugo-Slav migrations that overran the Balkans in the early part of the sixth century. Historically and numerically the Serbs and

Croats have been the most important of the five groups. Both had at one time or another been independent kingdoms. During most of the modern period, however, the Croats lived under Hungarian or Austro-Hungarian domination and the Serbs were subjects of the Ottoman Empire. Besides the environmental differences that grew between the two groups as a result of their separate historical administrative experiences, the most destructive seeds of dissension were sown with the coming of Christianity to the South Slavs. The Croats became Catholics and the Serbs a pillar of the Eastern Orthodox Church. The cleavage between the two was further widened by the Westernization of the Croats. Under the tutelage of the Austro-Hungarian Empire and the Catholic Church, the Croats were made a part of western Europe. Western influences only began seriously to penetrate Serbia after 1805 when the first Peter Karageorgević led a revolt which overthrew the Turkish rule of Serbia.

After the formation of the Yugoslav state in 1918, its Serbian leaders spent the next ten years trying to find a working compromise between their natural inclination to Serbianize their expanded kingdom and the insistence of the Croats upon some form of semiautonomy which would recognize what was in their eyes their superior culture. These efforts failed and all further attempts were brought abruptly to an end in 1929 when King Alexander closed parliament and wrote a new Constitution which made him virtual dictator within his kingdom. Exiled Croat separatists assassinated Alexander in Marseilles in 1934. At home the Croats continued their struggle against the Greater Serbia policies of the regent Prince Paul and his Serbian-staffed governments. Serb-Croat disunity culminated in the collapse of the Yugoslav Army after only twelve days of resistance to the Nazi invasion in 1941. The defection of Croatian troops had caused the rapid disintegration of the Yugoslav Army. The important Croat leaders made little or no protest to the formation of the Axis-sponsored kingdom of Croatia which immediately followed the Nazi victory over the Yugoslav Army. Anti-Serb feeling in Croatia was whipped up to a murderous climax by the fanatical Ustaša, the shock troops of the new kingdom of Croatia. The Ustaša mercilessly slaughtered thousands of Serbians whose only crime was to reside within the boundaries of the puppet state.

Tito and the other early Yugoslav Communists were far from novices in dealing with problems arising from nationalist incompatibilities within their own country. Soon after its formation in 1920 the Communist party of Yugoslavia was hopelessly split and often foundered on the issue of nationalism.[2] The problem continued to plague the Party until 1937, when Tito became its chief and skillfully unified the different national Communist organizations. For the first time the Yugoslav Communist party became a closely knit group of clandestine members able to operate with a singleness of purpose throughout the country. The Party had been outlawed since 1921.

Tito's talent for organization stood the Party in good stead when it took to the field against the Germans and Italians in June 1941. He built the Partisan army which by 1945 had defeated the invaders. By the end of the war he had firmly established the Communist minority as the rulers of Yugoslavia. Throughout the war, the Partisan leaders used to full advantage the differences between the national groups to swell the ranks of their army. The leaders promised each major group a form of sovereignty within a Yugoslav federation. They cleverly played down the Communist aspects of their movement. Instead they emphasized its role in the struggle for liberation from the foreign enemy and for a wide range of social reforms with an appeal to all nationalities.

By autumn of 1942, the Partisan army had achieved sufficient successes for its Communist leaders to decide that the moment was ripe to attempt the formation of a pro-

[2] For a short survey of the struggles of the early CPY with the nationalities problem, see Adam B. Ulam, *Titoism and the Cominform* (Harvard, 1952), pp. 10 ff.

visional government. In November of that year, they convened the first congress of the Anti-Fascist Council of the
National Liberation Movement of Yugoslavia (otherwise
known as AVNOJ) in the Bosnian town of Bihač. A con-
certed effort was made to include all racial, religious, and
social groups from all parts of the country among the representatives invited to attend the congress. However, the primary objective of the meeting was thwarted at the last
minute by a command from the Kremlin that under no cir-
cumstances should a provisional government be formed.[3]
The Bihač congress was thereby reduced to the role of little
more than a country-wide manifestation of solidarity.

A second AVNOJ congress was held in Jajce in November
1943. In the absence of orders to the contrary from Moscow,
the meeting this time laid the foundations for a new state.
Tito announced that the Karageorgević dynasty was pro-
hibited from returning to the country, and that the question
of whether Yugoslavia would continue as a monarchy or as
a republic was to be decided after the end of the war. Yugoslavia was now declared a federation. The equality of all
peoples and nationalities within its frontiers as well as the
equality of the component parts of the federation were guaranteed. The AVNOJ became the central organ of the National Liberation Movement and its highest legislative body;
it elected a Presidium entrusted with the power of nominating the Committee of National Liberation which was in turn
entrusted with the functions of a government. With Tito at
its head, the Presidium was composed of six Serbs, five
Croats, four Slovenes, one Montenegrin, and one Bosnian
Moslem.

The Constitution adopted by Tito's government in 1946
incorporated the federative principle as created by the
AVNOJ at Jajce. It recognized the sovereignty of the six
republics of Serbia, Croatia, Slovenia, Macedonia, Montene-

---

[3] See Vladimir Dedijer, *Tito* (New York: 1953), p. 189. The Soviet
leaders were apprehensive lest their Anglo-American allies—who supported
King Peter's London Government-in-Exile—would take offense.

gro, and Bosnia-Hercegovina, and gave a more limited form of sovereignty to the Autonomous Province of the Voivodina and the Autonomous Region of Kossovo-Metohija. Each republic, province, and region has its own Constitution (or basic statute in the case of the two autonomous areas), and each has its own government. The general lines of administrative authority within the federation were laid down by the 1946 Constitution, and are even more explicitly explained in the constitutional reform of 1953.[4] However, in contradistinction to the 1946 Constitution, the 1953 reform makes no mention of the sovereignty of the republics, mentioning only the independence and territorial integrity of the federal state.

By creating the six republics and the autonomous districts as the constituent parts of his new federation, Tito was deferring to the instinctive yearnings of the most important national groups for forms of autonomy and self-expression. But his federative policy was not entirely altruistic. Essentially, it must be regarded as a solution to the Serb-Croat disunity which had proved the main obstacle to the consolidation of political power by any previous Yugoslav Government.

The pressing need to remove as many as possible of the causes of Serb-Croat tension is the primary explanation for the creation of the Republic of Bosnia-Hercegovina and for the formation of the two autonomous districts. Instead of dividing Bosnia-Hercegovina between Serbia and Croatia as had been done by the desperate agreement of 1939 between Prince Paul's government and the Croatian leaders, the Titoists created a separate Republic of Bosnia-Hercegovina even though the population of this region consists essentially of Serbs and Croats.[5] In this fashion one of the

[4] The Constitution of 1946 and the reform of 1953 are discussed in greater detail in Chapter VII.

[5] Approximately 31 per cent of Bosnia-Hercegovina's population are Moslems who, though originally Serbs or Croats, adopted Islam during the Turkish occupation and are today more religously than nationally conscious.

most vicious quarrels between the Serbs and the Croats was effectively stilled.

The pre-World War II Belgrade governments had insisted upon pretending that the Macedonian Slavs were "South Serbs." Any and all protests to the contrary were consistently beaten down. While Tito's Republic of Macedonia exists as a recognition of the difference between Macedonians and Serbs, its establishment also serves to cut down the old territorial supremacy of Serbia. The formation of the Autonomous Province of the Voivodina, where only a little over one-third of the population is not Serbian, and of the Autonomous Region of Kossovo-Metohija, where Albanians are in the large majority, further serves to keep Serbia from being disproportionately larger than Croatia.

It would appear that the Serbs may have paid the lion's share in Tito's efforts to bring about a Serb-Croat equilibrium. But certain countervailing concessions helped to ease discontent among the Serbs. Both autonomous districts were placed under the guidance of the Republic of Serbia which was given the responsibility for approving their basic statutes and of exercising certain specific supervisory prerogatives therein. Then, Croatian influence in the government of the Republic of Bosnia-Hercegovina has been kept to a minimum. The composition of the republican government consists almost entirely of Serbs and Moslems. The Catholic Croats, who represent approximately 23 per cent of the total population,[6] do not have proportionate representation in the uppermost ranks of the Republic's leadership. Furthermore, the prewar orientation of the cultural relations of the Moslems of this area toward Zagreb was shifted to Belgrade. The large mosque built in the center of Zagreb in the interwar years as a symbol of this orientation has since the installation of the Titoist regime been converted into a Croatian folk museum.

[6] *Statistical Pocket-Book of Yugoslavia 1955* (Belgrade: April 1955), p. 28.

The federal parliament created by the 1946 Constitution contained a second house called the Council of Nationalities. It was composed of an equal number of deputies from each of the six republics, and a proportionately smaller number from each of the two autonomous districts. The consent of the Council was required for the passage of all laws, and in every other respect the Council was considered to have equal rights with the other chamber of the parliament. The 1953 constitutional reform merged the Council of Nationalities into the Federal Council, which was made upper house of the newly constituted National Assembly, but provided for the Countil of Nationalities to re-emerge as a separate body under certain specific conditions.[7] The purpose of the Council of Nationalities is to give assurance to each group therein represented that its national interest will not be slighted in federal policy. However, since the National Assembly itself is little more than a rubber stamp for policy outlined by the regime, the Council exists more for morale than for practical reasons. The real protection of nationality group interests rests more in the representation each has within the leading Party and government circles, and in the honest desire of the men who make up these circles to do away with all vestiges of intranational rivalry.

As a corollary to the federative principle, the Titoists have devised a policy aimed at assuring some semblance of economic equality among the six republics. This policy deliberately gives high priority to the development of the three poorer, most underdeveloped republics of Bosnia-Hercegovina, Macedonia, and Montenegro. The three richer republics pay a large share of the costs of this program. The economic equalization policy has, however, given rise to a reaction which the Titoists refer to as "localism": the desire of the advanced areas to evade their responsibilities toward the underdeveloped areas and to utilize their resources at home. Nevertheless, the policy of making the rich republics pay for the development of their poorer neighbors continues

[7] See Chapter VII.

in full force. Despite the "localism" it has engendered, the equalization program has also fostered greater intranational unity in Yugoslavia. As *The Economist* has remarked, to a foreign observer who has memories of the old Yugoslavia the Titoists' policy in this instance appears to be true statesmanship.[8]

One important indirect result of the need to put an end to Serb-Croat disunity is the stress which the Titoists place upon guaranteeing equal, often special rights to the non-Yugoslav minorities living within their country. Approximately 12 per cent of the total population of Yugoslavia are of non-Yugoslav origin.[9] From the outset the Titoist leaders knew that if their policy of equality amongst the Yugoslav national groups was to succeed, it had to be a total policy. This meant that equal rights had to be guaranteed to all citizens regardless of their race or religion. Therefore, one of the first laws enacted right after the Yugoslav Communists came to power in 1945 was the Law on the Prohibition or Provocation of National and Racial Hatred and Discord.[10] The intent of this law was considerably strengthened by the 1946 Constitution. It specifically provided for equal treatment and opportunity for all national minorities and assured them the right to their own cultural development and to the free use of their mother tongues. All of the pertinent fundamental laws since 1946 have provided for equal rights for all citizens without distinction of nationality, race, or creed. The mother tongues of the larger minority groups are official languages in the republics and autonomous districts where groups live in sufficiently large numbers to warrant it. The

[8] "Jugoslavia in Transition," *The Economist* (London: June 26, 1954), p. 1064.

[9] Table No. 3-5 *Statistički Godišnjak, op. cit.,* shows that of the total of 16,927,000 inhabitants of Yugoslavia, 2,038,000 are non-Yugoslavs. More than seventeen groups are represented in this figure, ranging from 752,000 Albanians to 1,000 Greeks.

[10] See Stojković and Martić, *National Minorities in Yugoslavia* (Belgrade: 1952), p. 57. This report gives a comprehensive review of the entire Titoist minorities policy. Most of the information contained in this report is reprinted in *QAS*, No. 11 (March-May 1952), pp. 123-46.

major national minorities are represented in proportion to their number in all the federal, republican, and autonomous district organs of government. Efforts are also made to see that non-Yugoslav minorities are proportionately represented in the local organs of government, the so-called people's committees.

Besides the purely legal and administrative aspects of the policy of making all minority groups free and equal citizens, what amount to special privileges in cultural development have also been granted these groups. Wherever possible special elementary, higher, and normal schools have been established for national minorities. Where it has not been practical to open such schools, classes given in minority languages have been added to the curricula of regular schools.[11] Minority group cultural organizations have been encouraged, and are often financed by official funds. Many of these groups now have their own professional and private drama societies, their own radio programs, and their own newspaper and publishing establishments.

By the time the Titoists drew up their 1953 Constitution, they were of the opinion that the principle of equal rights for all Yugoslav citizens was an accomplished fact in practice as well as in principle. The 1946 Constitution had contained several specific references to equal rights for minorities, but the new Constitution lays no special emphasis upon these groups. The 1953 Constitutional Law in fact refers to national minorities only once—in Article 9, which lists the specific rights and duties of the federal government. Amongst these are: the protection of the unity and equality of rights of the people of Yugoslavia, and the duty to insure the freedoms and democratic rights of citizens and their equality of rights regardless of nationality, race, or religion.[12]

[11] For a somewhat glowing report of the successes of this program, see Stojković and Martić, pp. 107-10 and 111-14. It should be noted, however, that many of the figures given as representing minority schools, actually include those regular schools which give some courses in a minority language.

[12] The text of the 1953 Constitutional Law appears in *New Fundamental Law of Yugoslavia* (Belgrade: Jurists' Association of Yugoslavia, 1953).

Tito's methods of solving his problems of intranational differences have not been confined to the reorganization of his state into a federation. Every care is taken to see that none of the major national groups has particular cause to feel slighted in appointments to the controlling body of the Party or to the various echelons of the federal administration. The armed forces are also used to foster the feeling of Yugoslav unity. The national origin of officers and soldiers has little or nothing to do with the formation of military units. Recruits are usually sent outside their native republic for training. Serbian and Montenegrin officers and men are serving in Croatia, Slovenes are in high army posts in Belgrade. Students are encouraged to attend universities outside their own republics. Members of youth organizations travel from one section of the country to another to assist in the special work projects which are made their responsibility. Workers are encouraged to take their vacations in republics other than their own. All such arrangements have done much to increase the feeling of Yugoslav national unity at the expense of attachment to separate minority loyalties. The most marked successes in these policies are with the younger generations who are naturally quicker to grasp the practical importance of being first of all Yugoslavs and not as in the past Serb, Croat, Slovene, Macedonian, or Montenegrin.

It cannot be denied that Tito has succeeded in diminishing Serb-Croat tension, but it is not possible to believe that he has miraculously wiped out once and for all their age-old mutual animosity. For one thing, the Ustaša massacres of Serbs and the Serbian retaliations against Croats during the last war are too recent a memory. By relentlessly enforcing the laws and procedures on ethnic and religious equality the Titoists have managed to push the mutual Serb-Croat dislike below the surface. But in older generations of Serbs and Croats the ill-feeling smolders just as virulently as ever. Nevertheless, if the Titoists can keep the friction suppressed long enough, the younger Yugoslavs, particularly those born since the war, should become more and more devoted to Yugoslav rather than separate racial unity.

It is ironic that mutual Serb-Croat hatred and mistrust today exists in its most violent form outside of Yugoslavia among Serbs and Croats who are refugees or who have become citizens of other lands. There is no real unity among such expatriate groups, not even in the face of the communism they claim to be fighting. Many Yugoslav politicians are supporters of ideas such as the future federation of Europe, through which they see the fulfillment of their fondest nationalist ambitions. These conceive European federation to mean an invitation to each nationality group to enter the future commonwealth as an independent entity. The Catholic hierarchy in Yugoslavia often looks upon such a solution as the ideal one.[13]

The Religious Problem

The dislike Communists in general feel for any kind of religion is given added impetus in Yugoslavia by the fact that differences in religion lie at the roots of the Serb-Croat problem. The Catholic Church had always exercised a strong and direct influence upon Croatian political leaders. Catholicism had been the official religion of the wartime Croatian kingdom, and the Ustaša massacres of Croatian Serbs were as often as not carried out in the name of Catholicism. While the Serbian Orthodox Church was not officially connected with the interwar Yugoslav state, it was in practice so connected. Its influence upon the Karageorgević monarchy was well known, and its privileged position in Belgrade was always painful to the Catholic Croats.

[13] In conversations with high Croatian church dignitaries in Yugoslavia during the period 1950-52, the author was often told that the only suitable solution to the Yugoslav nationalities problem was European federation. In such a federation, Croatia was to become independent; it was, of course, to receive almost all of Bosnia-Hercegovina, and many other territorial areas to which these Catholic leaders laid claim for Croatia. These churchmen considered that it would be in the best interest of the United States to make certain that the independent state of Croatia remained economically solvent.

After 1948, the Titoists' reliance upon the West to sustain their power forced them to decrease the intensity of their campaign against religion. The Moslem, Protestant, and Jewish religious groups came to terms with the Titoists a short time after the latter began to substitute persuasion for intimidation. The Orthodox Church followed soon thereafter. The Catholic Church is still resisting although with diminishing effectiveness. It has been the most violent in its fervor against the regime and consequently it has borne the major share of Titoist anti-religious zeal. Tito probably expected external Catholic pressure against his regime to relax after he released Archbishop Stepinac from prison at the end of 1951. If so, he soon learned of his mistake. At the end of 1952 Stepinac was elevated to the rank of cardinal. Belgrade testily reacted by severing official relations with the Vatican.

As the Titoists grew accustomed to their independence, their approach to the problem of religion became more rational. Gradually they evolved a policy of persuasion instead of intimidation in this field also. The religious communities of Yugoslavia, like the average individual Yugoslav citizen, are today free to go about their business if they steer scrupulously clear of politics. The official position was stated by Kardelj in 1953 when he told members of the Socialist Alliance, the Party's popular front organization, that their religious feelings were their own private concern but that the use of religion for political purposes would not be tolerated. He stressed that in the fight against church intervention in politics it was particularly important to strive "to guarantee, in actual fact, the unhindered exercise of religious affairs and customs on the part of all religious communities." [14] This leniency has not, of course, been extended to members of the Party. They are expressly forbidden to show a liking for any other religion than Marxism.

The census of 1953 showed that approximately 85 per cent of the population described themselves as belonging to some

[14] *YR*, II (March-April 1953), p. 18.

religion.[15] Worried by the increase and persistence of religious affiliation even among Party members, the Titoists
intensified the Party "house-cleaning" campaign begun in
1951, and put new energy into their drive to get priests to
join the associations the regime had earlier established with
the intention of counteracting from within the influence of
the Catholic and Orthodox churches. These priests' associations are a type of "professional" organization similar to
those formed for craftsmen, physicians, artists, and others.
They offer social security and other benefits to their members. The Vatican placed a ban upon such associations. Some
Orthodox bishops have attempted to resist them. Nevertheless, by the end of 1954, the associations were reputed to
have enrolled about 90 per cent of the officials and clergy
of both the Orthodox and Moslem communities.[16] At the end
of 1952, it was claimed that 60 per cent of Slovenia's Catholic
clergy belonged to associations.[17] The Croatian Catholic
clergy, however, were apparently under stronger ecclesiasti-
cal control; by the end of 1954, only about 10 per cent of
Croatian priests had signed up.[18]

In May 1953, the Law on the Legal Status of Religious
Communities was enacted.[19] It guaranteed freedom of conscience and confession to all citizens and expressly pro-
hibited the conversion of religious communities into political
organizations. Its primary impact upon the nationalities
problem came from its explicit guarantee of equal status to
all religions in the country. The Protestants and other religions whose congregations are relatively small in Yugoslavia were especially pleased with this provision. In the
past they had received decidedly shoddy treatment from the
all-powerful Catholic and Orthodox churches. The Orthodox,
the Moslems, and the Protestants had co-operated with the

[15] See Table 3-10, *Statistički Godišnjak, op. cit.,* p. 58.
[16] "Activities and Tasks of the Priests' Professional Societies," *RIA* (May
16, 1954), pp. 15-16.
[17] Kardelj, "The Policy of the Vatican against Yugoslavia," *YR,* III (Jan.
1953), p. 9.
[18] *New York Times,* Dec. 14, 1954, p. 8.
[19] The text of the law appears in *SL* No. 22, May 27, 1953.

government in drafting the new law. The Catholic clergy's co-operation had been sought but the Vatican forbade it.

Today the Yugoslav Communists feel that organized religion is politically on the defensive in their country. "Priests now have to ponder as to how to keep the people on their side," said a Titoist official in April 1955. "We are not required to conduct a large-scale political fight with them because for some time now we have had no need to keep them in mind." [20] Nevertheless, it is still very obvious that the Titoists are at heart adamantly against religion and count on its eventual disappearance. Stories of Communist-inspired mistreatment of individual priests on the local level, particularly of Catholic priests, are not infrequent and in general reflect the basic anti-religious bias of Party members. On the other hand, however, the Catholic Church in Yugoslavia, with its powerful international backing, makes little effort to conceal its desire to see Tito fail. The Titoist would usually argue that his Party cannot be expected to refrain from exercising the instinctive human prerogative of self-preservation.

Relatively few of the younger generation attend church in Yugoslavia today. This is to the ultimate advantage of the Communists. By such methods as making it possible for children to attend religious classes only after their regular school day is finished, the churches—particularly the Catholic Church which formerly held religious classes inside schools during regular school hours—are losing contact with the very young. While private church schools are still open, the difficulties they have in getting their graduates admitted to universities make such schools unpopular with children of secondary school age.

In brief, the Yugoslav Communist attitude toward religion may be summed up as one which tolerates religion so long as it is apolitical. The gradual disappearance of organized religion as such is simultaneously encouraged. Moves such

[20] Address by Dr. Vladimir Bakarić, the head of the Croatian republican government, *Vjesnik* (Zagreb), April 7, 1955, p. 1.

as those making it difficult for the religious organizations to instruct the young are particularly damaging to the previously privileged Catholic and Orthodox churches. As the Titoists weaken church influence on the younger generation, they are in fact weakening one of the most potent breeding places of Serb-Croat disunity.

If, however, the Serb-Croat problem is to be effectively solved, Tito will have to reach some satisfactory compromise with the Vatican. His policy of equality of religions cannot have its full impact upon Serb-Croat tension until the Catholic Church can be relieved of the special discrimination now shown against it. However, Tito holds a trump card in the game he is playing with Rome. The Yugoslav Catholic clergy are not in a position to withstand for long the temptation to join the government-sponsored associations through which they would receive old-age pensions, free medical treatment, income tax exemptions, rebates on railway tickets, and other such advantages. The Vatican is hardly in a position to match these benefits.

PART III

DECENTRALIZATION TO REMEDY OVER-BUREAUCRATIZATION

INTRODUCTION TO PART III

By 1950 the Titoists had concluded that decentralization of their Stalinist-type bureaucratic state was the most logical method of assuring their continued control. Expulsion from the Cominform had removed the Red Army as the ultimate source of their power. They had no choice but to seek a less oppressive system with which to rule. Two primary objectives were vital: to broaden the base of their popularity at home and to find a way to inject greater efficiency into their economy. Specifically, unless they achieved a substantial rise in productivity they could not hope to survive. Marxist theory requires the attainment of a highly industrialized society made up of politically sophisticated workers before the final stage of communism can be contemplated. There was little possibility of increasing productivity in Yugoslavia without increasing the individual Yugoslav worker's desire to co-operate with the regime.

By substituting indirect methods of control for the all-pervading direct methods practiced until 1950, the Titoists reached a compromise which permitted them to diminish their oppressively centralized supervision of every facet of Yugoslav life without discontinuing their careful direction of the struggle for socialization. Theoretically their decentralization reforms were presented as concrete examples of the Marxist concept of "the withering away of the state." In a more practical sense, however, decentralization created an administrative apparatus which, though it increased efficiency, gave the Titoists a less offensive method of control and restored much of the waning fervor of their socialist revolution.

As confirmed economic determinists, the Titoist leaders naturally considered decentralization of control over the economy to be the *sine qua non* of their new system. Therefore, the first positive step taken to decentralize their Stalinist state was the promulgation of the Workers' Council Law in June 1950. This revolutionary law technically transferred ownership of the means of production from the state to "society" as a whole. The workers of each enterprise, as the trusted representatives of "society" as the proprietor, were now given a role in the management of their respective organizations. The system of workers' self-management as created by the law was to engender an upsurge in the workers' incentive and initiative, sentiments so singularly lacking under the Stalinist-type rule. The Titoist regime's control of the Yugoslav economy was now to be exercised indirectly through fiscal measures influencing the market and through the supervisory responsibilities given over by the federal government to the political-administrative organs of the local community in which each enterprise is located. As it has developed in practice, workers' self-management has given real, although limited, management responsibilities to the workers. The system will remain the touchstone of Titoism. Even in its present limited form, the Titoists' program of workers' self-management represents a challenge to those in other types of political economies who are concerned with problems of management, especially with problems of workers' participation in management.

Workers' self-management as established by the Workers' Council Law automatically required freedom of action in the market. The Titoists had discovered that the laws of supply and demand were undeniable realities of modern economics. They therefore replaced their strictly controlled Stalinist-type market with a free-type market. This in turn forced a reformulation of their planning, fiscal, and financial systems. Reforms carried out in these sectors of control and administration have since produced greater realism and flexibility within the Titoist economy. Prices and wages are now more closely associated with the quality and quantity of production.

As Marxists, the Titoists readily succumbed to the standard practice of treating the agrarian sector of their society as though it were an unnecessary burden. Their energies and talents were almost entirely absorbed by their efforts to produce the industrial society required by Marxism to permit the ultimate transition to communism. In general, they merely tried to adjust the Stalinist patterns of agrarian reform to fit their own environment. But Yugoslavia even less than Russia itself was neither physically nor psychologically equipped to accept Stalinist agrarian methods. Eventually the passive resistance of the Yugoslav peasants forced the Titoists to adopt a more sensible attitude toward agricultural reform. Today collective farms are encouraged only in areas where they are practical. Voluntary co-operation in the parts of the country less adapted to collectivization is stimulated by indirect methods which cut down the profitability of the small private peasants' free participation in the local market. The Yugoslav peasant is now subjected to pressures similar to those that eventually brought peasants and farmers in Western democracies to the realization that they must seek more profitable methods of increasing their output or give up farming for a living. This battle has just begun in Yugoslavia. There is a world of ill-feeling between the peasant and the socialist regime. He is convinced that his resistance to the Titoists' inept attempts to force him to conform is primarily responsible for the soothing reforms of the past few years. In the final analysis, it is on the issue of socialization of the Yugoslav countryside that Titoism will stand or fall. The Yugoslav Marxists must eventually socialize the agrarian sector of their society or admit that socialization is not possible in their country.

Economic decentralization through workers' self-management demanded the complementary decentralization of the old administrative structure. Political-administrative reform began with the reorganization of the people's committees, the local and district organs of government. After 1952, these committees were entrusted with more and more responsibilities for supervising and co-ordinating the economic and social activities of their areas. They were given their own sources of revenue and permitted to draft their own budgets based upon estimated income and expenditure. In 1956, the people's committees were re-formed as "communes," the ideal type of self-government units recommended by Marx himself after the experience of the Paris Commune of 1871. The Yugoslav communes are to be given even greater autonomy in settling local economic and social problems. They are territorially larger than the local administrative units they replaced. Their territorial formation attempts to take into consideration the need to create a self-complementing geographical and social area. Theoretically such a homogeneous area permits the maximum practical opportunity for local self-government. However, the non-Marxist observer cannot help noticing that by reducing the total number of basic local units at the base of the Yugoslav political-administrative pyramid, the new commune system simplifies the supervisory responsibilities of the federal authority over the entire system.

The constitutional reform of 1953 reorganized the federal political-administrative structure so that it might serve more effectively the new systems of workers' self-management and people's self-government. One practical result has been to abolish the old dual-type federal apparatus in which the Yugoslav Communist party represented the "substance" government of Yugoslavia and the political-administrative structure merely the "shadow" government. Once again, the reform of the federal administrative structure is held by the Titoists to be a further example of the "withering away of the state." But, once again, the decentralization of this structure has merely substituted indirect for direct methods of control. It has created a more democratic method of administering the state, and in so doing has simultaneously presented the comparatively small group of men who rule Yugoslavia with a more efficient instrument with which to execute their will.

The Titoist regime has also relaxed its control over social

organizations. The social security system is run today by a hierarchy of supposedly self-administering units elected by the individuals who are members of the social security program. Since social security is a matter vital to socialization and at the same time not too closely involved with everyday politics, the amount of actual self-management permitted here is greater than in any other sector of economic, political, or social life in Yugoslavia. The educational system is more closely concerned with politics. It is responsible for the proper indoctrination of the Yugoslav youth. Nevertheless, the Titoists have worked out a compromise for the administration of their educational system which today permits educational institutions a maximum of freedom in their professional tasks while maintaining a careful minimum of control over institutional behavior.

The most interesting result of the Yugoslav Marxists' decentralization of control in state administration has been the correlative change it has in turn brought to Titoist jurisprudence. Economic, political, and social decentralization would have been a farce if the secret police and the courts had been permitted to continue as the mockery of justice they were in the Stalinist-type state. The Titoists have therefore attempted to substitute the rule of law for the arbitrary rule of force. Reform of the judicial structure was begun in 1951 with the promulgation of the new and comparatively liberal Criminal Code. Soon after there followed a law permitting citizens to bring questions of administrative misbehavior before the courts. This was another revolutionary "first" for the Titoists. Under Standard Marxist-Leninist-Stalinist practice, the administrative organs of government are responsible only to themselves for their public behavior. By 1954, the entire system of Yugoslav courts had been reorganized. Today it is possible for a citizen to obtain justice before these courts. The only exception, other than that arising from the possible incompetence of the officials of a court, is if the crime is of a political nature. As a minority government, the Titoist regime cannot always afford to submit its political practices to the dictates of an impartial court. Nevertheless, the Titoists' new emphasis upon legality has done much to restore some of the feeling of security which the average Yugoslav citizen lost completely during the dark days between 1945 and 1950.

In creating their "own road to socialism" the Titoists have leaned heavily upon the experiences and practices of Western liberal democracy. In theory at least the Yugoslav Marxists have woven many Western liberal democratic concepts into the pattern of their new social democracy. However, these concepts are only allowed full rein in practice where they cannot be used to challenge the total authority of the Titoist regime. These new concepts, even though they are honored in theory more than in practice, are of some value to the average Yugoslav, for at least they acquaint him with that higher standard of political existence which bred them.

Certainly, the Yugoslav Marxist leaders consider these Western liberal democratic concepts to be universal and have therefore clearly enshrined them in Titoist theory. In consequence, the average Yugoslav may one day bring himself to co-operate with the regime in an effort to create the society in which these concepts are supposedly to be practiced. However, he will soon find himself face to face with the destructive paradox of Titoism. The democracy which its relatively decentralized social system theoretically encompasses is ultimately self-negating. The Titoist leaders never intend their system to permit what they see as the "objective realities" of the Yugoslav struggle for socialism to be seriously challenged even by democratic differences of opinion. Tito himself spoke out against the anti-Communist revolutionaries in Hungary in November 1956.

CHAPTER V

Major Economic Reforms

In his Oslo address in the autumn of 1954, Kardelj stated that the Yugoslav system of democratic self-management of the economy was based upon two fundamental assumptions. The first was that no central leadership, no matter how wise, can control the entire economic and social development of a country. The second was that the maximum effort and initiative of the individual does not depend so much upon directives and control as it does upon the personal economic, social, cultural, and material interests of the worker who is working and creating in freedom. To ignore either assumption, Kardelj said, automatically leads to bureaucratic despotism.[1]

What Kardelj here offered as a profound discovery has been known to Western liberal thought for generations. Nevertheless, his "discovery" serves as an excellent illustration of the very real progress the Yugoslav leaders have made since 1950. Insofar as this progress is reflected in the Titoists' economic reforms, it has shown itself to be a growing willingness to recognize some of the beneficial realities of Western democratic practices and to weave these realities into the fabric of Yugoslav socialist democracy—provided, of course, that none of these imports threaten the regime's monolithic control of social and political development. In other words, the Yugoslav Marxists' experiences since 1950 have brought them to the free admission that all which is capitalist is not automatically bad.

[1] In Part III of Kardelj's Oslo speech, "Social Democracy in Yugoslav Practice," *Borba*, Jan. 1, 1955, p. 1.

Upon coming to power in 1945, the Titoists rapidly adopted every possible Stalinist method in organizing their economy. Each enterprise was directly supervised by an organ of the central government. The state plan included over-all production quotas as well as quotas for each individual enterprise. Prices, wages, profits, and investments were all planned and controlled from above. The state tried to resolve every conflict between the central plan and the inescapable realities of production by more and more systematic intervention and by placing greater restrictions upon the freedom of the market. Each step of this nature led to increasingly minute control by the federal government.

By 1950, the Yugoslav leaders recognized that their own state was over-bureaucratized. This was the deadly disease of Stalinism which unavoidably caused the perpetuation of the total monopoly of power by the small group of men who headed the administrative hierarchy. Decentralization, the Titoists concluded, was the only possible remedy. They therefore decided that Marx had never regarded nationalization as the socialist panacea or even as a practical necessity. Their own experience showed that the nationalization of industry all too readily bred a power-hungry, top-heavy, inefficient, undemocratic bureaucracy which stifled workers' incentive and piled up deficits.

The desire to decentralize their economy presented the Titoist improvisers with a formidable riddle: how, without resorting to purely capitalist forms, could the role of the state as the proprietor of the means of production be reduced and the individual producer's interest in increasing his productivity be inspired? The problem consisted in finding a way to organize a type of "free enterprise" which would not interfere with the essential plans for continued socialization. Thus, a second riddle grew automatically from the first: how could the need for a central plan be reconciled with the laws of supply and demand which the

Titoists now accepted as an objective reality of modern economics?

To solve these two riddles a somewhat tendentious formula was devised whereby "society" as a whole replaced the state as proprietor of the means of production; "society" in turn then entrusted the workers of each economic enterprise with the responsibility of management. This formula is commonly referred to as the system of workers' self-management. It was formalized by the Workers' Council Law of 1950, and has been proving its limited validity in practice since 1951. To a certain extent, Yugoslav workers now manage their own enterprises. Apart from some basic raw materials and semifinished goods, the enterprises compete on the open market for production materials. In the main the enterprises fix the prices of their own products in accordance with the laws of supply and demand. Wages now have some slight relation to profits. Formerly profits were fixed by the state. They now depend upon success in the competitive market, and therefore enterprises must now pay stricter attention to costs and to efficiency in production.

In order to permit the freedom of the market required by the policy of workers' self-management, the entire financial system had to submit to corresponding forms of decentralization. The old centralized systems of budgeting and taxation had likewise to be decentralized. Planning is now a two-way process. The federal government produces a yearly plan limited to fixing the "basic proportions" of economic development. Each republican, district, and local unit produces its own individual plan. Every effort is made to leave most of the administrative and technical detail to the plan of the lowest possible political-administrative planning unit. At the very bottom of the planning structure are the individual enterprises which are responsible for drawing up their own detailed production plans. The socio-political control which the planning system exercises over the economy is supposedly kept from becoming a power monopoly in the hands of the federal government by the role assigned to the market. Under the laws of supply and demand, the market is theoretically responsible for regulating prices.

In brief, Titoist economic decentralization has created a system which is a compromise between the free and the strictly controlled markets. The compromise attempts to synthesize what the Titoist leaders consider the indispensable or most advantageous features of each of the two types of markets. However, the Yugoslav economy is still insufficiently industrialized to meet Marxist requirements and the "level of socialist consciousness" of most Yugoslavs is still extremely low. Therefore, the major emphasis within the contemporary Titoist economic system lies on the side of control, indirect though this control may now be. In the final analysis, decentralization has acted to bring greater efficiency to government planning and management within the economy. At the same time, there is no doubt that the decentralized economic system is infinitely more realistic and less painful to the individual worker than the Stalinist form previously practiced. Hence, the Titoists' economic decentralization policy must be considered at least a limited success. It has produced favorable results both for the central administration and for the worker.

WORKERS' SELF-MANAGEMENT

In June 1950, the Titoists introduced their most revolutionary reform, "The Basic Law on the Management of State Economic Enterprises and Higher Economic Associations by the Workers' Collectives," [2] subsequently referred to as the Workers' Council Law. In essence, this law was the earliest expression of the new Titoist creed. It furnished the framework for wider participation of the Yugoslav

[2] The text of the law appears in SL No. 43, July 5, 1950. Translation of text: NYL, I:2-3 (1950), pp. 75-83.

working masses in their revolution. It was to be the keystone of the Yugoslav Marxists' campaign to divest their system of the curse of Stalinist revisionism and to return to the "true path" of Marxism-Leninism.

In presenting the new law to the National Assembly, Tito recalled that Marx, Engels, and Lenin had taught that the state begins to wither away at the moment "when the proletariat should really be in power." This withering away, Tito wanted it clearly understood, is gradual and begins first of all in the economic functions of the state. In Yugoslavia, he said, the process had already begun, first with the administrative decentralization started at the very end of 1949, and second with the new law then being presented to the Assembly. "From now on," Tito announced, "state ownership of the means of production [in Yugoslavia] . . . is gradually passing on to a higher form of social ownership. State ownership is the lowest form of social ownership and not the highest as the leaders of the U.S.S.R. consider it to be." [3]

The administrative decentralization to which Tito referred was a series of steps taken to abolish many of the federal ministries formerly responsible for the direct management of the various branches of the economy. Their functions were transferred to the six constituent republican governments which in turn shifted some of their former industrial management responsibilities to local administrative organs. In effect, this reorganization did not change the form of the existing system but merely rearranged its content. Because of the vastness of the fundamental theoretical and practical changes then being worked out by the Yugoslav leaders, these early attempts at administrative decentralization were not much more than stopgap measures all too often marked in practice by confusion and delay. In the history of Titoist economic decentralization, the

[3] Tito, *Workers Manage the Factories in Yugoslavia* (Belgrade: "Jugoštampa," 1950), p. 41.

period from 1950 through 1952 is best described as a process of continuous trial and error. It was not until the complete reorganization of the state administrative apparatus by the 1953 constitutional reform that comparative order and tranquillity were brought to the hitherto mercurial economic administrative structure. Before 1953, the deluge of economic laws and decrees[4] was carried out in practice mainly by the will of responsible officials, all of whom were Communists with the power to improvise wherever necessary.

To Yugoslav Communists, the Workers' Council Law represents the beginning of the third phase of their postwar economic development. The first had been the period in which their revolution transferred the means of production from private to state ownership and simultaneously created the conditions necessary to socialist development. The second phase brought the consolidation of the administrative organizational forms and methods which would assure the economic progress required to sustain socialization. And the third phase is that of passing to what the Titoists call the superior socialist stage of producer-owner relationships wherein workers' self-management is achieved. The Workers' Council Law is meant to symbolize this third stage. To the Titoists this law is the beginning of the realization of one of the fundamental principles of communism as expressed by Marx—the management of the means of production by the workers themselves.

The basic ideological principle of the system of workers' self-management is expressed as follows in Article 1 of the Workers' Council Law: "The factories, mines, transport, commercial, agricultural, forestry, communal, and other state economic enterprises, as the common property of the whole nation, are administered in the name of the social

---

[4] For example, in the summer of 1952, the government admitted that there were some 3,500 economic decrees, orders, regulations, and instructions still in force, many of them contradictory. (*Borba*, July 17, 1952, as quoted by Alex Dragnich, *Tito's Promised Land* [New Brunswick, 1954], pp. 224-25.)

community by the working staffs within the framework of the state economic plan and on the basis of the rights and duties established by the law or by other legal prescription. Each working collective realizes this management through a workers' council and management board in each enterprise." [5]

According to the law, the workers' council of each enterprise is elected for a one year term by all of the workers and employees of the enterprise by means of general, equal, and direct suffrage expressed in a secret ballot. Each council consists of from 15 to 120 members, depending upon the size of the enterprise; in enterprises employing less than thirty persons, the entire staff constitutes the council. The list of candidates for election is drawn up by the trade union branch of the enterprise, but alternate lists may be submitted by a definite number of workers and employees.[6] Once elected the council chooses a chairman from amongst its members; this chairman is not eligible for a position on the management board. Meetings of the council must be held at least once every six weeks; there is no other limitation upon the number of times it may meet. The chairman must call a meeting of the council upon the request of the management board, of the trade union branch, of the director of the enterprise, or of one third of the council membership. Meetings of the council are attended by the management board

[5] For one of the better detailed discussions of the Workers' Council Law and its intentions, as well as a short review of the Titoist system of economic management prior to the installation of the law, see Jovan Djordjević, "Essential Characteristics of the New System of Managing State Economic Enterprises and Higher Economic Associations," *NYL*, I:2-3 (1950), pp. 13-28.

[6] Article 13 of the law states: "In enterprises of up to 500 workers and employees a list of candidates may be put up by one-tenth of the workers and employees who have the right to vote, on condition that the number of signers is not less than five. In enterprises which have more than 500 workers and employees, a list of candidates may be put up by a number of workers and employees equal to the number of members of the workers' council to be elected. Among the signers there must be equal representation of the various sections or units of the enterprise."

and the director. Every member of the council has the right to put questions to the management board and to the director, who are theoretically obliged to answer all such questions to the best of their ability. The council's decisions are taken by majority vote of the members present, and are binding only if over half of the council's membership are present.

The rights and duties of the workers' council as listed by the law make it responsible for supervising the over-all management and operation of the enterprise and for approving the periodical accounts and production plans. Originally the law gave the council the right to dispose of that portion of the excess profits left to the enterprise at the end of a fiscal year. This privilege was considerably curbed after 1953 when many workers' councils, left to their own devices, distributed excess profits more according to the needs of the worker than to those of the community.

The workers' council elects and recalls the members of the management board. The board can consist of from three to eleven members, depending upon the size of the enterprise. Its members are chosen from amongst the workers, the technical staff, and other employees. They do not necessarily have to be members of the workers' council. In order to make certain that the technical and administrative staffs are not in a position to monopolize the work of the board, at least three-quarters of the board's membership must be workers directly engaged in production. As a further guarantee against the possible growth of a permanent management bureaucracy, only one-third of the board members are permitted to succeed themselves and then for no more than two successive terms. The director of the enterprise is an ex officio member of the board, but he may not be its chairman. The board reaches its decisions only at meetings called by its chairman. Its decisions are taken by majority vote of the members present. A dissenting member may communicate his objections to the workers' council.

The rights and duties of the management board as they

are defined in the Workers' Council Law make the board responsible for the day-to-day management of the enterprise. In general, the board is subject to the supervision of the workers' council and is required to carry out all suggestions voted upon by the council.

Members of both the workers' council and the management board are expected to continue their regular jobs while serving on the council or the board. They are not to receive additional remuneration for their services. However, the duties of the management board are extensive and often time-consuming; therefore members are entitled to indemnification to the extent of the earnings they might lose while occupied with the business of the board.

The 1950 law provided that the director of each enterprise be appointed by the higher economic association or by the competent government administrative organs.[7] The workers' council or the management board may propose the removal of a director. According to the law, the director is the executive officer empowered by the state to act within the enterprise. He is responsible to the management board and to pertinent government administrative organs. He is held responsible for the realization of the state economic plans insofar as they concern his enterprise. He is directly responsible for the legality of the actions of the management board and the workers' council. He concludes all of the concern's business agreements and legal transactions. Workers and employees are responsible to him for their work, and he is in turn responsible for the discipline of the enterprise.

[7] By 1954, directors were appointed by a commission composed of representatives of the workers' council and representatives of interested professional associations appointed by the people's committee or, in the case of larger enterprises, appointed by republican or federal organs. But this method has not proved entirely satisfactory since it often happens that workers' council and local government representatives reached compromises which paid too little attention to the capabilities of the individual chosen. By 1956, official circles were searching for a formula which would permit the use of competitive examinations to be given by a committee composed of representatives of the workers' council, the people's committee, the professional associations, and the trade union branch.

As the leader and organizer of labor within the enterprise, the director exercises extensive rights in the employment and discharge of personnel, and he decides upon the placement and promotion of most of the workers and employees. However, workers and employees have the right to appeal to the management board for a final decision in cases of dismissal and of questionable work orders coming from the director. He is responsible for placing into effect the decisions of the management board. Should the board reach a decision which appears contrary to the law, the director can suspend action and present the matter to the local people's committee or to a competent government agency. He may not, however, take upon himself the duties of the management board, except in instances where it is not practical to wait until the board can be consulted. In such cases, the director may take the necessary action on his own initiative, but he must inform the management board of his action at its next meeting.

The Workers' Council Law also contained a section devoted to the organization, rights, and duties of the so-called higher economic associations. These were originally envisaged as pyramids of worker self-managed associations within each branch of industry beginning at the lowest individual enterprise level and working up to the federal level. In most instances, these higher associations were never formed, however. The constant changes in the administrative structure and the enormous difficulties encountered in trying to find a satisfactory method of seeing that both large and small enterprises were properly represented in the association hierarchies caused the plan to be abandoned almost before it was begun. In some respects, a vestige of the higher economic associations was maintained in the more easily organized industrial branches. But, until 1954, these voluntary associations had no official responsibilities other than those specific incidental tasks government officials may have assigned them. Since 1954, however, a new importance has been given to the ladders of vertically linked self-managed industrial and trade associations.[8] They are now the primary means used by the regime in its efforts to establish more efficient lines of communications between the central authority and the individual enterprises in order to bring greater unity to the economic system and to counteract the many incidents of selfish "localism" springing from the greater independence fostered by decentralization.

It was not until well into 1951 that effective moves were made to turn all enterprises over to the workers. Even then, the development of the new system as formulated by the Workers' Council Law was a slow process. Regulatory measures were constantly required both to implement and to improve the system and to keep it from seizing the initiative and bolting the Titoist economy much further down the road to freedom than the Yugoslav leaders could safely permit. The reluctance of the Party organization within each enterprise to relinquish its management privileges was unquestionably one important cause for the delay in implementing the system of workers' self-management. However, at the Sixth Party Congress, held in November 1952, the Party rank and file were given their orders to change their tactics from intimidation to persuasion. As Party members were made aware of the meaning of these orders they began to interfere less in their authoritative capacity in the management of economic enterprises. Today it is not unusual to find that Party members constitute only a minority of the membership of workers' councils and management boards.[9] On the other hand, in almost every instance, the director, the chairman of the workers' council, and the officials of the trade union branch within all enterprises are Party members.

The transition from direct control of the economy by the central government to the indirect methods envisaged by

[8] The status and role of these voluntary associations will be discussed in detail in Chapter X.

[9] For example, in one of the larger factories the author visited in spring of 1955, of the fifty-one members of the workers' council only one-third were Party members, and of the eight members of the management board none were Communists except the director.

the workers' self-management system was more or less successfully completed by the spring of 1954.[10] By the end of that year over 600,000 workers and employees had participated in the basic self-management agencies of economic and administrative organizations.[11] The 1954 elections for workers' councils followed the regular procedure of choosing candidates from lists drawn up by the trade union branches, but the prerogative of groups of workers to submit non-union-sponsored lists had been exercised in 281 cases. Of the 111,734 individuals elected to councils in industries of thirty or more in personnel, 3,234 had been proposed from non-union lists. There were 4,378 enterprises employing from seven to thirty persons (in each of these the entire collective is considered to be the workers' council) and when these are added to the number of council members elected in the larger enterprises, the total workers' council membership in 1954 came to 185,829. These figures do not include: enterprises employing less than seven persons, the defense industries, or the postal, telegraph, telephone, and railway system. The self-management principle had been extended in 1954 to include this last-named group, but pertinent statistics were not available when those quoted above were compiled. It was later estimated that by the end of 1954 one out of every seven persons employed by self-managing organiza-

[10] See Jovan Djordjević, "Four Years of Workers' Self-Management in Yugoslavia," *RTA*, V (July 1, 1954), p. 13.

[11] The statistics used in this paragraph are taken from *Report of the Federal Executive Council for 1954*, Joint Translation Service (an agency of the American and British Embassies in Belgrade) Supplement, April 25, 1955, pp. 2-3.

Workers' council elections were suspended in 1955. The practicality of the one-year tenure of the council was being examined throughout 1955 by the federal authorities. Often the single-year term meant that management efficiency was lost in that it took several months to train new council members. Elections for one-year terms were once again held in 1956. However, the federal authorities were still looking for a method of avoiding the loss of efficiency from yearly changeovers without diluting the system's primary aim to permit as many workers as possible an opportunity to take part in the mangement of their enterprise. The most practical and popular solution suggested so far is that the council term be extended to two years but that half of its members be elected each year.

tions was directly included in the management agencies of his enterprise.[12]

By 1954, the Yugoslav Communists looked upon workers' self-management as a basic characteristic of their country's social development, and, in one form or another, as the indispensable element of social democracy. There is no doubt that the Workers' Council Law of 1950 ushered in a new period of socialist development not only for Yugoslavia but for all interested groups throughout the world who consider the careful adjustment of existing worker-management problems to be vital to progress. To liberal Marxists particularly, the Yugoslav experiment adds valuable experience to the practice of Marxism and gives new validity to the slogan "the factories to the workers." Socialists like the British Fabians look to the Yugoslav experiment to produce clues as to what should be their own future theoretical development.

There is likewise no doubt whatsoever that the Titoists' system of workers' self-management has had a certain amount of real success in Yugoslavia.[13] The power of the agencies of workers' self-management in Yugoslav economic enterprises is genuine, if limited. The system has helped to bring about an upsurge of productivity and worker morale by bringing about a more rational organization of work in

[12] In a speech delivered March 24, 1956, Kardelj said that the 1954 workers' council elections had been held in 10,350 enterprises whose staffs included 1,308,533 workers and employees. These had elected 201,296 workers and employees to their workers' councils. ("Our State Administration under the New Conditions," *NYL*, VII: 2 [April-June 1956], p. 5.)

[13] This conclusion is generally admitted by most foreign observers. See for example:

H. Tennyson, "Marx in Illyria," *New Statesman* (Nov. 28, 1953), p. 666.
New York Times, Jan. 5, 1954, p. 74.
G. E. R. Geyde, "Djilas Case," *Contemporary Review* (March 1954), p. 135.
Kathleen Stahl, "Too Much New Industry," *Manchester Guardian*, Jan. 17, 1955, p. 6.

The author's own opinion results from visits paid in 1955 to factories in Belgrade, Zagreb, and along the Dalmatian coast, as well as from conversations with friends and acquaintances employed in industrial and other self-managed enterprises—some of these friends and acquaintances were Titoists and others decidedly not.

the enterprise.[14] Workers' councils have been responsible for rooting out inefficiency and have often been known to dismiss state-appointed directors and other unworthy members of the administrative staff.

But it would be quite erroneous to accept at 100 per cent of face value all of the Titoists' glowing reports of the successes of their workers' self-management system. All too few Yugoslav workers are sufficiently endowed either by capacity or by experience to fulfill the role the system theoretically calls upon them to play. A constantly increasing proportion of the labor force is made up of peasants whose environmental and hereditary backgrounds leave them ill-equipped to deal with the full meaning and spirit of the new system.[15]

---

[14] See Vukmanović-Tempo's report to the National Assembly on the characteristic features of economic development in 1954 and the economic policy for 1955, *Borba*, Dec. 28, 1954, p. 1.

Analyses of statistics on the social product and national income are given in Section VI of *Statistički Godišnjak FRNJ 1955* (Belgrade: July 1955), pp. 101-7.

The Statistical Pocket-Book of Yugoslavia 1955 (Belgrade: July 1955), p. 47, gives the following index figures for industrial production (1939 = 100):

1947—121	
1951—166	(These figures do not include the output
1952—164	of purely defense industries.)
1953—183	
1954—208	
1955—240	

Note: The completion of many key industrial and power projects in 1954 undoubtedly accounts for much of the 1954 rise. Nevertheless, some of the the credit is also due to the workers' self-management system which began to function more or less normally by the end of 1952.

The Federal Social Plan for 1956 claimed that total industrial production for 1955 represented an increase of 16 per cent over 1954. (See *Supplement to Joint Translation Bulletin No. 1824*, Joint-Translation Service, [Belgrade], p. 2.)

The Federal Social Plan for 1957 states that total industrial production for 1956 represents an increase of 10 per cent over 1955. (See *Supplement to Joint Translation Bulletin* [Belgrade: Jan. 25, 1957], p. 1.)

[15] By 1953, Yugoslavia's agricultural population had been reduced from approximately 66 per cent of the total in 1945 to approximately 61 per cent. Almost all of this decline represents a shift to industry. It is estimated that between the years 1945-50 the urban population of Yugoslavia had increased by two millions (See Ruth Trouton, *Peasant Renaissance in Yugoslavia 1900-1950* [London: 1952], p. 218). During the author's 1955 visit

Ignorant and inexperienced workers are often elected to positions of relative authority in their enterprises. This is at least partially responsible for the tremendous waste and inefficiency existing in Yugoslav industry. It is also partially responsible for the unusually large amount of *economic* crime. The power which the workers' self-management system places in the hands of many untrained and incapable workers, when combined with the feeling the system has unwittingly fostered that the enterprise is now the property of the workers themselves, often makes it difficult for them to resist temptation. Yugoslav newspapers are constantly reporting cases of skulduggery and theft. The latter crime reached such proportions that, in April 1955, a Slovenian court issued the death sentence to a railway worker who had stolen over four million dinars' (then approximately $13,500) worth of material from his workshop.[16]

The success or failure of the system of workers' self-management in individual enterprises—and of the enterprise itself—depends to a large extent upon the skill of its director. A good director is able to make the system work efficiently in his enterprise through the strength of his diplomatic tact. If he is sufficiently endowed with this talent and is able to gain the respect of the personnel of his organization, he has no trouble in adhering to the letter of the self-management laws and regulations and in keeping the hydra-headed apparatus of authority from working at cross-purposes with what he considers to be the best interests of the enterprise. But all enterprises do not have directors able to perform such a delicate mission of leadership. Nor do all of them have tractable management boards or workers' councils. This is obvious from remarks made in the spring of 1955 by one of the most competent Titoist improvisers, in which he pointed out that a major problem of workers' self-management is to find ways

to Yugoslavia, he was told by a local demographic expert that approximately 25 per cent of the individual working force in 1955 were part-time peasant employees.

[16] *Borba*, April 19, 1955.

and means to improve the relationships between the workers' councils and management.[17]

The need for highly qualified directors is great. At the same time, the Party often has grave doubts about entrusting economic enterprises, particularly large undertakings, to the direction of non-Party members. Some of these doubts unquestionably arise from the fact that many lesser Party members see in such a policy the withering away of their privileged positions in the face of their own comparative incompetence.[18] Nevertheless, the trend today is away from considering Party membership as an absolutely indispensable qualification for the directorship of an economic enterprise. This in turn is a reflection of the fact that the Titoist leaders, in their efforts to bring greater efficiency to their system, have consciously caused a certain withering away of the influence of the Party as such.[19]

Incompetence and crime within the self-managed economy are partly responsible for the federal government's cautious "re-centralization" activities begun in 1954.[20] Re-centralization in this instance does not, however, mean a lessening of the principle of workers' self-management. Rather, it means recognition of some of the basic facts of life which come hard to the average Marxist. The experience of the past few years of workers' self-management has taught the Titoist leaders that the average Yugoslav worker needs much more "cultural advancement" before he will be able to fill the ideological role which their theory has in mind for him. Steps

[17] See *ibid.*, April 28, 1955, p. 1.
[18] Several Party members discussed these doubts with the author in 1955. They admitted that they were on the horns of dilemma since they knew that success in the economy depended upon getting the most capable men into leadership positions within the economy, and that most such men were not Party members and were seldom likely to join the Party. These informants felt that if these capable individuals did join the Party, their influence therein would probably challenge and diminish the importance of most of the existing lower-ranking Party leaders. Furthermore, these informants expressed a general feeling of insecurity in entrusting the economy to persons who did not swear by the "objective truths" of Marxism-Leninism.
[19] See Chapter XII.
[20] See Chapter X.

are being taken to see that the education period does not continue to pile up costs beyond the ability of the Yugoslav economy to pay. In other words, the Titoists have now come to realize that more efficient supervision from above might be able to eliminate many of the endemic weaknesses of the workers' self-management system and thereby bring more efficiency not only to the development of the system itself but to the economy as well.

It should not be concluded from these critical remarks that the workers' self-management system in Yugoslavia is even a passive failure. Such a conclusion would be far from the truth. The system represents the dynamic framework of a policy which can yet develop into the establishment of Titoism as a successful new form of socialist government. Especially when compared with the Stalinist-type organization of the Yugoslav economy prior to 1951, the workers' self-management system represents an almost immeasurable improvement. That the system has raised worker morale and the quantity and quality of production is proof of at least its partial success. Furthermore, it furnishes the best possible training school for those workers who have the urge to acquaint themselves with all aspects of industrial management and development. Hence, it might eventually produce a sizeable new class of industrially-minded workers in Yugoslavia who in turn would be in a position to do much for the economic advancement of their country.

The system of workers' self-management will remain the touchstone of Titoism. If it continues to be strengthened in practice, it is more than likely that it will represent an increasingly potent challenge to worker-management relationships in all types of economies.

PLANNING, BUDGETING, AND TAXATION

If workers' self-management and the new respect for the laws of supply and demand were to have practical meaning, the Titoists' highly centralized system of planning had to

be modified. The Yugoslav Five Year Plan, inaugurated in
1947, had served as the controlling blue-print for the entire
Titoist economy. Despite the Plan's inherent lack of realism
and the setbacks it had received from the Cominform's economic blockade and from the droughts of 1945, 1946 and
1950, the Titoists were grimly determined to complete as
many as possible of its original goals, particularly those concerned with the development of heavy industry. For this
reason, in the latter part of 1950, it was decided to extend the
Plan to the end of 1952 and thereafter to have no further such
plans. In the meantime, in December 1951, three new laws
were passed to prepare for the eventual decentralization of
the planning system. These laws were: the Law on the
Management of the National Economy, the Law on Budgets,
and the Basic Law on Social Contributions and Taxes.[21] They
furnished the framework for the Titoist planning, budgetary,
and taxation systems as they exist today.

The Law on the National Economy provided that the
national economy shall be managed on the basis of: the
federal social plan, the individual social plans of the republican, district, and local governments, and the independent
production plans drawn up by each enterprise. According
to the law, the federal plan is to confine itself to only the
most "basic proportions." The plans of the lower governmental administrative organs are to be somewhat more
specific, wherever practical leaving the most detailed planning to the lowest possible administrative organ or to the
enterprises themselves. Within the restrictions of the basic
proportions fixed by the social plans, the economic enterprises are to plan and to conduct their business independently in conformance with the rights and duties determined
by laws and other legal prescriptions.

The 1951 planning law defined "basic proportions" as
those required to determine the direction and development

[21] For texts of the first two of these laws, see *SL* No. 58, 1951. For text
of the third, see *ibid.*, No. 1, 1952. For a translation of all three texts, see
Collected Yugoslav Laws, No. 3 (Belgrade: Union of Jurists' Associations of
Yugoslavia, 1952), pp. 36-59.

of material productive forces and to effect the basic distribution of national revenue to consumer funds (mainly salary and bonus funds), to capital construction, and to other general requirements of the social community. The law lists as follows the basic proportions to be dealt with by the yearly federal social plan: First, the fixing of the general obligatory production minimum in the different branches of the economy; these figures are fixed for each branch, broken down by republics. As it has developed in practice, the yearly federal social plans have called for basic production minima which are slightly below the actual minimum production capacities of the different branches of the economy. The second basic proportion is the fixing of the amount of obligatory capital expenditure considered necessary for the development of the country's material productive forces as a whole. Provisions for all other capital construction are left to the republican, district, local, and enterprise plans. The third basic proportion determines the basic wages to be paid by each branch of the economy, broken down by republics. This basic proportion was modified by a new wage law enacted in December, 1954. The fourth basic proportion fixes the average taxation and contribution rates to be paid by all production, transport, and trade enterprises into the "social funds," viz. the amortization fund, the social security fund, the wage fund, and so on. This basic proportion is the real economic and social core of the entire federal social plan in that it determines the surplus of production which should be realized by the different branches of production, transport, and trade. It consequently determines not only the basic distribution of the national income but the country's basic economic policy as well. The fifth and last basic proportion mentioned in the 1951 law is closely related to the fourth. It establishes the average rates which are to be assessed in the form of contributions or taxes to be paid into the various government administrative funds. This basic proportion determines what part of profits are to be at the disposal of society as a whole through the state apparatus and what part is to remain at the direct disposal of the workers' collectives themselves.

All of the social plans drawn up at the different levels of government are yearly plans. Legally the draft plans are the independent responsibility of the elected representative bodies at the level at which they are drawn up. All of the yearly plans are co-ordinated during the drafting process. Under the method presently in use, the drafting process generally begins in the individual enterprises and works up through the local, district, and republican levels to the federal level, and then works back down again once the federal social plan is officially adopted. Co-ordination of the federal and the six republican social plans is the responsibility of the Federal Institute of Economic Planning.

In the general reorganization of the federal administrative apparatus which took place at the beginning of 1953, the Federal Planning Commission (one of the most powerful federal agencies until its functions were curtailed by the administrative reforms of 1951 and 1952) was disbanded and the less authoritative Federal Institute for Economic Planning created in its place. The Institute is composed mainly of experts. Its directorate is made up of three federal officials and the heads of the planning commissions of the six constituent republics. It is directly responsible for advising and co-ordinating the work of the republican commissions. In 1954, it was given the additional task of following the day-to-day progress of the total economy and drafting periodical surveys and special analyses for the Federal Executive Council (the highest executive organ of the federal government).

If the workers' self-management system and the new planning system were to succeed in reducing the federal government's direct role in the economy, supplementary reforms in the financial system were required as well. These changes were brought about by the Law on Budgets and the Law on Social Contributions and Taxation enacted in December 1951 at the same time as the new planning law. In accordance with the aims of the new economic decentralization policy, these first two laws attempted to draw a fundamental distinction between funds at the disposal of state organs and those at the disposal of the economy, or between state-owned property and that supposedly belonging to the people. Only state-owned property was now to be controlled through the federal budget; all relationships between state-owned and socially owned property were now to be precisely regulated by laws on taxation, contributions, and subsidies. Here the Titoists were attempting to create conditions in which the socialist forms of property under workers' self-management could continue to develop as freely as possible, and in which more and more state property could be easily transformed into social property. The Yugoslav leaders look upon this transfer as one of the key methods of defeating bureaucratic tendencies in economic life and in worker-management relationships.

In the Titoist system up to 1952, all state and local requirements were financed through the federal budget. The budget, in its role of a single, central treasury, accumulated all the country's financial means and attempted to distribute them according to requirements. It was a general state budget which included the budgets of the lower administrative units. After 1951, the new federal social plan was to be the instrument which would insure economic unity and integrate the entire economy into an economic whole. The reform law of December 1951 abolished the general state budget and provided that each representative body, from the National Assembly down to the local people's committees, would henceforth adopt its own budget independently and on the basis of its own estimates of revenues and expenditures. The law also provided that each of the different levels of political-administrative organs was to be allowed to allocate independently, through its own social plans, all of the revenues granted to it by law.

The Law on Social Contributions and Taxation attempts to differentiate between the various sources of private and corporate—or "social"—profit as well as between the methods of assessing these profits. According to the law, all enterprises pay a contribution to the social community at an equal rate calculated according to the payroll of each enterprise. Thus, every enterprise and its workers' collective is obligated to the social community in equal proportion to its payroll. But some branches of economic activity are more favored than others, either by nature or by state aid, and are thereby able to extend their payrolls over and beyond a planned limit. A supplemental social contribution at a sliding rate is levied upon such enterprises on the ground that they have a correspondingly greater debt to the social community.

The Law on Social Contributions and Taxation designated the turnover tax as the principal instrument for governing and regulating market relationships and for manipulating the distribution of the national income. This tax was found to be incompatible with the new economic system and was abandoned entirely in 1953. At that time it was replaced by instruments more in keeping with a market-type economy such as interest on fixed and circulating capital, a tax on natural wealth, and a tax on profits. However, by 1955 it was decided that these indirect methods were unable to control inflation and the growing "bourgeois tendencies" of certain enterprises to take advantage of the free market. The turnover tax was therefore revived as the primary instrument of taxation, although it was now to serve along with certain indirect market-type control procedures.

The law of 1951 provided that income taxes were to be paid by private farmers, artisans, private professional men, and private property owners deriving income from their property. No such tax is collected on income derived from service as an employee. The law also provided for inheritance and gift taxes, the rates of which are to be determined progressively according to the value of the inheritance or gift and according to the degree of relationship between the taxpayer and testator or donor and according to the economic status of the taxpayer. It also made provisions for surtaxes which might under special conditions be levied by local people's committees for meeting local needs or requirements.

According to the law, the assessment and levying of taxes is, in the main, to be carried out by the financial organs of the district and local people's committees. However, in practice, the district and republican governments assume the primary responsibility and merely hand down most of the assessments to the local committees for collection. The federal social plan, it will be recalled, fixes only the *average*, or minimum-maximum, rates of contribution and taxes for the entire country. Therefore, these rates can, and do, differ from one local area to the next depending mainly upon the degree of wealth or poverty of each area. A kind of national uniformity is maintained by the supervisory responsibilities given by the planning and taxation laws to federal and republican fiscal agencies.

WAGES

The relative freedom of the economy envisaged by the workers' self-management system required at least a token decentralization of control over wages. Prior to December 1952, all wages had been fixed administratively by the central government. The Law on the Planned Management of the Economy enacted at that time prescribed the fixing of only a general wage fund for each branch of industry. To implement this requirement a new wage system was evolved which at first seemed to be more in keeping with the spirit of decentralization. In practice, however, it proved unsatisfactory and was replaced in December 1954.

Like all other decentralization reforms, the 1952 wage system attempted a compromise between freedom of action to encourage individual incentive and centralized control to assure continued socialization. Workers' wages were divided into two fundamental parts: the "constant" wage and the "variable" wage. The constant wage contained both an element of control and an element of free incentive. It consisted of both a "basic" wage fixed by law and a "supplemental" bonus-type wage regularly paid for extra or unusual services. The "variable" portion of wages was created purely as an incentive to the worker to interest himself in the overall success of his enterprise. Variable wages were to consist of the worker's share in the profits of his enterprise once it had met all its obligations. Thus, under the 1952 wage system a worker's total wages were to depend upon three factors: his qualifications entitling him to a fixed rate of basic wages, his own output, and the over-all success of his enterprise.

The 1952 wage system had the federal government guarantee payment of 80 per cent of the basic wage if the enterprise was unable to meet its basic wage obligations. The federal government also fixed the limits within which the supplemental wage might fluctuate. The republican or local social plans fixed the total amount each enterprise was to use as its wage fund. This fund could be disbursed in any manner the workers' collective of each enterprise saw fit except that no worker or employee could receive less than the minimum fixed by the federal government for his category of work.[22] The enterprise was free to form its own variable wage fund from its surplus profits.

In 1953, the workers' councils of many successful enterprises ordered the payment of variable wages to their workers and employees. Extra wage payments in the Belgrade area that year were equivalent to from one to four months' salary. Since 1953, however, variable wages have

[22] The 1952 wage decree divided workers into highly skilled, skilled, and semiskilled categories. There was no "unskilled" classification. Such a distinction was still considered to be unsocialist. Employees were broken down into the following classifications:

Jobs requiring higher professional qualifications
  "   "   intermediate   "   "
  "   "   lower   "   "
Auxiliary jobs.

The text of this decree is given in SL No. 11, 1952. A résumé of the text is given in NYL, III:1-2 (1952), pp. 47-48.

in most cases been conspicuous by their absence, or, if granted at all, have been merely token payments. The regime had never intended variable wages to attain the proportions reached in 1953. It rightly feared inflation, and preferred to see most extra profits used for planned industrial improvement and expansion or for community projects. Therefore, in 1954, the major responsibility for disposal of surplus profits in the form of variable wages was shifted from the workers' councils to the local political-administrative authorities, the people's committees. The workers' council remains technically responsible for the disposal of surplus profits, but it must now obtain the permission of the people's committee before it can take action. The source of temptation was weakened when early in 1954 the government ordered enterprises to lend it 50 per cent of their unused surplus profits. The government claimed it had no other way to obtain the funds it required for the liberalized investment credit system then being inaugurated. In 1955, an excess profits tax was established to permit the central government to maintain constant control over the surplus profits of economic enterprises.

In December 1954, the Federal Executive Council issued a decree reorganizing the wage system. The 1952 reform had failed to meet expectations in stimulating labor productivity, and it was now admitted that one of its principal objectives had been to assure an equilibrium between commodity supply and monetary circulation. But in practice the system had proved entirely too inflexible and hence had acted to retard initiative, particularly after the government had clamped down on the liberal distribution of variable wages.

The 1954 decree makes wages depend more upon each enterprise's earning capacity. It decentralized control of wages so that these are now fixed almost entirely by the enterprise in conjunction with the local people's committee. Each enterprise draws up its own wage scales according to units of working time. Wherever possible work norms are established. The system of work norms was a typical Com-

munist appurtenance which had been largely dropped in
Yugoslavia after 1952. Draft wage scales drawn up by the
management board of each enterprise are submitted to the
entire collective of the enterprise for discussion and approval. They are then submitted for final approval to a commission composed of representatives of the workers' council, the local people's committee, and the trade union branch
involved.[23] Work norms are fixed by the director and professional staff of each enterprise with the approval of the
workers' council. The people's committee is not permitted to
interfere with the fixing of work norms.

The new system legally places the major responsibility for
wages upon the local people's committee. Besides taking
part in fixing the actual wage scales, it is allowed to fix the
limits on premiums and allowances paid by the enterprise
to workers who are exceptionally efficient, or who distinguish
themselves in their work. It determines what proportion of
the enterprise's income is to make up the wage fund, and
since, in the main, the committee decides upon the disposition of surplus profits, it also controls the payment of variable wages. Its role in assessing and levying taxes and its

[23] The following are the wage scales fixed in a boiler factory in Zagreb
(May 1955); they differed only slightly from the scales of similar factories
the author visited in Serbia:

(300 dinars = $1.00 at the official rate of exchange)

Workers

Highly skilled	—50 to 75 dinars an hour
Qualified	—35 to 55 " " "
Semiskilled	—35 to 45 " " "
Unskilled	—32 to 38 " " "

Employees (According to educational qualifications)

1.	—13,500 to 28,000 dinars a month
2.	— 7,000 to 15,000 " " "
3.	— 6,500 to 10,000 " " "
4.	— 6,500 to 8,000 " " "

These are *basic* wages. To them are added supplemental wages paid for
outstanding efficiency, extra output, prizes for cutting down losses in
production, and other such bonuses.

50 per cent of the basic wage is paid as overtime to workers permitted to
work on weekdays more than the regulation eight hours; they are permitted
to work no more than four hours overtime a day. 100 per cent overtime
is paid for Sunday work.

right to levy special taxes gives the people's committee still another indirect control over workers' income. However, the people's committee also has a responsibility toward the workers in that it must guarantee payment of 60 per cent of each basic wage fund in the event that the enterprise itself is unable to meet its basic wage obligations.

The 1954 wage decree established permanent district, republican, and federal wage commissions in which representatives of the people's committees and the trade unions serve along with administration officials. These commissions supervise the continuous functioning of the wage and work norm systems and make suggestions for their improvement. It is through these permanent commissions, and through the trade unions which are also organized on a national scale, that a kind of national uniformity of wage rates and work norms is maintained.

The Titoists feel that their 1954 wage system should inspire workers to increase their productivity since they are to be paid according to the results of their work. Furthermore, workers are expected to exhibit greater interest in the success of their enterprise because they are to participate in its income either directly through drawing fixed and additional wages from this income, or indirectly when this income is used for increasing productivity, the erection of suitable living quarters, for health institutions and schools, and for other such purposes aimed at raising the standard of living of their local communities.

In March 1955, the chairman of the Federal Wages Commission pointed out two of the outstanding flaws in the 1952 wage system which the 1954 reform was expected to correct.[24] He remarked that the new wage-scale system sought to foster greater differences between skilled and unskilled wage rates and thereby to encourage workers to strive to become skilled. In all previous wage systems these differences had been insignificant and there had been little

---

[24] See the interview with Nikola Mincev, chairman of the Federal Wages Commission, *Borba*, March 24, 1955, p. 1.

incentive to qualify as a skilled worker. In fact, in the early years of the Titoist revolution it was frequently considered "anti-socialist" to permit too great a gap between the salaries of skilled and unskilled workers. Although the 1956 Federal Social Plan prescribed that wage scales for that year were to be the same as those extant in 1955, the plan also promised that methods would be sought to bring greater flexibility to the wage system. The chairman of the Federal Wages Commission was also highly critical of the numerous people's committees that had been extremely niggardly in distributing excess profits to the workers, and had thus devitalized an important incentive to increased productivity.

Considering the official source of these criticisms, it can be assumed that the Titoists are at least aware of the fact that increased productivity is more directly connected with the worker's desire for personal rewards than with his devotion to his community. This awareness can only mean that in the future the worker in successful Yugoslav enterprises is to be given more of the fruits of his labor in the form of fatter pay envelopes. However, the realities of the current economic situation in Yugoslavia would seem to indicate that, until inflationary tendencies and other major illnesses of the Yugoslav economy are cured, the workers' share in excess profits, despite the Titoists' new awareness of the real source of individual incentive, will be maintained at more or less a token level.

PRICES

Late in 1951, a high Yugoslav Communist official described the role the Titoist planners assigned to the market in their decentralized economic system. The role of the market in Titoist social democracy, he said, is not to be an "anarchistic one as in capitalism" since the operation of the economic laws of supply and demand within the Yugoslav market are to be restricted by such means as the basic proportions of the social plan, the system of contributions and taxation, and the wage system. He spoke of the market as a "planned market" in which the prices of those basic raw materials and "those key products which cannot be allowed full freedom chiefly because we cannot import them in sufficient quantities" would have to be determined by the federal government, but in which finished goods would in the main be allowed to seek their own price levels.[25] As the system has developed in practice, the government has controlled the distribution of those raw materials and semifinished goods the supplies of which are insufficient to meet demand. All other products have, more or less, been allowed to seek their own price levels in the open market, with the government exercising the right to create specific price controls whenever it may consider them necessary.

In preparation for the return to a market-type economy, the rationing of consumer goods was completely abandoned at the end of 1951. Forcible delivery of quotas or agricultural produce by the peasants was also stopped. Currency devaluation, an essential move in creating greater freedom in both the domestic and foreign markets, was carried out in 1952. Before devaluation there had been two levels of internal prices, an extremely low rate for goods purchased with ration tickets and an extremely high rate for those goods which might be found in the open market.

By the end of 1954, there had been a considerable rise in prices of food and other consumer items.[26] These continued to rise until the very end of 1955 when they reportedly began

[25] Milentije Popović, "Concerning the Law on Budgets and the Basic Law on Social Contributions and Taxation," *NYL*, III:1-2 (1952), p. 35.

[26] The retail price index (1953 = 100) for industrial products had risen from 91 for 1952 to 102 for December 1954; for agricultural products it had risen from 79 for 1952 to 104 for December 1954. (*Statistical Pocket-Book of Yugoslavia 1955* [Belgrade: April 1955], p. 80.) For a complete breakdown of retail price indices, see Table 20-6 *Statistički Godišnjak FRNJ 1956* (Belgrade: July 1956), p. 266.

The *Federal Social Plan of 1956* (*op. cit.*, p. 4) states that wholesale prices of industrial and agricultural products rose 6 per cent between December 1954 and December 1955. Retail prices during the same period rose by 10 per cent.

to level off.[27] Price rises were often the natural consequence of the regime's policy of creating monopolies. To assist the building of basic industries, these monopolies were protected from foreign as well as domestic competition. But much of the blame could also be traced to the latent "bourgeois tendencies" which easily manifested themselves in the freer atmosphere created by the decentralized economy. As *Borba* described the situation, an unsocialist "business spirit" or "speculation" often caused certain monopolistic enterprises, especially trading concerns, to take advantage of their position and of the freer market to create surplus profits not by increasing productivity or by greater turnover but by fixing higher prices.[28]

In March 1955, it was announced that a Price Control Bureau was to be established for the purpose of studying price and tariff problems and fixing prices for certain key products. It was admitted that, even though the system of workers' self-management had prospered precisely because there had been relatively few administrative controls of the free market since 1952, "price control, as an independent form of administrative interference, is fully justified when the disturbances in the economy are due to subjective factors." [29] Two of these "subjective factors" were listed as the "insufficient sensitivity of enterprises to shifts in prices of production and investment materials," and the tendency of enterprises to realize too high a profit.

"We must organize a trade which will know how to satisfy freely the needs of the market but which, however, will not work for profit, but will function as a specific social service," Kardelj had proclaimed at the end of 1953.[30] The realization of such a dream world must have seemed extremely remote to Kardelj by mid-1955. No matter where the blame for rising prices might justifiably lie, one thing was clear: it was

[27] See p. 5, *The Federal Social Plan for 1956, ibid.*, p. 5.
[28] Quoted in the *New York Times*, Oct. 17, 1954, p. 3.
[29] *Ekonomska Politika* (Belgrade), March 10, 1955.
[30] Kardelj, "Le Rôle du Citoyen dans Notre Système," *QAS*, No. 22 (Jan.-Feb. 1954), p. 115.

obvious that the Titoists had counted upon their market to have a higher "level of socialist consciousness" than it actually had. By the end of 1955, the Titoists had awakened to the fact that their social plans and their fiscal and other administrative measures of control as they then existed were insufficient to insure the working balance originally envisaged as possible between centralized control and the free market. More control was required to make certain that the free market did not run away with the entire system. The extension of price controls was one method used to curb inflation and misuse of the market. But the creation of a series of vertical ladders of so-called self-managed industrial and trade associations was the major tactic to which the Titoists turned.[31]

CREDIT AND BANKING

Centralized administrative control was maintained longest in the fields of investment and banking, mainly because the over-ambitious capital development program had absorbed most of the available investment funds. Since 1950, however, the capital investment program has been steadily pared down in the face of practical necessity.[32] By 1954, many of the remaining key projects had been completed. It was then possible to take steps to decentralize the investment system so that it might be brought into closer accord with the other economic decentralization policies which aimed at substituting monetary and fiscal measures for purely administrative control.

The theory behind the 1954 reforms decentralizing investment and banking has been summed up by a responsible Titoist official as follows:[33] Titoist economic theory considers

[31] See Chapter X.
[32] For a comprehensive, statistically annotated review of the capital development program, see Rade Niketić, "Investments in Yugoslavia," *RIA,* VI (July-Aug., 1955), pp. 33-36.
[33] Serge Krajger, "Le Rôle de la Gestion Ouvrière dans Notre Système Économique," *QAS,* No. 25-26 (July-Oct. 1954), pp. 99-100.

money, as "capital," to be the property of no one in particular but of society in general. The right to dispose of money,
as "capital," belongs to the workers' collectives, the local
administrations, the republics, and the federation by virtue
of the right of the people's representative agencies to supervise the distribution and use of that part of his labor which
each worker dedicates to society. The workers' self-management system has made each enterprise an independent
entity. If this independence is to have real meaning, each
economic organization must be permitted a certain autonomy in seeking credits from banks for working funds and
for investment. At the same time, it is necessary that these
credits be controlled in order to permit the federal government to influence the economy and, if necessary, the work of
each enterprise. Therefore, the Titoist spokesman concluded,
the banks, as the "treasuries of society," must serve as
the intermediaries between the freedom the market-type
economy demands if it is to function properly, and the control the Titoist-type of socialism must maintain if it is to
progress in accordance with the dictates of the Yugoslav
Marxists.

All private banks were liquidated when the Titoists came to
power. In their place was established a simple pyramid of state
banks in which the federal branch controls the six republican
branches, which in turn control the branches on the local
level. The National Bank is responsible for the ultimate collection of all contributions and taxes assessed by the federal,
republican, and local social plans. It is also the repository
for all the current and long-term funds of economic enterprises. It is responsible for collecting and distributing the
funds of the federal, republican, and local budgets. In 1954,
the Bank was given the additional duties of compiling
periodical statistics on the movement of prices and savings
and key investments and of collecting data on the final balance sheets of all economic enterprises. Thus, the National
Bank serves as one of the most important means through
which centralized supervision and control of both the econ-

omy and the different levels of state administration are effected.

In 1954, it was decided that 45 per cent of the total amount in the federal government's General Investment Fund was to be turned over to the branches of the National Bank for their independent disposal. Each bank has since been given a yearly allotment from the fund and is permitted to dispose of this allotment as it sees fit, subject only to the general supervision each higher bank regularly exercises over the accounts of the lower banks within its area. Economic and social organizations not otherwise granted special credit facilities by the state must now compete for the amounts of capital investment credit available. The issuing bank is expected to exercise its discriminatory powers by granting loans to those applicants showing the greatest possibility of repaying them.

Besides the amounts granted them from the General Investment Fund and the amounts of investment credit available to them from their own deposit funds, the banks now receive from the state regular quotas of short-term credit funds for which economic enterprises are permitted to compete. Discriminatory interest rates on such credits are fixed by the federal government for each of the short-term credit quotas it issues to the banks. In this way the central authorities had originally hoped to influence the short-term trends of the economy. However, this type of control produced meager results.

In practice the new liberalized credit system was often grossly misused. For example, funds supposedly borrowed for industrial projects found their way instead into such things as community development and housing projects. Furthermore, because local banks could now issue credits without referring applications to higher branches, they frequently were subjected to undue pressure from local authorities pushing their own pet projects. Once again the human factor, with which Marxists seem to have so little acquaintance, rose to haunt the Titoists. By 1955, it was admitted that the local people's committees had generously given guarantees for both long- and short-term credits without questioning the real need of the applicant. People's committees had often guaranteed a total amount of credits far in excess of their own assets. One people's committee guaranteed credits in 1954 which were 1,643 per cent higher than its own total funds.[34] To put a stop to the abuse of the liberalized credit facilities, the Federal Executive Council in March 1955 decreed that all administrative organs, social institutions, and other guarantors of credits to economic enterprises would henceforth have to support their guarantees by depositing with the lending bank collateral amounting to a fixed percentage of each loan granted. The decree has had a sobering effect upon the easy generosity formerly exhibited by local administrative organs.

It became obvious that the highly centralized banking system was not equipped to cope with the realities of the reformed credit and investment facilities. In February 1955, it was announced that consideration was to be given to plans for the reorganization of the entire banking structure. By the late spring of that year, tentative plans called for the eventual establishment of separate and independent banks, such as agricultural banks, commercial banks, communal banks, and savings banks, all of which would be related to the Central Bank through ties strongly resembling those of the American Federal Reserve System.[35] The Central Bank would issue all currency, and would attempt to control circulation and credit by changing the amounts of obligatory reserves maintained by the independent member banks, by manipulating the rediscount rate, and by fixing the maximum use which could be made of individual types of deposits in granting credits. Under the proposed system individual banks are to receive the largest portion, if not all, of their funds from the revenues and savings of the institutions

---

[34] See *Borba*, March 20, 1955, p. 1.

[35] The information in this and the following paragraph comes from a personal interview in April 1955 with Mr. Janko Smole, an assistant director of the federal branch of the National Bank.

and individuals in the community which they serve. Each bank will then have its own investment and credit funds to disburse with little supervision from outside other than that provided by local authorities and by the requirements of the various social plans. It is expected that the new system will eliminate one of the greatest faults of the old centralized banking system: the tendency of lower branch banks to grant loans beyond their own practical capacities, knowing that any insufficiencies in their own funds will eventually have to be covered by the higher branches ultimately responsible for their accounts. Under the reformed system, the Central Bank will supposedly grant loans to member banks only if they are able to submit acceptable documentation of their need.

The Titoist planners feel that, with independent banks as part of the communal organization, the people's committees will automatically find themselves more or less responsible for the accumulation of the bank's resources and for the allotment of its credits. This responsibility is expected to curb the prevalent tendency of the people's committees to push over-ambitious and impractical investments. It is believed that the new responsibility will also cause both the banks and the people's committees to exercise greater initiative in carrying out thorough investigations of the credit potentialities of enterprises applying for assistance. Failure to make proper investigations has been one of the primary shortcomings of the banks under the centralized system.

The implementation of the banking reform will unquestionably be a slow and cautious process. The "level of socialist consciousness" of the average Yugoslav seeking banking and credit assistance, not to mention that of the average person trusted by the Titoists to serve as a banker, is still too low to permit a rapid changeover from the old rigidly controlled system to the indirect supervision envisaged by the reform. Before a general banking reform law is enacted, the planned changes in the banking structure will probably be experimented with in those sections of the country and the economy where they might be expected to be received with the fullest understanding. Nevertheless, it would seem that the Titoists have in mind the recruitment of a group of men who will be talented bankers in every capitalist sense of the word but without the desire for personal gain. Like every other worker in the society the Titoists are theoretically building, Yugoslav bankers are to ply their trade with the utmost personal skill for only a modest recompense.

FOREIGN TRADE

The system of workers' self-management could not logically be applied only to production for the domestic market. Decentralization of the Titoist economy automatically had to apply to foreign trade as well. Nevertheless, until the end of 1953, foreign trade was the exclusive province of the federal government. To encourage export, the government in 1952 began to permit economic enterprises to dispose independently of a percentage of the foreign exchange they managed to earn. As a direct result of this policy, the quality, quantity, and variety of Yugoslav-manufactured exports increased. Furthermore, the policy had a favorable effect upon imports to the extent that the private purchases made abroad by individual concerns were generally related to real rather than theoretical needs—a decided improvement over the old import system directed entirely by the all-encompassing centralized plan. However, many Yugoslav export enterprises began to accumulate their own foreign currency surpluses, and by using these surpluses to manipulate the domestic foreign exchange market were able to realize unfair profits. In 1955, the right of exporting enterprises to keep quotas of their foreign exchange earnings was abolished. They were now given only 1 per cent of such earnings to cover their business expenses abroad.

At the end of December 1953 and at the beginning of 1954, the federal government issued a series of decrees aimed at the decentralization of its control over foreign trade.[36] Whenever practical, direct administration was replaced by indirect methods of supervision. The decentralization of foreign trade techniques did not, however, mean the decentralization of foreign trade policy. This remains the exclusive province of the federal government. One of the decrees established a Foreign Trade Board and gave it certain regulatory and control powers over the new foreign trade system. New regulations permitted any firm able to meet minimum governmental requirements to be entered in the register of firms with permission to buy and sell abroad. Previously, only those firms arbitrarily designated by the government had such permission. Export and import permits were largely done away with; but the Federal Executive Council retained the right to control the export and import of specifically named products. Prices in foreign trade were now to be a matter of free agreement between the exporter and importer. Trade enterprises were authorized to engage in export business either on their own behalf or on behalf of other domestic buyers and sellers. The federal government, however, retained the privilege of deciding upon and naming those branches of the economy or those specific articles barred from foreign trade. Agencies who wished to serve as domestic representatives of foreign firms were now to be permitted to import goods on consignment without special permits; but private persons were expressly forbidden to enter this type of business.

Foreign exchange had been handled exclusively by the National Bank until March 1954, when it was decided to establish a Foreign Exchange Settlement Center, a sort of clearinghouse at which concerns were to buy and sell more or less freely. The government was to meet its own needs by taxing foreign currency incomes. However, as might have been expected, this system only created instability in the foreign exchange market, and by the end of the year a new series of regulations restored some of the control lost in the

[36] For a review of these decrees, see Stane Pavlić, "Innovations in the Yugoslav Foreign Trade Regime," *RIA*, V (Feb. 16, 1954), pp. 18-19.

previous period of excessive decentralization. The National Bank once again became the principal distribution agency for foreign exchange. All foreign currency not permitted by law to be retained by the earning enterprise had to be sold, generally at rates highly favorable to the seller, to the Bank for deposit in its Central Foreign Exchange Fund. From the fund periodical allotments were made to the Foreign Exchange Center. The Exchange Center then sold foreign currencies at special meetings attended by importing concerns. Importers were classified into groups whose respective priorities to purchase foreign currencies at the clearinghouse meetings had been fixed by the federal government. Each meeting was open only to the specified importing groups especially invited to attend. Certain categories of importers and exporters received special rates (in the form of coefficients) and other privileges in the purchase of foreign exchange.

Since demand is much greater than supply at almost every Foreign Exchange Settlement Center meeting, bidding for the currencies available became the only possible means of deciding distribution. Consequently, the rates rose to ridiculous heights. Often rates for the less valuable were greater than those for the more valuable currencies simply because of the momentary demand. Firms with foreign currency balances were freely entitled to sell all or any part of their supply at the Exchange meetings. They often withheld or offered their supplies when they knew there was an urgent need, and thus manipulated the rates to their own advantage. In this way certain firms were able to recover even large local currency losses. It was due to this misuse of the Exchange meetings that the federal government decided in 1955 to forgo the advantages of permitting exporters to keep quotas of their foreign earnings. By 1956, exporters were required to turn all but 1 per cent of their foreign earnings over to the National Bank. The Central Foreign Exchange Fund was abolished, and the National Bank became the only authorized seller of foreign currency at the

Foreign Exchange Settlement Center meetings. Decentralization of control over foreign exchange had brought out the selfish "bourgeois" trading instincts of Yugoslav exporters and importers. Freedom in the foreign exchange market had to be postponed until such time as Yugoslav traders reached that "level of socialist consciousness" where they would willingly sacrifice their own personal interests for those of the socialist community.

The defects and shortcomings which have appeared in the practice of the other reforms decentralizing foreign trade may also be traced to the human factor. One Yugoslav analyst complained in the spring of 1955 that Yugoslav exporters sold in high-price markets without regard for their own importers who consequently had to buy in high-price markets if they were to use the currency made available to them from exports.[37] This same analyst spoke of the need for a better control of the quality of exports; there were too many instances in which goods shipped abroad were not up to the standard called for by the contract. Furthermore, there were many cases where foreign currency had been spent for goods already available in Yugoslavia, and articles scarce at home had been exported. Once again the Yugoslav Marxists are plagued by unawareness of or unwillingness to recognize the phantom haunting all their decentralization reforms, the shadow of "bourgeois tendencies" or, ideologically speaking, of the "low level of socialist consciousness"—known outside Yugoslavia as human nature.

The success of Yugoslavia's export trade is of vital importance to the Titoists. The success of the entire concept of rapid industrialization will, in part at least, be judged by the success achieved in exports. The shortcomings of the freer foreign trade policies therefore cause the Titoist leaders serious concern. For one thing it is not possible to write off the costs of exporters' mistakes or carelessness by using funds

[37] *Borba*, April 21, 1955, p. 5. This is the third and last in a series of penetrating articles by Ladislav Gonda discussing foreign trade problems. The first two appear in *ibid.*, April 19 and 20, 1955, respectively.

from another sector of the economy as can be done to cloak failures in internal trade. A system of inspection and control was required to counter the errors of haphazard decentralization of the techniques of foreign trade. Gradually the Foreign Trade Board established by the 1953-54 reforms has come to exert closer control and supervision through the newly emphasized ladders of self-managed foreign trade associations. The centralized control network was further strengthened in 1956 with the creation of the Foreign Trade Bank. These two institutions are now expected to work together with the pertinent government inspection agencies to raise the quality, quantity, and general standard of Yugoslav foreign trade.

ARTS AND CRAFTS

Most arts and crafts trades and services are by nature small and highly personalized businesses. Because of the Yugoslav Marxists' doctrinal mistrust of private enterprise, the situation in arts and crafts services in Yugoslavia has steadily deteriorated. Despite the fact that the transition to a market-type economy had created more favorable conditions for these services, there is still a very serious gap between their supply and the needs of the economy and the population.

Arts and crafts were not excluded from the Titoists' determination to collectivize all producers. Members of these groups are constantly urged to form or to join existing producing, processing, and service co-operatives. But artisans and craftsmen have so far resisted. Only a very small percentage not already included within other collectivized branches of the economy, as for example in industrial enterprises and agricultural co-operatives, have joined arts and crafts co-operatives.[38]

[38] By Sept. 1954, approximately 5 per cent of the total number of artisans and craftsmen in the country belonged to the 924 producing, processing, and services co-operatives then extant; see Table 10-1, *Statistički Godišnjak FRNJ 1955* (Belgrade: July 1955), p. 160.

The producing, processing, and service co-operatives consist of groups of artisans or craftsmen who band together and sell or lease their tools and equipment to the corporate entity which they form. Each member may purchase one or more shares in his co-operative. Artisans, craftsmen, and assistants (journeymen and workmen) owning no equipment may join such co-operatives by purchasing at least one share. All members have equal rights within the co-operative no matter how many shares they hold; each member has but one vote in settling co-operative business. The earnings of those co-operative members who choose to maintain their separate establishments are turned over to the co-operative. Remittances and shares in the profits are paid to members in accordance with the number of shares each holds. The meeting of the entire collective is the organization's highest authority. This meeting elects yearly a management board and a supervisory board to carry out the responsibilities of day-to-day management. The chairman of the management board is considered the president of the co-operative. Members of producing, processing, and service co-operatives are entitled to social security benefits, tax reductions, and other such privileges generally reserved for the socialized sector of the economy.

To encourage artisans and craftsmen to increase their services the 1955 Federal Social Plan exempted the trades from paying the federal profits tax.[39] The plan also shifted the entire responsibility for determining the social contribution and taxes to be paid by artisans and craftsmen to the individual people's committees. It was intended that this shift in authority would permit local administrative bodies to encourage the development of those specific trades and services for which their individual communities had the greatest need.

The highly personalized, small-business nature of most arts and crafts trades and services makes it extremely diffi-

[39] See Federal Social Plan for 1955 (Part I, Sect. 6), *SL* No. 56, Dec. 30, 1954.

cult to find a suitable method of collectivizing this sector of the economy without stifling the individual initiative upon which its effectiveness depends. To find a solution to this riddle is today an important preoccupation of the Titoists. They must eventually discover a suitable compromise if they are not to be forced into the embarrassing admission that there is one sector of social existence which is better served by private enterprise than by socialization.

TRADE UNIONS

With the advent of economic decentralization, Yugoslav trade unions lost their role as the defender of the worker and of the Five Year Plan. In fact, there are today many observers who see no reason for the continued existence of trade unions in Yugoslavia now that the workers themselves, through their workers' councils, are in a position to see that their own best interests are protected. But the Titoists argue that the unions still have a responsibility to protect the interests of the workers and to serve wherever necessary as the intermediary between the workers and the political-administrative authorities. Whatever the Titoists may say, however, under the system of workers' self-management the primary official responsibility of Yugoslav trade unions is to sponsor educational and cultural programs. The formal task of all unions is to raise the "level of socialist consciousness" of the workers to the point where they will no longer doubt the so-called objective truths of Titoist ideology.

Trade unions had a stormy career in prewar Yugoslavia. Some managed to evade government opposition by becoming tools of the government. Some survived by becoming an integral part of the machinery of strong political factions. All others were suppressed. The Communist party of Yugoslavia, outlawed in 1921, had to content itself with relatively ineffectual, clandestine syndicates. During the last war, the Communist leaders of the Partisan movement lost no time in organizing new trade unions in each area of the country as it was liberated. At the time of the first national conference of Yugoslav trade unions, held in January 1945, there were 225,000 members. In December of the same year there were 622,432 members, and by the middle of 1954 membership had reached 1,700,000 or approximately 85 per cent of the total number of employed persons.[40]

There are no state laws or regulations governing the general rights and spheres of activity of Yugoslav trade unions. Some specific duties are assigned to them by laws and regulations pertaining to other matters (their right to draw up the candidates lists for workers' council elections, for example). This privileged position of the trade unions is unquestionably due to the important fact that Communist party members furnish almost 100 per cent of the unions' leadership at all levels.[41]

Trade union membership is considered to be voluntary. Any employed person can become a member by paying dues which average a little less than 1 per cent of his salary. Apprentices pay even less, and unemployed persons pay only one dinar a year. The unions are organized on an industrial basis, hence only one union usually exists in each enterprise. Unions are organized both horizontally and vertically, each of the two hierarchies containing a community, district, republican, and federal branch wherever practical. The so-called horizontal organization is confined to each single industrial union, organized on a national scale. The vertical organization creates the pyramid making up the Federation of Yugoslav Trade Unions, from the

[40] From a mimeographed handout entitled *The Yugoslav Trade Unions,* prepared in the summer of 1954 by the central office of the Federation of Yugoslav Trade Unions. It contains a detailed history of the development of Yugoslav trade unions from 1900. It also shows that every category of employed person from miners to museum personnel had, in 1954, his own separate union. There was even a separate union for pensioners.

[41] In a meeting with Dr. Ivo Vivoda, then the director of the central office of the Federation of Yugoslav Trade Unions, the author asked what percentage of the leadership of trade unions were Party members. Dr. Vivoda replied that no figures were available on this, but that it was certain that almost all trade union leaders were members, especially since most of the contemporary leadership had belonged to the prewar clandestine syndicates.

community organizations composed of representatives of the separate industrial unions functioning within each community, through similar district and republican organizations to the central office in Belgrade. Officers of both structures are elected by the periodical assemblies held by each organization. Every member of a trade union is technically eligible to become an officer at any level of both structures. Most officers of the separate industrial union organizations are not paid salaries for their work.[42] Most officers of the Federation are salaried. Both hierarchies work on the principle of "democratic centralism"; the lower branches must submit to the decisions of the higher ones, but they supposedly have the right to criticize decisions from above and to request that they be changed, or to take steps to recall the leaders of the higher branches.

During the war and in the period immediately following, the main task of Tito's trade unions was to "protect the workers' interests" against the vicissitudes of private ownership. As soon as the Yugoslav means of production had been safely nationalized, the role of the unions changed to that of "arousing" the working class to fulfill the requirements of the Five Year Plan. Because union leadership was entirely Communist, the unions played a primary role in factory management during the period from 1945 to 1951. It was not unusual during this period for unions to oppose workers' demands for higher wages.

After the inauguration of workers' self-management, the intended conversion of the unions from militant organizations into less powerful educational and social clubs apparently did not progress as smoothly as the regime had anticipated. For one thing, the introduction of workers' self-management and the policy of substituting persuasion for intimidation had combined to lose many a union stalwart his privileged position in his place of employment. In the

[42] Dr. Vivoda said that only 430 officers of all the trade unions and of the Federation were paid salaries. These were usually the president and secretary of federal branches of individual unions and of the Federation, and the highest officer of each of the branches at the republican, district, and sometimes at the community levels.

summer of 1954, Tito spoke bluntly to the trade union laggards.[43] Trade unions are no longer a political movement, he said, and under the new philosophy there is no need for them to retain their old form and content. Instead, he continued, the unions in the new Yugoslav system are a factor working within the Socialist Alliance, the political front organization, to help it pursue its socialist objectives. He warned the unions to accept this point and to concentrate their energies in the lower rather than the higher echelons of their organizations. In stressing the role of the unions as educators of the toiling masses, Tito wanted it clearly understood that no one was setting the unions the task of teaching workers "the rudiments of Marxism-Leninism," rather unions were to devote themselves to teaching men how to manage the means of production and how to avoid such unsocialist pitfalls as "localism."

Observing the letter of democratic centralism, the Third Congress of the Federation of Yugoslav Trade Unions, held in May 1955, emphasized the growing importance of the communal and district branches of the Federation. It also approved of the increasing extent to which decisions and solutions were being formulated in the Federation's local councils and in enterprises themselves.[44] The Congress decided that, since the unions' basic functions now took place at the level of the community and the enterprise, it was perfectly logical for the operative functions of the higher trade union branches to diminish. The Congress accordingly adopted a resolution to decrease the number of component unions within the Federation by unifying some of the separate branches. The Congress was further of the opinion that in their future development the Yugoslav unions would acquire the character of organizations satisfying the concrete necessities of the life and work of their members, and

---

[43] Tito, "Trade Unions Should See to Individual Welfare, but Also Concern Themselves with the Collective," *Yugoslav Trade Unions,* a publication put out by the Federation of Yugoslav Trade Unions (Belgrade: Aug.-Nov. 1954), p. 3.

[44] See "Conclusions of the Congress of Trade Unions," *YR,* IV (May-June 1955), p. 19.

would essentially occupy themselves with supporting practical measures for the improvement of the health, housing, and cultural welfare of the workers.

Most of the duties assigned to the trade unions in Yugoslavia today could easily be carried out effectively by the individual agencies of workers' self-management. However, with the exception of the Party itself, the unions, because of the purely Communist nature of their leadership, represent the most loyal single group of Titoist supporters within the country. Hence the trade union federation is of very real use to the regime in maintaining effective control of the workers' self-management system. Futhermore, the Federation's existence considerably simplifies the problem of creating national unity within the workers' self-management system, a unity which would be difficult to duplicate by purely administrative means without detracting noticeably from the goal of decentralization.

The Titoists are becoming increasingly aware, despite the obvious value of the trade union federation to the regime, that an individual's talents are at least as important a qualification for economic leadership as is Party membership. The ideal solution would be to entice capable individuals to join the Party. But the talented do not always want to join the Party. The desire on the part of the Yugoslav leaders to reduce Party interference in running the economy is unquestionably one of the principal reasons for their present efforts to diminish the importance of the higher organizational echelons of the Federation of Yugoslav Trade Unions. Henceforth the Federation will have to exert most of its influence at the local level. Most of the Federation's higher officials are prewar clandestine syndicate workers who frequently do not possess the new talents required in the age of workers' self-management. The attack on the Federation's upper echelons does not mean that the nation-wide organization is to be disbanded or even structurally weakened to any major degree. Only the Federation's power to interfere in top-level policy is being curtailed.

CHAPTER VI

Major Agricultural Reforms

Bitter experience has taught the Yugoslav leaders that power tactics alone are incapable of achieving either the agricultural output needed to ease the burden of rapid industrialization or the respect for socialism that must infiltrate the Yugoslav peasantry if total socialization is to be accomplished. Titoist agrarian policy has run the gamut from gentle cajolery to brutal intimidation, and back again. It began with land reform and a voluntary collectivization program. By 1949, the voluntary aspect of this program was superseded by relentless coercion. The peasants resisted passively. The need to halt the disastrous decline in agricultural production led to the abandonment of the entire collectivization program in 1953. In the following year, the Titoists were trying to win back peasant confidence by allocating greater investment and credit facilities to both the private and the socialized sectors of agriculture. By 1955, the "intensified agriculture" policy had been inaugurated. In essence this policy attempts by use of the free market to force the private peasant to the realization that he must either voluntarily seek modern means to increase his productivity or give up farming altogether. "Intensified agriculture" represents a strategic retreat from standard Marxist-Leninist-Stalinist agrarian tactics to the more liberal forms of agricultural concentration historically arrived at in Western democratic societies. But the Titoists have not executed their retreat gracefully. In their subborn withdrawal they have built up an enmity amongst their peasants which today represents their greatest theoretical and practical challenge.

Marx had not intended his system to be applied to agrarian societies. He had meant the proletarian revolution to take place in highly industrialized societies where industrial workers made up the majority of the population. Ironically, however, a Marxist system has only succeeded in installing itself in predominantly agricultural countries. In all instances where it has come to power of its own accord, it has ridden to victory on the backs of disaffected peasantries. The minority Communist group has always managed to convince the peasants that they were serving their own best interests in assisting in the overthrow of existing authority. Once the Communists were established, however, the peasants soon found themselves reduced from the status of comrades-in-arms to that of the target of Communist oppression.

The Yugoslav revolution has in no way been an exception to this pattern. When the Yugoslav Communists took to the field in 1941, 68.4 per cent of their country's total population was directly employed in agriculture, forestry, and fishing.[1] The 1953 census showed that the proportion of the total population in those categories was slightly less than 61 per cent.[2] The Partisan forces during the war consisted almost entirely of peasants. Most Yugoslav workmen stayed on at their regular jobs or were shipped off to Nazi labor camps. Throughout the war, the Communist leaders of the Partisan movement carefully explained the movement's goals in terms which catered to the main yearnings, antagonisms, and aspirations of the peasantry—that is, to their undying attachment to their land, to their anti-bureaucratic and anti-militaristic sentiment, and to their longing for peace and self-government.

In the interwar period, the two largest Yugoslav peasant parties, those of Serbia and Croatia, had become so strong as to represent a challenge to the exclusive authority of the

[1] Milun Ivanović, "The Development of Yugoslav Agriculture," *RIA*, III (Oct. 1, 1952), p. 18.

[2] See Table 3-15, *Statistički Godišnjak FRNJ 1955* (Belgrade: July 1955), p. 61.

military group which ruled the country.[3] In fact, the increasing electoral strength of the intensely nationalistic Croatian Peasant Party so impressed the ruling Serbian military clique that in 1928 it arranged the assassination of the party's powerful leader, Stjepan Radić. Aided by the army and leading business circles, King Alexander then dissolved parliament, abolished the Constitution, and organized a rigorous dictatorship which was heartily despised by most peasants—particularly by the Croatian and Macedonian peasants who bitterly resented the "Greater Serbia" policies of the ruling group. In their political battle the peasants had relied exclusively upon their voting strength. Hence, in the showdown they were no match for the military who all too readily resorted to their weapons. By the time the Yugoslav Communists decided to resist the Nazi and Italian invaders in 1941, most peasants were the willing supporters of the Partisan movement which promised democratic self-government when the war was over. As soon as liberation was won, however, the peasants found that once again their ballots were impotent in the face of bayonets—this time wielded by the Communists.

During the Yugoslav war of liberation the Partisan leaders, like Lenin at the time of the October Revolution, promised their peasants a land reform. Land reform was a standard Leninist operational technique to placate the peasants while the Communists were busy consolidating their hold over the state. The Titoists therefore had their provisional National Assembly pass a land reform act in August 1945.[4] Even the Leninist slogan "the land belongs to those who cultivate it" served as the rationale for the

[3] For a survey of Yugoslav history 1918-41, and of the role of the peasants therein, see Dinko Tomasevich, *Peasants, Politics, and Economic Change in Yugoslavia* (Stanford: 1955), pp. 233-61.

[4] The text of The Law on Land Reform and Colonization of August 28, 1945, appears in *SL* No. 64, 1945. The law was confirmed by the permanent National Assembly elected in 1946 (see *ibid.*, No. 24, 1946). It was amended in 1947 and 1948 (see *ibid.*, No. 105, 1948). For résumé of text and its amendments, see *NYL*, I:2-3 (1950), pp. 47-49.

Titoist reform. The law confiscated all peasant holdings over forty-five hectares. It limited the amount of arable land a peasant could own to no more than twenty-five hectares. In the case of the existing family co-operatives, the traditional "zadrugas," the maximum could be increased. The law also confiscated all land belonging to banks, enterprises, corporations, monasteries, and other lay and religious groups and funds, and all arable land exceeding from three to five hectares belonging to persons who did not work this land. Explicitly included in the land pool formed by the law was all land confiscated under a wartime law against enemies of the state and absentee landlords.[5] Arable land from this pool was to be distributed to landless and poor peasants to become their own property, registered in the receiver's name, at the rate of from eight to twelve hectares per family. Such land could not be ceded, sold, rented, or mortgaged for a period of twenty years; it could be exchanged for other land in order to bring a family's holdings into a single, unified plot.

Relatively few peasants suffered from the land reform act. Only 7.8 per cent of the total amount of all kinds of land taken into the pool as a result of both confiscation and the land reform law came from peasants owning more than the maximum fixed by law.[6] Of the total amount of arable land brought into the pool, approximately 80 per cent was distributed to poor and landless peasants and to veterans. The remainder went to state farms, to economic enterprises whose workers desired to cultivate it collectively as a private source of raw materials or food, to persons willing to form co-operative farms, and to the state forestry and afforestation fund. Many of the peasant and veteran recipients were transplanted bag and baggage from the poorer areas in which they lived to the well-built villages confiscated from

[5] The Law on State Appropriations of Enemy Property and on Sequestration of the Property of Absentee Persons was passed in Nov. 1944. The text appears in *SL* No. 2, 1945. Text of amendment appears in *ibid.*, No. 63, 1946. A résumé of amended text is given in *NYL, op. cit.*, pp. 46-47.

[6] See Table 7-1, *Statistički Godišniak, op. cit.*, p. 109.

the German minority groups in the most fertile parts of the country—the Voivodina, the Srem, and Slavonia.

In addition to the land reform, the provisional National Assembly passed a law late in 1945 canceling all peasant debts. About one-third of the total peasantry were thereby released from indebtedness amounting to some nine billion dinars.[7]

The land reform and redistribution represented the completion of the important second phase of accepted Marxist-Leninist theory prescribed for agrarian revolution in backward countries.[8] The first phase, the prerevolutionary fomentation of class conflict between the workers and poorer and landless peasants on the one side and the large landowners and capitalist peasants on the other, had been bypassed by the success of the wartime Partisan revolution. With the completion of the second phase, coinciding with the victorious revolution and ending with the distribution of land to small and landless peasants as a necessary concession to their "property-owner fanaticism," the Titoists were ready to proceed with the third phase: to organize the peasantry on a co-operative basis. In July 1946, the Basic Law on Co-operatives was passed by the National Assembly.[9]

As has often been the case with land reforms in agrarian countries, the Titoists' reform merely perpetuated all of the defects of individual subsistence farming by increasing the number of small holdings. Population density per hectare of arable land in Yugoslavia had long been one of the highest in Europe.[10] Therefore, co-operation of some kind

---

[7] Ivanović, *op. cit.*

[8] For a discussion of the four phases of this policy, see David Mitrany, *Marx Against the Peasant* (Chapel Hill: 1951), pp. 187 ff.

[9] The text of this law is in *SL* No. 47, July 1946.

[10] Population density per 100 hectares of arable land in Yugoslavia in 1954 was 114, compared with 97 for Rumania, 91 for Poland, 72 for Hungary, and 30 for Great Britain. (*Yugoslavia* [Belgrade: "Jugoslavija" Press, 1954], p. 103.) From 1931 to 1939 population density per 100 hectares of arable land had increased from 103.5 to 114 (Ivanović, *op. cit.*).

As for the size of individual landholdings, of the total number of peasant landowners before World War II, 67.8 per cent owned farms of less than

amongst the Yugoslav small landowners has been a long-standing necessity if they are to succeed in a modern world. Communal co-operation is not entirely new to them, however. For centuries Yugoslav peasants lived in varying forms of communal organizations known as "zadrugas." [11] These zadrugas were organized on a family basis, often with whole villages belonging to members of a single clan. With the infiltration of Western ideas during the eighteenth and nineteenth centuries, the zadrugas began to break down and the land became parceled into smaller and smaller units. Nevertheless, many family zadrugas continue to exist even today. When the Titoists were seeking a way to avoid the psychological stigma of the Soviet word *kolkhoz* to describe the type of collective farms they intended to sponsor in Yugoslavia, they quite naturally seized upon the word "zadruga" as the proper compromise.

The Titoist leaders were both unwilling and unable to follow purely Stalinist techniques in pursuing their objective of agricultural collectivization. In the first place, it was both economically and politically impossible to exterminate resisting Yugoslav peasants with the same reckless zeal Stalin had used against the Russian kulak. More important still, much of the congenital hostility and distrust which the average Marxist feels for the peasant was—in the earliest years of Titoist rule at least—tempered by the fact that Tito and many of his closest associates were themselves of peasant origin. Furthermore, the peasants, since

---

5 hectares; 20 per cent farms of from 5 to 10 hectares; and 11.7 per cent farms of over 10 hectares (*Yugoslavia, op. cit.*). By the end of 1951, when approximately 25 per cent of the country's arable land was collectivized, 65.5 per cent of the remaining private farms were smaller than 5 hectares, 21.3 per cent between 5 and 10 hectares, and 9.2 per cent larger than 10 (*YR*, I [Jan. 1952], p. 10).

A detailed breakdown from a sample of the 1953 census shows that the 1951 figures had not changed to any worthwhile extent; see Table 3-15, *Statistički Godišnjak, op. cit.*, p. 62. (*Note:* This census was taken just prior to the collectivization and land reforms of 1953.)

[11] For a history of the development of the zadruga system in Yugoslavia, see Dinko Tomasic, *Personality and Culture in East European Politics* (New York: 1948).

they had formed the large majority of the Partisan forces during the war of liberation, had come to be a strong class faction within the Yugoslav Communist party.[12] Even as late as 1948, they represented 49.14 per cent of the Party's total membership.[13] The Titoists' cautious approach to agricultural collectivization also took into account the fact that a large part of Yugoslavia's arable land consists of small plots scratched from the unyielding rocky soil of the mountains. Such land does not readily lend itself to collectivization.

The Basic Law on Co-operatives of 1946 provided for centralized planning in agriculture. It established state tractor stations and designated the co-operatives as the main outlets for the distribution of town-made goods in the village. To achieve this distribution the law formed what are known in Yugoslavia as "general" co-operatives, purchase and sales organizations to which peasants can belong merely by paying membership fees. In effect, these general co-operatives replaced, unified, and expanded the network of independent procurement, sales, and credit co-operatives which had existed prior to the war.[14] The emphasis of the 1946 law was on the formation of four different types of "peasant working co-operatives." These ranged from a purely *kolkhoz*-type farm in which members shared equally in the organization's earnings, to a farm in which members were paid shares of profits according to the amount of land and equipment they brought into the organization. In most instances, mem-

[12] The Party had entered the war with 12,000 members, of which 3,000 survived. At the close of the war, membership had been increased to 141,000 (Ranković, *Borba*, July 23, 1948). Most of the wartime recruits must have come from the peasant ranks of the Partisan forces.

[13] From Alexander Ranković's address to the Fifth Party Congress (1948), *Borba, op. cit.* By 1956, the proportion of peasants had been reduced to 18 per cent of the total membership. (*Komunist*, No. 11-12 [Belgrade: 1956].)

[14] By 1939, there were 9.813 rural co-operative organizations in Yugoslavia. These were mainly independent organizations formed for procurement, sales, processing, and credit purposes (from: "General Agricultural Co-operatives," *Bulletin*, I:2 [Belgrade: Glavni Zadružni Savez FRNJ, 1952], p. 1).

bers were permitted to sign a three-year contract at the termination of which they might withdraw from the collective, taking with them their own land and equipment. The law also provided that the assembly, composed of the entire membership of the co-operative, was to be highest organ of authority in each collective farm. Technically, government authorities had no right to interfere in the internal affairs of the collective farms. Unlike the Soviet *kolkhoz,* whose president-manager was appointed by the central authorities, each Yugoslav co-operative was to be headed by officials elected by its assembly alone.

Unfortunately, however, during the first six or seven years of Titoist development it was not the practice of the authorities to feel in any way constrained even by the laws they themselves made. The law on agricultural co-operatives was no exception. The assembly of all types of co-operatives was a mere formality. The plans and policies of each organization were in practice handed down as unchallengeable orders from the local authorities. Co-operative officials were persons chosen by the local Party authorities with little or no thought as to their agricultural experience or qualifications. The tractor stations which the law had promised were few and far between. Furthermore, the shoddiness and scarcity of consumer goods completely hamstrung the "general" co-operatives in achieving their theoretical as well as their practical purposes.

Until their expulsion from the Cominform, the Titoists stressed no point more regularly than that agricultural co-operatives should be formed through voluntary action on the part of the peasants. Even those peasants who received land from the state land pool were not urged to form co-operatives unless they seemed so inclined. Almost all the recipients of land had actually established themselves as private farmers.[15] The only positive tactics used to foster

[15] Table 7-1, *Statistički Godišnjak, op. cit.,* p. 109, shows that only 2.6 per cent of the arable land distributed by the pool was used by individuals to establish co-operatives.

collectivization were subtle forms of economic coercion which made it difficult for the wealthier peasants to obtain seeds, fertilizers, and other farming equipment. The instruments of taxation and the forcible collection of agricultural produce, initiated in 1947 as a part of the Five Year Plan, were sparingly used.

Of all the Kremlin's captious charges against the Titoists' policy of collectivization, only one had any real claim to Marxist-Leninist validity: that the Yugoslav leaders had departed from the true path by failing to assert the supremacy of the proletariat over the peasantry, to whom Tito had openly referred as "the strongest pillar" of the Yugoslav state.[16] It was true that the Titoists had failed to bring class warfare to the village. There had been no discrimination against the rich peasant. If he wanted to join a working co-operative he was free to do so provided that he brought in all his land and equipment and obeyed all the organization's rules and regulations. Tito himself had said that the test of being a kulak in Yugoslavia was not the size of a man's holdings, but whether he was for socialism or against it.[17]

Apparently the Kremlin's criticism and the subsequent Cominform excommunication shook the Titoists' faith in their ability to wheedle their peasants into voluntary collectivization. By the beginning of 1949, the regime was resorting to what was later referred to as "publicity action" to step up the pace of agricultural collectivization. Mass propaganda was directed at all private peasants to get them to join the working co-operatives. All who resisted—it made no difference if they were rich or poor—were badgered and intimidated at every turn. Taxes and assessments for delivery of surplus produce to the state were fixed at impossible rates in order to drive into bankruptcy all peasants who held out against collectivization. The number of peasant

---

[16] See *The Soviet-Yugoslav Dispute* (London: Royal Institute of International Affairs, 1948), pp. 9-10.
[17] See Mitrany, *op. cit.*, p. 201.

working co-operatives rose from 1,318 at the end of 1948 to 6,964 at the end of 1950.[18] Even so, the 1950 figure represented in area only approximately 25 per cent of the country's total arable land (this included collectivized land owned by the state) and 17 per cent of the total number of peasants.[19] The percentages were much lower in the extent of pasture land, meadows, orchards, and vineyards collectivized.

The forced collectivization drive embittered the large majority of the peasants. Production dropped, land went out of cultivation, and livestock inventories decreased or at least failed to increase. The peasants' mood of sullen defiance was strengthened by the severe drought which struck in the summer of 1950. The priests, particularly in Slovenia where resistance to the drive had been the most successful and in Croatia where the memory of the once strong peasant movement still persisted,[20] did not fail to indicate to the

[18] "From the Report of the Managing Board of the Glavni Zadružni Savez FRNJ," *Bulletin,* III:2 (Belgrade: 1954), p. 25.

Note: Published statistics pertaining to the number of peasant working co-operatives extant at the end of 1950 are frequently conflicting. Since the General Co-operatives Union (the Glavni Zadružni Savez) was the highest government agency most directly concerned, its figures have been included here. No matter what the variation, however, it is generally accepted that the figure 6,900 is not far out of the way on either side. The figure quoted for 1948 seems to be generally accepted as correct.

[19] Ivanović, *op. cit.,* p. 17. On p. 18 he gives the following breakdown for all types of farm land (1951):

	per cent in state sector	per cent in co-op sector	per cent in private sector
Arable land & gardens	4.9	20.3	74.8
Meadow land	2.3	11.0	86.7
Pasture land	3.1	13.7	83.2
Orchards	1.9	7.7	90.4
Vineyards	2.4	9.1	88.5

[20] The drive brought the total collectivized arable land to 11 per cent in Slovenia, and to 14 per cent in Croatia; in the Voivodina and Macedonia, the total reached 50 per cent at the end of 1950, and although the drive slackened in 1950 in all other parts of the country, it was continued in Macedonia until mid-1951 when the percentage of arable land in collectives reached 63 per cent. (From Hugh Seton-Watson, *East European Revolution* [London], 1952, p. 274.)

peasants that God was using the drought as a sign that He was with the peasants in this struggle. The United States, Britain, and France stepped in to save the regime from possible collapse and sent shipments of food to Yugoslavia to keep the population and livestock from starvation.

The rapidly deteriorating situation caused the Titoists to call off their collectivization drive. In all parts of the country except Macedonia, the campaign ground to a halt in 1950; in Macedonia it lasted until mid-1951. The authorities now concentrated their energies upon trying to consolidate the gains already made. As an incentive to agriculture in general, the government promised to lighten the burden of the forced collection of surplus produce. By the end of 1951, it had canceled the collection of meat, milk, and fodder, but it still insisted upon delivery to the state of large quotas of all cereals.

In June 1950, a new Basic Law on Agricultural Co-operatives[21] replaced the 1946 law. It laid renewed stress upon the voluntary principle as essential to the formation of all co-operatives and insisted upon the principle of total self-management within both the general co-operatives and the working co-operatives. In theory, the socialized agricultural sector was to be brought into closer conformity with the new methods then being worked out for putting the workers' self-management system into practice. The new law emphasized the development of the general co-operatives as the lead horse of the entire collectivization system. It widened the gaps established by the 1946 law between the Yugoslav working co-operatives and the Soviet *kolkhoz* prototype. According to the new law, members were to keep title to the land they brought into co-operatives. They could, if they chose, receive a fixed land rent as compensation besides their shares in the organization's profits. In all four types of working co-operatives authorized by the new law, members were to be permitted to keep up to one

[21] The text of this law appears in *SL*, No. 49, June 9, 1950. A résumé is given in *NYL* I:2-3 (1950), pp. 67-74.

hectare of their land for their own private use. They were to be compensated for the buildings, equipment, and livestock they brought into the organization. In brief, the 1950 law tried to find a suitable compromise between the peasant's traditional respect for ownership and the contrary dictates of socialization.

The 1950 law also dealt in detail with the hierarchy of agricultural co-operatives unions. The General Co-operatives Union was a prewar institution which the Titoists had reformed immediately following liberation. In its new form the General Co-operatives Union became a pyramid with the federal branch at its apex, descending through the six republican branches to the district unions at the lowest level. The new law on co-operatives tightened the organizational structure of the General Co-operatives Union and required all general and peasant working co-operatives, the family-type zadrugas, and all other agricultural enterprises to become members of their respective district unions.

The expressed intention of the 1950 law on co-operatives was to bring greater freedom and self-management to the agricultural co-operatives. However, right up to the abandonment of collectivization in the spring of 1953, the local Party authorities continued to run the collective farms just as arbitrarily as before the enactment of the 1950 law. Eventually, the Titoists guilelessly admitted why the entire agricultural collectivization policy had failed: "In the operation of the peasant working co-operatives, breaches were committed in the democratic principle of management. There were failures in making payment for the inventory and livestock. In addition, in the majority of cases the co-operatives were guilty of default in connection with different other obligations toward the co-operators." [22] In so many respects this was a masterpiece of understatement.

At the end of 1951, thousands of peasants—particularly in Macedonia—gave the three months' notice of withdrawal

[22] "From the Report of the Managing Board of Glavni Zadružni Savez," *Bulletin*, III:2 (Belgrade: 1954), p. 26.

stipulated by the contracts they had signed on joining their collectives. The government, although it had every reason to be fully conscious of the peasants' general mood of defiance, was shocked by the vast number of withdrawal notices. It reacted in the fashion still most natural to it by forcing peasants to remain in the co-operatives in spite of their legal right to withdraw. However, the crisis did cause the regime to order a thorough re-examination of its entire collectivization policy. This re-examination led to a shift in emphasis from the working co-operative to the general co-operative as the keystone of future agrarian policy.[23]

Titoist apologists began to explain that the leaders had never meant collectivization to be the ruthless affair it had turned out to be. They explained that the policy had been "wrongly interpreted by some local government bodies, thus leading to a departure from the principle of voluntary membership" and to the formation of co-operatives in regions where they were impractical.[24] They now admitted that of the total number of peasant working co-operatives in existence at the beginning of 1952, one-third were working at a loss, in some cases at a considerable loss, one-third showed a profit, and the remaining one-third were on the borderline.[25] Co-operatives which were obviously impractical were, from this time on, gradually dissolved. Little by little those which remained were granted some of the independence the laws supposedly meant them to have. Soviet

[23] At the end of 1951, the Central Committee of the CPY issued instructions entitled "On the Further Course of the Socialist Transformation of the Village" which were sent to all Party organizations throughout the country. It emphasized the CPY's point of view that the general co-operative should serve as the "fulcrum in the struggle for promoting agricultural production and for the socialist reconstruction of agriculture." It talked of the liquidation of obligatory deliveries of produce surpluses to the state and of the abolition of the system of rationing of both industrial and agricultural products. It suggested that taxation be used to attack the "residual village rich." It explained the new self-management and accounting systems which were to be set up in each working co-operative, etc. The text of this instruction is given in *Bulletin*, I:1 (Belgrade: 1952), pp. 16-27.

[24] See Ivanović, *op. cit.*, p. 17. See also the instruction of the CC of the CPY, *Bulletin*, *op. cit.*, p. 23.

[25] *The Economist* (London), May 24, 1952, p. 526.

methods, such as calculating members' shares in "labor days," were dropped wherever they had proved unsuccessful. Co-operatives were ordered to set up profit-and-loss bookkeeping systems. The budget of the central government would no longer include the profits and losses of each individual co-operative. The success or failure of each co-operative was now to be the concern of the co-operative itself and of the local political-administrative organ responsible for the supervision of the local economy. To clear the way for the new cost-accounting system, the government canceled debts incurred by the working co-operatives to the extent of over nine and one half billion dinars.[26]

These reforms in no way meant that the Titoists were abandoning their ultimate ambition to collectivize all Yugoslav farming land. On the contrary, most of the reforms were inspired by necessity alone. An apt illustration of the confusion between necessity and desire was the order handed down by the regime at the end of 1951. This order instructed local authorities to heap taxes upon the private peasant to force him to give more serious consideration to "voluntary" collectivization. However, the peasants' reaction was so vociferous that the central authorities beat a hasty retreat. The taxation tactic was called off. In June 1952, the government reduced by six-sevenths the amount of cereals the peasants were to turn over to the state. Consequently, free market trading in wheat, corn, and other cereals was restored. By 1953, the forcible collection of all agricultural produce was entirely abandoned. However, the private peasant realized that these were not concessions made to him, but that they were merely steps which were required to restore the free market as an integral part of the new decentralized economy.

In the summer of 1952, Tito, alarmed by the drought which was developing, informed the peasants that they were not to be coerced in any way into joining collectives. At the same time he reminded them that Yugoslavia's future

[26] See *Bulletin*, III:2 (Belgrade: 1954), p. 28.

unquestionably lay in collectivized agriculture.[27] By the end of that year, Titoist officials admitted frankly that their attempts at wholesale collectivization had been a dismal failure. Yet they still clung doggedly to eventual collectivization as the final goal. In the meantime, they were busy liquidating those co-operatives that were economically unsound. Of the 6,964 peasant working co-operatives extant at the end of 1950, only 4,697 remained at the end of 1952.[28]

In spite of the regime's moves to liberalize its agrarian policy, the situation in the Yugoslav countryside continued to deteriorate. More and more agricultural land lay fallow because many collectivized peasants were completely demoralized by the government's refusal to recognize their legal right to withdraw from collectives, and most of the private peasants were ruffled by the abortive attempt at coercive taxation. The desire to resist passively was encouraged by the feeling among the peasants that the constant dribble of official reforms showed growing weakness on the part of the regime. The peasants saw these reforms as the result of pressure on the government by the Western powers who had since 1951 been underwriting Tito's trade deficits and equipping his armed forces. As these sentiments grew, even the most gentle efforts to prove to the peasants the superior advantages of collectivization were met with scorn.

In the end, the peasants won their battle. In March 1953, the Decree on Property Relationships and Reorganization of Peasant Working Co-operatives[29] was announced. It permitted the dissolution or reorganization of all peasant working co-operatives. Except for those individuals who had formed co-operatives from government-owned land, all peasants were now free to leave their collectives and to take with them the land, buildings, inventory, livestock, and other such items they had originally turned over to the

[27] See *New York Times*, July 28, 1952, p. 4.
[28] See "From the Report of the Managing Board of the Glavni Zadružni Savez," *Bulletin*, III:2 (Belgrade: 1954), p. 25.
[29] The text of this decree appears in *Borba*, March 20, 1953, p. 1.

organization. Those who withdrew, however, had to reimburse their co-operative for any improvements it might have made on the property returned to them. They had likewise to assume a share of the co-operative's indebtedness in proportion to the value of the property they removed from the organization. A mortgage was to be placed upon their property pending payment of these debts.

Although this decree described in considerable detail the reorganization of working co-operatives, once all individual withdrawals had been effected, it was essentially concerned with establishing the new basic principles for socialized agriculture. It left the internal operational details of each collective to be settled by regulations drawn up by the members. The local people's committee was given the task of making certain that each collective's self-determined operational rules and regulations conformed with the basic principles of the decree. No attempt was made to define organizational patterns for peasant working co-operatives. These patterns were now to be permitted to vary to any extent which the members and the local authorities might consider compatible with the aims and purposes of the individual collectives and of the new collectivization policy. Essentially, the basic principles of internal organization and management of the peasant working co-operative were to parallel those of self-management in economic enterprises. Each member was to share authority and responsibility in the work of his collective. Both general and working co-operatives were now to be free to plan their own work in accordance with the needs of the different yearly social plans and of the market. All collectives were now free to make their own contracts with their workers and with outside concerns. In most instances, the former government subsidies for almost every purpose were to cease. Co-operatives were to work out most of their own financial problems and were to seek their own credits from regular banks.

By the end of 1953, there were only 1,258 peasant working co-operatives as against the 6,964 reported just three years earlier.[30] The number of general co-operatives (most working co-operatives were automatically members of general co-operatives) grew from 6,973 in 1952 to 7,114 in 1953,[31] and embraced over 85 per cent of the country's peasantry.[32] The decree of March 1953 had reorganized the general co-operatives along lines more in keeping with the self-management techniques then being perfected in the industrial sector.

General co-operatives now have an assembly of members which elects both a management board and a supervisory board. The first board is charged with the management of the daily business of the co-operative and the latter supervises the work of the management board. General co-operatives still deal mainly in buying and selling services, although efforts are being made to have them expand into specialized agricultural pursuits such as stock breeding, food processing, and artisan and crafts services. Almost every rural community in Yugoslavia today has a general co-operative with its general store which makes manufactured goods and necessary raw materials available to its members.

As the richer peasants withdrew from the co-operatives once the law of 1953 was enacted, the poorer members, having brought little or no land or equipment into their organizations, found themselves faced with the possibility of becoming laborers working for peasants who had formerly been their colleagues. In May 1953, the government answered the nation-wide complaints of these poorer and

[30] "From the Report of the Managing Board of the Glavni Zadružni Savez," *op. cit.*

In the most fertile districts the least number of working co-operatives were disbanded, and, conversely, in the poorest areas, almost all were broken up. Thus, only 22 per cent were dissolved in the Voivodina while 100 per cent were dissolved in Montenegro. From: *Report of the Federal Executive Council for 1954*, Joint Translation Service (of the American and British Embassies in Belgrade) Supplement, April 25, 1955, p. 42.

[31] See Table 7-24, Statistički Godišnjak, *op cit.*, p. 132.

[32] "From the Report of the Managing Board of the Glavni Zadružni Savez," *op. cit.*, p. 24.

landless peasants with a new land reform bill, the Law on the Agricultural Land Pool.[33] All of the confidence which the March decree disbanding co-operatives might have restored to the peasants was immediately wiped out by this new land law which reduced to ten hectares the maximum amount of arable land an individual peasant family could own. The 1945 land reform had previously set this limit at twenty-five hectares. It was now explained that, since the mechanization of agriculture had yet to be achieved in Yugoslavia, the amount of land a single owner could reasonably cultivate without the help of hired labor was ten hectares. Only arable land was brought within the scope of the new law; pastures, forests, and wasteland were excluded. Owners could decide which surpluses they wished to turn over to the Social Land Pool created by the law. The state was to pay for surplus land at the rate of from 30,000 to 100,000 dinars a hectare.[34] Buildings and other installations on such land were to be assessed separately. According to the law, all payments were to be made in the form of state bonds payable in yearly installments spread out over a period of twenty years.

The land ceded under this reform was in most instances to be handed over to the local administrations. They were to form their own land pools to be used in settling as many as possible of the 180,000[35] peasants who at that time were landless or who owned only very marginal plots. But these peasants were not to receive this land for the purpose of establishing individual farms as had been permitted in the 1945 distribution. According to the new law, they were to have land only if they formed peasant working co-operatives or specialized agricultural co-operatives. Whatever land remained in the Social Land Pool was to be used, if eco-

---

[33] The text of this decree appears in SL, No. 37, June 1953. A discoursive article on the law is presented in *Bulletin*, II:3 (Belgrade: 1953), pp. 3-6.

[34] This was generally considered to be a fair price. As it worked out in practice, the average price paid per hectare was 60,500 dinars. See *Report of the Federal Executive Council for 1954, op. cit.*, p. 42.

[35] *YR*, II (June 1953), p. 7.

nomically plausible, for the formation of new state farms, working and specialized co-operatives, experimental farms, and breeding stations.

There is little doubt that one of the primary reasons for the 1953 land reform act was the need to appease that faction within the Yugoslav Communist party which saw the abandonment of the old collectivization policy as the severance of the last remaining tie with orthodox Marxism-Leninism. That the 1953 land reform had more political than practical substance is obvious from the fact that it affected only approximately 2 per cent of the total peasant population, and only approximately 3.7 per cent of the country's total arable surface.[36] Despite the relatively small number of peasants affected, however, the reform served to confirm every peasant's fear that the regime ultimately meant to divest him of all his land. Therefore, agricultural production continued to lag. It has been estimated that by mid-1953 approximately one-half million hectares less land was being farmed in Yugoslavia than before the war.[37]

In October 1953, Tito announced the inauguration of a new program aimed at increasing agricultural production by 50 per cent over the next ten-year period.[38] This was the first sincere effort made by the Titoists to focus their serious attention upon the development of agriculture. The program planned the investment of a total of 640 billion

[36] See *Report of the Federal Executive Council for 1954, op. cit.*

[37] See "Land Reform in Jugoslavia," *The Economist* (London), July 4, 1953, p. 36.

In spite of the fact that 1953 was a bumper year for Yugoslavia, the index of agricultural yields that year stood at only 109 (1930 = 100), even though orchards had increased by 25 per cent, vineyards by 20 per cent, and meadow land by 4 per cent; even though most crop yields per area had reportedly increased; and even though it was estimated that tractor power had increased by 314 per cent, threshers by 1 per cent, sowers by 53 per cent, and reapers by 87 per cent. Livestock production, with the exception of cattle which in June 1954 was 2 per cent greater, had also declined from the 1930 figures: horses by 15 per cent, pigs by 11 per cent, sheep by 8 per cent, and poultry by 3 per cent. (See Milun Ivanović, "Agricultural Perspectives," *YR*, II [June 1953], p. 12.)

[38] See "New Deal for Jugoslav Farmers," *The Economist* (London), Oct. 10, 1953, pp. 109-10.

dinars in agriculture during the following ten years (compared with the 116 billion invested in industry during the previous five years). In 1954, substantial amounts of credit funds were for the first time made available to private peasants. The 1955 Federal Social Plan included provisions for raising investments in agriculture and the food-processing industries, and provided large credits and facilities for such things as the increased use of chemical fertilizers and pesticides. The 1956 plan called for a 17 per cent reduction in industrial investments and an over-all increase of 19 per cent (over the 1955 total) for investments in agriculture. Land reclamation and water conservation projects were now being emphasized. Since 1954, all of the Federal Social Plans have called for the republican and local social plans to include maximum assistance to all phases of agricultural development.

The 1954 Federal Social Plan also changed the system of taxing income earned by private peasants. The old system of having local authorities attempt to assess the private peasant's yearly earnings had become a highly subjective and arbitrary process since it was practically impossible for officials to obtain honest income statistics from the peasants themselves. The new tax system is based upon assessments made in advance. These are founded upon supposedly objective, uniform standards based upon the size of each peasant holding, the quality of the land, the type of crop grown, the average earnings of all producers in a given area, and so on. In this way all private peasant producers within each area are placed on an equal footing. They pay taxes on their average and not on their real incomes. The basic tax rate fluctuates from area to area, the peasants in the richest farming areas paying the highest amounts.[39] According to Titoist reasoning, given the quality

[39] The 1956 Federal Social Plan fixed the basic agricultural tax rates at not less than 10 per cent and not higher than 44 per cent of cadastral income. It also ordered the local people's committees to fix a surtax of 3 per cent upon such income. See Chapters XX and XXI of the *Federal Social Plan for 1956*, Supplement to Joint Translation Bulletin 1824 (Belgrade: Joint

of land and the other fixed determinants, each peasant producer has the same obligation to society under this new tax system. Therefore, if a peasant realizes a larger than average income, he has a larger surplus profit to keep as his own. If he has a lower than average income, he is paying the penalty for his backwardness or laziness.

The provisions of the 1954 plan for short-term credits to assist private peasants with their out-of-season purchases of raw materials and equipment were accompanied by the expansion of their rights to contract freely for the future delivery of produce to industrial and trading concerns. Peasants were also given the right to ask for advances in cash. It was hoped that the contract privileges would encourage production since it would serve as assurance to the farmer that he would be able to market his produce at fixed prices. Furthermore, it would permit him to obtain seeds, fertilizers, and other necessary equipment without paying interest as he would have to do if he borrowed the money.

A law passed in June 1954 permitted the free purchase and sale of real estate,[40] including agricultural land (within the maximum limits fixed by the 1953 land reform). This right to free trade in land was another major development resulting from the shift in Titoist agrarian policy away from the Soviet pattern to the more liberal trend essentially aimed at winning the peasants' confidence in order to have them increase production.

Despite the regime's *volte-face* in 1953 in its collectivization policy and its subsequent concern for agricultural development, the much-needed increase in production was not forthcoming. The drought of the winter 1953-54 crystallized peasant apprehensions that the government would eventually revert to the old policies of compulsory deliveries

Translation Service), pp. 43-44. The 1956 plan appears in *SL*, No. 14, March 30, 1956.

The actual rates, within the limits fixed by the plan, are established by the six republican governments.

[40] For a discussion of this law, see Chapter VIII.

of produce, of further reduction in private landholdings, and of forced collectivization. Rumors became so prevalent that Tito himself spoke out in spring of 1954 to dispel them. He publicly criticized Party members who clung to their "old views" concerning the village, and declared that the peasants were no danger to socialism and that, after all, socialism could not be built upon industrial workers alone. At the same time, he let it be understood that the regime did not look upon the independent peasantry as a permanent institution in Yugoslavia.[41] Once again the left hand immediately took away what the right hand had given. The result was merely the *status quo ante.*

The 1954 wheat crop was the worst the country had had for thirty years.[42] The over-all agricultural output for the year was only 86 per cent of the 1953 yield.[43] The Titoists' explanations of the failure mentioned the bumper crop of 1953 as an unsound basis for comparison and blamed the unfavorable weather conditions of the preceding winter and spring. However, these weather conditions had not been half as severe as the droughts of 1950 and 1952. Much of the real cause for the dismal showing of agriculture in 1954 (and in each of the subsequent years as well) lay elsewhere—undoubtedly in the peasants' distrust of the regime.

In the spring of 1955, Dr. Vladimir Bakarić, the head of the Croatian republican government and one of the leading "liberal" thinkers in the uppermost ranks of the Yugoslav Communist party, publicly clarified for the first time the regime's latest efforts to increase agricultural output without abandoning plans for the eventual socialization of the village.[44] He was particularly critical of the Titoist theorists'

[41] See *New York Times,* April 29, 1954, p. 10.
[42] *Ibid.,* Nov. 12, 1954, p. 4.
[43] See Ivanović, "Agriculture in 1954," *RIA* V (Belgrade: Jan. 1, 1955), p. 17. Every agricultural category of production, except livestock which had an 11 per cent increase, turned in a decrease when compared with 1953 yields; cereals were the lowest, representing only 62 per cent of the 1953 total, wheat and rye together representing only 56 per cent of their 1953 performance.
[44] See *Borba,* May 1, 2, 3, 1955, p. 3.

past failure to understand what he considered the realities and the "dynamics" of the Yugoslav agrarian situation.

Dr. Bakarić did not question that in theory large estates are more profitable than small landholdings. But, he pointed out, the truth of this theoretical proposition in no way guaranteed the actual profitability of large estates nor did it even guarantee the most rapid development of the economy. The dismal failure of many Yugoslav state farms was sufficient proof of this. The "theorists'" approach to agrarian over-population lacked understanding of the actual "dynamics" of the Yugoslav situation. The preoccupation with agrarian over-population, he said, had been "created" by those theorists who insisted upon rapid development of large agricultural estates by "Prussian" methods, and by those who constantly stressed the need for large agricultural investment programs. He believed that Yugoslavia's economic development was so geared that such programs were impractical. The policy of increasing agricultural investments aimed at expanding collectivization and thereby forcing surplus farm labor into non-agricultural pursuits had the cart before the horse. The important first step, Dr. Bakarić insisted, was to make certain that industry would be in a position to absorb surplus farm labor as it became available. To date, Yugoslav industry is not in a position to absorb completely even that amount of surplus farm labor which is presently available.

Dr. Bakarić was of the opinion that, under present conditions in Yugoslavia, the Titoists would best serve their own interest by working "to change the structure of the village in the least painful manner." Or, in other words, only those steps should be taken which do not require the direct departure of surplus labor and which at the same time do not raise the per capita income of the households too much above the average of the present peasant standard of living." [45] It is true, he pointed out, that if the peasant becomes a part-time worker in industry, his farm will not be

[45] *Ibid.*

properly exploited. Nevertheless, such an interlacing of the industrial and agricultural sectors is a much cheaper way to change the present structure of peasant farming and to raise the "level of socialist consciousness" of the village than the policy of indiscriminate collectivization. Practice had shown that the latter policy caused only ruinous upheaval in the countryside.

Dr. Bakarić admitted that the present Yugoslav structure of small landholdings could not hope to secure a profitable and progressive agricultural development.[46] The most profitable crops, wheat for example, cannot be produced effectively under the present structure. It is still more profitable for the Yugoslav farmer to produce livestock, milk, poultry, eggs, or wine, since these crops permit him the maximum participation in his local market. Dr. Bakarić reasoned that the proper policy for the government to pursue, given the existing structure of Yugoslav agriculture, is one which will encourage in every way possible the small farmer's intensification of production of those very crops which bring him the most profit. Simultaneously, the government must concentrate upon increasing the efficient production of these same products by the socialized sector of agriculture, upon improving the communications networks between rural areas and urban markets, and upon expanding refrigeration and other storage facilities. Eventually the investments required by the private peasant to increase his productivity in the face of collectivized competition in the local market will be beyond his resources. He will find the breeding of pigs, the production of milk, and such pursuits, much more expensive than the prevailing market prices warrant. He will then discover that he is able to earn higher recompense for his efforts in some other manner. He will either begin to consider some form of closer collaboration with his neighbors in order to raise the productivity of his land or he will begin to seek non-agricultural employment.

The tactic Dr. Bakarić described above came to be known

[46] See *ibid.*, April 28, 1955, p. 4.

as the "intensified agriculture" policy. Although it was not generally publicized, the government had been experimenting with this tactic since the latter half of 1954. The sum total of the theory behind "intensified agriculture" is that, instead of attempting to bring about agricultural collectivization by force or by pouring large sums of money into the collectivized sector and ignoring the private sector, collectivization is to be encouraged indirectly by the creation of market conditions which will show the small landholders the practicality of voluntary co-operation. The new policy includes the right of the peasant to work part-time in industry and part-time on his land. Such an interpenetration of agriculture and industry is expected, as Dr. Bakarić has indicated, to play an important role in raising the "socialist consciousness" of the village. As more and more peasants work alongside urban workers, the old antagonisms between these two groups are expected gradually to disappear. Furthermore, the "intensified agriculture" policy does not force the sudden flow of large masses of village surplus labor into the urban areas as would a successful collectivization drive. Instead, the new policy makes possible a gradual influx more in keeping with the real absorptive capacities of Yugoslav industrialization.

The "intensified agriculture" policy bears a marked resemblance to the standard historical experience of Western democracies. It intends competition in the free market to force the private peasant to modernize or to give up farming. Its Marxist content seems conspicuously lacking. Like all other Titoist reforms, however, the policy is one of trial and error. It is a compromise designed to bring about the reformation of the structure of Yugoslav agriculture to have it serve both theoretical and practical necessities. If "intensified agriculture" fails, there is no assurance the regime will not return to the old methods. The Yugoslav peasants know this and consequently are wary of all Titoists bearing gifts. They have had ample opportunity since 1950 to observe the Titoists' tendency to make a concession with one hand and to withdraw it with the other.

The constant "zigzagging" of Titoist agricultural policy is due primarily to the fact that this policy has been a particular bone of contention between the "liberal" and "ideological extremist" factions within the top leadership of the Yugoslav Communist party. The somewhat turbulent progress of the Titoists' agricultural reforms since 1950 is due almost entirely to the struggle between these two factions. The ideological extremists held the field from 1945 to 1950. During that period all of the oppressive measures such as the compulsory delivery to the state of agricultural produce and the forced collectivization drive were the order of the day. As a result, production gradually dwindled almost to the peasants' own subsistence level. For some time it looked as though the Titoists were consciously attempting the complete ruination of the Yugoslav countryside.

The 1950 drought and the serious danger of the collapse of the entire Titoist structure in the face of impending starvation gave the liberals their chance. It was at the end of 1950 that the Politburo of the Communist party first ordered the Ministry of Agriculture to consider practical reforms for the collectivization policy.[47] However, the majority of the officials within the Ministry at that time belonged to the ideological extremist faction and remained steadfast in their faith in the Soviet agrarian ideology and methods then being followed. When the rash of petitions to withdraw from the co-operatives came at the end of 1951, the Politburo met to consider what must be done. The ideological extremists had their way and the petitioners were suppressed. But the arguments of the liberals were given added impetus by the rapidly declining productivity. Eventually, the liberals, under the leadership of Dr. Bakarić, worked out the profit-and-loss accounting methods and the other reforms which lead to greater self-management within the co-operatives. By the spring of 1952 these reforms were adopted by the government.

[47] This and the remaining information in this paragraph came from a conversation the author had with several high-ranking Communists in January 1952.

Though the 1952 reforms were meant to appear as sops to the peasants to get them to increase production, in reality they were essential agricultural adjuncts to the general economic decentralization reforms then being carried out. The peasants were not impressed by these "concessions." It was the drought of 1952 which gave the liberal faction the lever it needed to pry loose the tight grip the ideological extremists still held on agricultural policy. To increase agricultural production at almost any cost became an irrefutable necessity. By the end of 1952, impractical and uneconomical working co-operatives were disbanded. In March 1953, came the decree permitting any and all peasants to withdraw from the working co-operatives. This decree represented a serious blow to the ideological extremists and a very rude awakening to those Party sycophants who had soft jobs within the agricultural co-operative system. It was unquestionably partly because of the need to placate these two groups that much of the good which might otherwise have resulted from the dissolution decree was almost immediately nullified by the land reform which was promulgated in May 1953.

But, if the ideological extremists were stunned, it did not take them long to recover. During the latter half of 1953 and the first half of 1954, they renewed their struggle with the liberals over agrarian policy. The extremists fought for the concentration of all available resources upon mechanizing the remaining co-operatives as the only means short of force to bring socialization to the villages. The liberals wanted the regime to adopt the "intensified agriculture" policy.

Dr. Bakarić did not wait for a decision. He began to work out methods of encouraging the Croatian small landowners to intensify production of livestock, milk, wine, and other such products which brought them the greatest profit and participation in the local market. Simultaneously, he began to take steps to increase the productivity of Croatian state farms and to improve the Republic's transportation network. When the showdown between the liberals and the ideological extremists finally came, Dr. Bakarić had several important practical results to show for his pains.[48] In the end these practical results carried the liberals to victory. In the autumn of 1954 Tito placed his stamp of approval upon the "intensified agriculture" policy and appointed Slavko Komar, a friend and supporter of Dr. Bakarić, to head the Federal Executive Council's agricultural section.

Thus, contemporary Titoist agricultural policy may be summed up as follows: The immediate emphasis is upon finding suitable ways to induce peasants to raise productivity. Nevertheless, the Yugoslav leaders do not for one moment lose sight of the fact that the present small landholding structure of Yugoslav agriculture must eventually be replaced by larger farms organized in various types of collectives. The peasant is now more or less able to enter or to leave a co-operative of his own free will. The emphasis in collectivization is upon increasing the nature and scope of the general co-operatives in order to have them demonstrate to the peasants the advantages of co-operation. As it concerns the working co-operative, Titoist agricultural policy seems to be based primarily upon the economic practicality of such organizations and not upon the formation of a working co-operative merely for the sake of increasing the extent of the socialized sector. Last, but probably first in theoretical importance, is the new approach represented by "intensified agriculture," a tactic through which socialization of the Yugoslav villages is to be reached by evolution rather than by revolution.

[48] One such "practical result" was as follows: In the autumn of 1953, the government imported a number of pedigreed English pigs to improve the breed in Yugoslavia. Serbia received 3,000 of these pigs, Croatia only 500. However, following the Bakarić approach, most of the Croatian allotment were turned over to private peasants who took the pigs into their homes where they were treated almost as cherished members of the family. The Serbian allotment, in accordance with the ideological extremists' dictum, were turned over to the state farms. By spring 1954, there were no English pigs left in Serbia. In Croatia, on the other hand, their numbers had grown considerably and their pedigree had been kept. The Serbians therefore had to come to the Croatian market to buy English pedigreed pigs, and by mid-1955 these pigs brought from four to five times the price of ordinary pigs.

In the end, however, Titoist agricultural policy, no matter how liberal it becomes, cannot avoid the ever-present fundamental impasse of peasant-Communist relationships. The intelligent peasant, who does not deny the need for closer co-operation in order to raise his standard of living, insists that this co-operation be left more or less to his own initiative and control. The Communist insists that agriculture, like industry, be run by the central "representative" authority, or, when he reasons on his highest level of generalization, that it be run by selfless society.

The Titoist regime, in its dealings with peasant reluctance to accept social reform, has so far made all the concessions. The peasants have made none. The peasants dislike and mistrust the regime's ultimate aims and aspirations. Therefore, if the Titoists are to bring about the eventual socialization of their villages—without which Yugoslavia can never be considered a completely socialist country—they will have to display extraordinary patience and fortitude in their dealings with the peasants. The Yugoslav Marxists will have to give continuous and searching thought to those of their theoretical concepts which today conflict so violently with the peasants' most basic instincts. This means that in the future the Titoists will have to make even greater compromises on private property, religion, and individual freedom. But if the regime continues to make such concessions, what remains of Marxism? Yet if the regime fails to bring its peasants to socialism, what can possibly remain of its plans for total socialization? The Yugoslav peasants have superior numbers and an age-old technique of resistance. They are today bolstered by the knowledge that resistance has forced important concessions from the Communist regime. On the other hand, the regime controls the primary instruments of political power. If a common meeting ground is to be found, both the peasants and the Communists will have to give and take alike. The peasants, in the final analysis, are Titoism's greatest challenge.

CHAPTER VII

Major Political-Administrative Reforms

It was neither practical nor possible to decentralize control of the Yugoslav economy without decentralizing the political-administrative machinery of the state. To employ the proper Marxist terminology, Titoism's superstructure, its state government, had automatically to be overhauled so that it could reflect the changes in its substructure, its worker-owner relationships. In purely Titoist terms, workers' self-management in the economic sphere had to be matched with workers' self-government in the political sphere. When combined, workers' self-management and workers' self-government were to represent the essence of what the Yugoslav Marxists call "social democracy."

The very first political-administrative reforms were makeshift arrangements adopted mainly to facilitate economic decentralization. As the system of workers' self-management began to take root, more comprehensive reforms were invented to give the individual working citizen greater responsibility in matters of his own civic welfare. Early in 1952, a new basic law on the people's committees reorganized the system of local government and gave the people's committee greater independence and responsibility in local affairs. This in turn prepared the way for the constitutional reform of January 1953 which completed the political-administrative reorganization by modernizing the existing structures of the federal and republican governments.

In their search for a non-Stalinist yet Marxist rationale for the new system they hoped to build, the Titoists took as their guide the lessons supposedly taught by the Paris Commune of 1871. Marx had hailed the commune as the means through which decentralized forms of authority could be substituted for the centralized state.[1] Lenin's cry of "all power to the soviets" carried on the tradition of the commune. But when this tradition proved impractical in Russia it was snuffed out by the most stringent form of Party dictatorship. The Titoists searched for a way to restore what Soviet practice had lost. As explained by Kardelj in 1951, the essential kernel of the new Titoist theory of the ideal democratic state was as follows: "At the top, a small apparatus, highly qualified and subordinate to the central *representative* organs, with its rights and duties strictly defined. At the bottom, in the sense of the 'commune' of Marx, the real basis of social activity, the social organs of the districts, localities, factories, institutions, etc., and, as the center of gravity of all of these a qualified apparatus of professionals responsible to the social organs and fulfilling its tasks within the framework of strictly determined rights and duties." [2]

When considering the political-administrative structure of the Titoist state, it is well to keep in mind that, as in all authoritarian political organizations, there often seems to be an unbridgeable gap between the legally constituted rights and duties of the state apparatus and those which that apparatus actually performs. Without the genuine consent of the large majority of the people, a minority government requires

[1] The Titoist theorists frequently quote the following from Karl Marx, "The Civil War in France, 1871," *Selected Works*, II (New York: 1933), p. 500, as the inspiration for their post-1950 political-administrative reforms:

"The rural communes of every district were to administer their common affairs by an assembly of delegates in the central town, and these district assemblies were again to send deputies to the National Delegation in Paris, each delegate to be at any time revocable and bound by the *mandat imperatif* (formal instructions) of his constituents. The few but important functions which still would remain for a central government were not to be suppressed, . . . but were to be discharged by Communal and therefore strictly responsible agents. The unity of the nation was not to be broken, but, on the contrary, to be organized by the Communal Constitution, and to become a reality by the destruction of the state power which claimed to be the embodiment of that unity independent of, and superior to, the nation itself, from which it was but a parasitic excrescence."

In this statement, Marx was giving a rough sketch of national organization which the Paris Commune of 1871 had planned, but did not have sufficient time to implement.

[2] Kardelj, "Dix Ans de Revolution Populaire à la Lumière de l'Histoire," *QAS*, No. 5-6 (July-Sept. 1951), p. 22.

force to maintain itself. Official references to democratic principles and practices are thereby frequently reduced to theoretical rather than practical importance. The Titoist leaders have at no time had the consent or even the tacit approval of anywhere near the majority of the Yugoslav people, except perhaps when they openly defied the Soviet Union. Their primary ambition on seizing control of Yugoslavia in 1945 was to create their own state and its administrative structure and practice as much in the Stalinist image as local conditions would permit. The desires of the majority of Yugoslavs were not solicited or even considered.

The determination of the Titoists, once they had been expelled from the Cominform, to find a Marxist yet non-Stalinist form of political and social organization has been tempered by the full realization, in theory at least, that socialism can succeed only if it is firmly allied with most of the fundamental Western democratic concepts. Hence, valid—though perhaps still visionary—democratic principles form the theoretical basis of much of the Titoists' current philosophy. While developments within Titoist administrative practice since 1950 still fall short of democracy as understood by Western liberals, these changes at least tend toward a more lenient form of statecraft than Stalinist Yugoslavia knew.

In contemporary Yugoslav administration, from the federal to the lowest local levels, there are in reality two governments: the "shadow" government and the "substance" government. The former is the administrative apparatus established by constitutional and other fundamental structural and administrative laws and regulations. The real government, the "substance" government, is made up of the "conscious socialist forces," or, in other words, of the leading members of the Communist party of Yugoslavia. These men make the laws and regulations. They head all important government and administrative organs from the Federal Executive Council at the top right down to the base of the people's committees and the agencies of workers' self-management within the individual enterprises. They are in all the controlling defense and police positions from the highest to the lowest echelons of command. They supervise and control the judicial system.

The period prior to 1950 was the high noon of the "substance" government; its "shadow" was the least evident. Since 1950, however, the decentralization policies have given new emphasis and consequently greater importance to the "shadow." There is no doubt that the Titoist leaders would prefer to have the "shadow" become the "substance." They continue to assist this process wherever it cannot threaten their total control. Hence, much of the tension between the governed and the governors has been eased in the past few years. But the process is still in its infancy and will remain there until the Titoist system has brought a much greater feeling of security and well-being to the average Yugoslav or until it has been overthrown. The "substance" is still clearly to be seen, but it has complied with the orders to make itself less obtrusive. Today the assistance of non-Party members in the settlement of vital government problems is solicited and the more capable young Yugoslavs are invited into the Party itself. Nevertheless, as long as the "conscious socialist forces" form but a minority within the country, the Party will be required to serve as the "substance" of any Titoist government.

The 1946 Constitution

The first Titoist Constitution, that of January 31, 1946,[3] established the Federative People's Republic of Yugoslavia, the foundations of which had been laid at the anti-Fascist Council of the National Liberation Movement (AVNOJ) meeting held by the Partisans at Jajce in 1943. This Con-

[3] A translation of the 1946 Constitution has been made by the Department of State Office of Research and Intelligence, publication No. 3726 (Washington, D.C.: April 10, 1946).

stitution received its inspiration almost entirely from the 1936 Stalinist prototype.[4] It created what Communists like to call a "people's democracy." The rights it guaranteed to Yugoslav citizens were extensive, yet the state machinery which it formed was authoritarian since it theoretically assured the total omnipotence of a single state organ, the National Assembly.

The Constitution declared that all power stemmed directly from the people and belonged exclusively to them. They were, however, to exercise this power through duly elected representatives serving in the people's committees at the local level, in the national assemblies on the level of the six constituent republics, and in the National Assembly at the federal level. Political liberty existed mainly in the right to vote, granted to all citizens of eighteen years of age and over, regardless of sex, nationality, race, religion, or creed. Referendum and recall were alluded to in the Constitution, but enacting legislation was not passed until 1953, and then only for recall. A long list of civil liberties to which all citizens were to be entitled was included within the Constitution. Except for the fact that this list was an integral part of the Constitution, it represented no oustanding departure from, nor did it contain any original additions to, those forms of civil liberties usually offered by liberal democratic governments.

As established by the 1946 Constitution, the Titoist state was a federation.[5] Theoretically, the six republics were sovereign and had the explicit right to secede from the federation. But this right existed only in theory since the republics were expressly forbidden to maintain their own armed forces or

---

[4] An excellent analysis of the 1946 Constitution is made by Henri Fabré, *Revue du Droit Public et de la Science Politique*, LXII (Paris: Librarie Général de Droit et de Jurisprudence, 1946), pp. 456-59. He points up some of the basic similarities to the 1936 Stalinist Constitution as well as some of the essential differences such as those concerning private property and the fact that the Yugoslav Constitution did not specifically prescribe the predominance of a single political party.

[5] *Ibid.*, pp. 462-68 is devoted to a penetrating analysis of whether or not the Titoists had a right to refer to their state as a federation. Fabré concludes that they did not.

to deal with foreign governments. The unity and supremacy of the federal state was achieved by the fact that the Constitution listed the specific rights and duties which the republics technically ceded to the federal state as its exclusive province. The enumerated federal rights and duties were so extensive that little other than administrative detail was left to the exclusive initiative of the republics. The Constitution prescribed the organization of the power and administrative structures of the republics (and of the two autonomous districts: the Voivodina and Kossovo-Metohija), modeling these structures insofar as practical after their federal counterparts. Most republican ministries were to be supervised by the appropriate federal ministries. Even the matter of local structural organization was fixed by the Constitution. Federal control over the entire administrative apparatus was assured by the express provision permitting higher government organs to suspend or to abrogate illegal acts of lower organs. Thus, the real chain of command of the Titoist state ran from top to bottom and not vice versa as the Titoist theorists were wont to claim.

The Constitution outlined the judicial structure of the entire country, and prescribed the most general rights and duties of the system of courts and public prosecutor's offices which it created.[6]

The National Assembly as created by the 1946 Constitution was bicameral institution, containing a Federal Council elected by all of the citizens on the basis of one deputy for each fifty thousand inhabitants. The second house was the Council of Nationalities, composed of thirty deputies from each of the six republics, twenty from the Autonomous Province of the Voivodina, and fifteen from the Autonomous Region of Kossovo-Metohija, each delegation elected by the voters of their respective areas. Both houses were elected simultaneously for a term of four years. Both had equal rights. No legislation could become law without the full consent of both houses.

[6] See Chapter XI.

The Presidium of the National Assembly was created to serve as the Assembly's executive organ. It was elected by both houses in joint session from amongst the Assembly's own membership. Its rights and duties as outlined by the Constitution made it a kind of collective chief of state, legally responsible to the Assembly for its work, and legally subject to recall either collectively or individually by the Assembly.

Apart from the Presidium, the Constitution also provided for the creation of a Government (the Cabinet) which was to be the supreme executive and administrative organ of federal power. The Government was composed of a Prime Minister, Vice-Premiers, all heads of federal ministries, and the heads of the Federal Planning Commission and of the Federal Control Commission.[7] Each of these individuals received his appointment from and was technically responsible to the National Assembly.

The Constitution made the National Assembly omnipotent. Even the Constitution itself was a law within and under the competence of the Assembly since only that body could revise or amend it. No consent of the people was required for revisions and amendments. Furthermore, there was no constitutional check upon the laws passed by the Assembly. The Presidium was only charged with seeing that republican and local laws, ordinances, decisions, etc., were constitutional. The courts were given no jurisdiction over the consitutionality of laws, either federal or republican. The federal legislative function was to be the exclusive province of the Assembly. Although it turned its executive powers over to the Presidium and the Government, the Assembly technically controlled both of these agencies by its right to appoint and recall their members. In a similar

[7] The Federal Control Commission was one of the important Soviet-type agencies the Titoists adopted in the earliest stages of their development. Its task was to examine the efficiency and honesty of the administration and to investigate complaints of abuses. In practice it showed less zeal for the defense of the citizens against bureaucratic abuse than for protecting the interests of the government against both private individuals and subordinate officials. It was abolished in 1951.

fashion, the Assembly controlled the judicial function, although the Constitution maintained that the courts were to be independent in the administration of justice.

Each of the six republics drew up a Constitution which was a miniature of the federal prototype wherever practical, except that the republican assemblies were unicameral since they had no need to consider the nationalities problem. Each republican assembly elected a Presidium and a Government as its dual executive organ.

It was this duality of the executive organs of government which was one of the chief targets of the 1953 constitutional reform. It was claimed that the split made it impossible for the national and republican assemblies to exercise proper control over the executive functions, and that this in turn permitted an inordinate growth of bureaucracy. However, in actual practice the assemblies had no independent power whatsoever—they were merely rubber stamp congresses. Furthermore, most of the members of the federal and republican Governments were also members of their respective Presidiums. With one or two exceptions at the federal level who were used as window-dressing, all of these officials were members of the top echelons of the Communist party. Until the implementation in 1950 of the policy of substituting persuasion for intimidation, the Party made little effort to hide the fact that it alone was the real government of the country.

During the period from 1945 to 1950, there was a steady increase in the number of federal ministries and committees created to deal with each facet of total administration as the Titoists became aware of each new need. Reforms begun just before the enactment of the Workers' Council Law in June 1950 dissolved many federal ministries directly concerned with the economy and replaced them with councils which were given the duties of supervising and co-ordinating rather than directly administering. But these early reforms were only temporary expediencies until a more basic and comprehensive reorganization of the state administrative apparatus could be worked out. One of the first reforms of a more general nature was the abolition of the State Control Commission in February 1951. Its functions were supposedly transferred to the local organs of self-government and self-management. However, in practice the Commission has been replaced by a series of inspection agencies attached to the different branches of the federal government or to the Federal Executive Council. Although increasing reliance is being placed upon the inspection agencies to assure unity of purpose and practice throughout the entire Titoist administrative system, these agencies do not operate in the same police-state fashion as did the old Commission. Rather, contemporary inspection agencies are more in the nature of government accountants.

Piecemeal political-administrative decentralization was finally ended on January 31, 1953, when the National Assembly adopted the new Constitutional Law. Steps were immediately taken to implement the changes and reforms envisaged by this fundamental statute. Under a special law passed the same day, the old Assembly proceeded to elect Tito to fill the newly created office of President of the Republic and a group of men to serve as the Federal Executive Council (which now replaced the Presidium and the Government). Both of these new offices had been created by the 1953 law as executive organs. Their officers were to be elected by the newly constituted National Assembly from amongst the members of its upper house. The constitutionality of a soon-to-be-extinct parliament's electing the officers of a reformed parliament which had yet to be convened did not disturb the Yugoslav rulers. They merely had the outmoded parliament pass a law to make the election possible. The new National Assembly was not elected until November 1953. Until it held its first session in January 1954, the President of the Republic and the Federal Executive Council continued to function technically under the supervision of the old National Assembly which constitutionally had no authority to perform the task.

LOCAL SELF-GOVERNMENT: THE PEOPLE'S COMMITTEES

All of the "people's republics" formed after the last war claim that their states are built upon the precedent that all power comes from and belongs exclusively to the people. The Titoist state is no exception. But the Titoists argue that from the beginning there had been conditions peculiar to the development of their state which made it a foregone conclusion that the evolution of Yugoslav administrative practice would differ from that of the Soviet Union and its other satellites.[8] The Yugoslav revolution, unlike the Russian revolution, had not begun by destroying the old central organs of power and replacing them with the central power organs of the working class. From the outbreak of the Yugoslav war of liberation, it had been the inferior organs, the Liberation Committees formed by the Partisans in each liberated village and district, which had exercised administrative power. These Liberation Committees had been elected by the people, generally at meetings of voters. They functioned more or less independently, directly administering the people within their individual jurisdictions. Even though a centralized state apparatus had been created by the AVNOJ of 1943, it was not until after the cessation of hostilities in Europe that this apparatus was able to consolidate its control over the entire country.

The Liberation Committees served as the model for the people's committees which the early Titoist state theoretically made the fundamental organs of the people's power and of state administration. However, there was one essential difference between the Liberation Committees and the postwar people's committees: the former were created during a time of uncertainty when the Partisan leaders, for practical reasons, were careful to hide their preference for Stalinist methods of administrative organization.

[8] See Leon Gershković, "L'Organisation d'État de la Règublique Federal Populaire de Yougoslavia," *QAS*, No. 7 (Oct. 1951), p. 108.

The organizational structure and the basic terms of authority of the people's committees were delineated by Chapter XII of the 1946 Constitution. There followed a series of laws, decrees, and regulations setting forth the specific rights and duties of the committees. In July 1949, a law designed to co-ordinate and improve the previous laws and regulations was enacted.[9] One of the express purposes of the 1949 law was to do away with the smallest village committees and to group several of these into a more manageable and efficient single "municipality" committee. But the primary aim of the law was to create the district committee which would co-ordinate and control a number of municipality and/or town committees. The previous system in which the village and town committees were directly under the republican government had proved too cumbersome to centralized control. The newly created district committee was to serve as a much-needed intermediary.

From the time of its creation, the people's committee was hailed as the highest organ of state authority within its own territory. It was meant to be the effective representative body of the local population in administering communal affairs. All higher organs, excluding those specifically excepted by law (such as the secret police), were theoretically subordinate to the people's committee when carrying out their business at the local level. But no matter what the theoretical intent, as in all other administrative echelons lower than the federal government during the period from 1945 to 1950, the people's committee merely served in actual practice as the local administrative minion of the central organs of authority.[10] Most of the local committees became the private preserve of lesser Party members whose talents were too insignificant to earn them more coveted sinecures.

[9] For the text of this law, see *SL* No. 49, 1949. For a résumé of text, see *NYL*, I:4 (1950), pp. 30-36.
[10] A frank appraisal of the servile status of the pre-1950 people's committees is given in Jovan Djordjević, "Local Self-Government in Yugoslavia," *American Slavic and East European Review*, XII (April 1953), pp. 188-200.

The effect on local self-government was disastrous. As Kardelj declared—once the regime had decided to frown upon such mismanagement—some people's committees had shown a tendency to transform people's self-government into a "pashalik" of local officialdom.[11]

On April 1, 1952, the General Law on People's Committees[12] was enacted. It reorganized the structure and function of the entire system of local self-government to make it conform more logically with the economic decentralization reforms and to bring it into closer accord with the general philosophy of Titoist social democracy. The new law was to lay the foundations for the more general constitutional reform then under consideration. In addition, the Titoist planners expected that the structural and functional reforms proclaimed by the new people's committee law would facilitate the eventual transition of local self-government units into the more advanced "communes" visualized as the ideal units of local government in a social democratic state.

The 1952 law described three regular types and one special type of people's committees: municipalities, made up of a group of villages or smaller towns; town municipalities, consisting of single towns large enough to have a committee of their own; districts, which include a varying number of municipalities and/or towns; and the special city municipality existing in cities of approximately fifty thousand or more inhabitants. City and larger town municipalities were divided into subordinate wards, each of which has its own people's committee. Republican laws were to fix the territorial boundaries of each of the four types of committees and to establish the detailed regulations for their organization and operation.

According to the 1952 law, the independent authority of the people's committees is based upon their right to draw up and to execute their own social plans, budgets, and instru-

---

[11] Kardelj, "Dix Ans de Revolution Populaire à la Lumière de l'Histoire," *QAS*, No. 5-6 (July-Sept. 1951), pp. 31-32.

[12] The full text of this law appears in *NYL*, II:1-2 (1952), pp. i-xvi.

ments of finance—within the limits established by republican and federal laws and regulations. Since 1952, these material rights of authority have been substantially supplemented by new laws and regulations such as those which placed the major responsibility for the supervision of economic enterprises upon the people's committees.

Besides introducing basic changes aimed at increasing the real authority of the people's committee, the 1952 law also altered the structural composition of the people's committee. The most significant change was the creation of a council of producers as a second chamber of the town, city, and district committee. The municipality committee, however, was not given a second chamber, undoubtedly because municipal committees existed mainly in rural areas. The theory behind the creation of this second chamber lies in what Kardelj called the foremost principle of Titoist state organization: the leading role in governing belongs to the working class; this being the sum and substance of what Marx meant by the "dictatorship of the proletariat." [13] Kardelj believed that by creating the producers' councils as second chambers of the people's committees, the new local self-government law permitted representatives of the agencies of production to take part directly in their own communal government. The system of workers' self-management had given the worker some control over the distribution of the wage fund within his own enterprise since he technically controls his own workers' council and management board. With the creation of producers' councils as part of his local government, the worker was now to be in a position to exercise some control over the size of the wage fund of his enterprise since the size of each wage fund is largely determined by the local people's committee.

The producers' council is meant to be the lower chamber of the people's committee. Its membership is generally not to exceed one-half of the number elected to the upper

---

[13] See Kardelj, "On the Law on People's Committees," *NYL, op. cit.,* pp. 14-16.

chamber, the people's council. The upper chamber is elected every four years; the producers' council every two years. Both chambers have equal responsibility for local statutes and for all matters which in any way involve local economic affairs. All other responsibilities of local authority fall within the exclusive competence of the people's council.

Members of the local producers' councils are elected by the individual producers themselves from the various general branches of production, such as manufacturing, agriculture, arts and crafts, in direct proportion to the percentage which each branch contributes to the "total social product" [14] of the town, city, or district electing a council. The definition of a producer at the local and district levels legally makes no distinction between the socialized and the private sectors of production. However, that distinction *is* made in the republican and federal producers' councils formed after the 1953 constitutional reform; at those levels only the socialized sector is represented. The total number of agricultural members of local and district producers' councils is supposed to be divided between the specialized and private sectors in accordance with each sector's participation in the total agricultural product of the pertinent area.[15]

The first chamber of the local people's committee, the people's council, is elected by free, universal, and secret ballot. According to the 1952 law, candidates may be proposed either by a group of voters submitting a written petition with a fixed number of names to the local authorities, or they may be proposed and nominated at open voters' meetings held specifically for this purpose. However, in practice,

[14] Total social product is gross product, which means the total value of new produce without deduction of any kind. (See Leon Geršković, "The System of Producers' Councils in Yugoslavia," *International Labor Review,* LXXI [Geneva: Jan. 1955], footnote No. 1, p. 42.)

[15] In this respect, it is interesting to note that prior to the creation of the new districts under the 1955 law on the organization of communes and districts, the system of choosing representatives to the local producers' councils resulted in the agricultural sector's having the majority of representation in both local and district councils when these were considered on a nation-wide basis. (See Geršković, *op. cit.,* p. 42.)

this latter procedure is severely restricted by legal technicalities which give almost insurmountable advantage to members of the "conscious socialist forces." [16] An innovation of the new law was the provision that final lists of candidates for the people's council must contain at least twice as many names as there are positions to be filled. The law also contained provisions for the recall of members of the people's committee either by the voters or by the people's committee itself.

The 1952 law abolished the Executive Committee of the people's committee. Under the old system this agency had become the all-powerful "politburo" of each committee. The functions of executive authority which it had so consistently abused were now transferred either to the people's committee as a whole or to permanent and *ad hoc* subordinate committees created by the new law to supervise the various specific tasks of local administration. These committees, called "citizens' committees," are generally to be composed of private citizens whose professional experience or individual aptitudes can contribute to the improvement of local services. All such members are elected by the people's committee. They are not paid for their services. The citizens' committees are meant to decide in principle upon the policies to be followed within the areas of their competence. The actual administrative tasks arising from such policy decisions are carried out by the committees' individual secretaries, who are usually members of the people's committees, and by the permanent local administrative apparatus.

The permanent administrative apparatus of each people's committee is, according to the 1952 law, composed of personnel appointed by the people's committee. At the head of this administrative body is the secretary of the people's committee. He is appointed by the committee as an employed official strictly accountable to the chairman of the committee. The secretary is in effect the highest official of local government.

[16] See the final section of this chapter.

The 1952 law does not emphasize the role of the chairman of the people's committee. It gives him no powers other than those necessary to insure the constant, lawful, and proper operation of the committee and of its various subordinate agencies. He is elected by the committee from among its own members to serve for the four-year term for which the upper chamber of the committee is elected. He may not be elected to the chair for more than two successive terms. He is paid a salary, but other committee members, except for the vice-chairman of some of the larger committees, receive no regular remuneration apart from reimbursement for expenses and losses of regular income incurred while doing committee work.

Because of the de-emphasis which the 1952 law placed upon the role of the chairman of the people's committee, the leading Communist party official in the local area is now more likely to be the secretary rather than the chairman. On the surface, at least, this lends respectability to the Titoists' claim that the former practice of placing the local Party secretary in charge of the local administrative apparatus had been abandoned in the search for more democratic forms of administration after 1950.[17]

The institution of the voters' meeting was created by the 1952 law to assure the widest possible participation of citizens in local affairs and to make it easier for them to exercise direct control over their people's committee. These meetings, besides drawing up lists of candidates at election time, serve as regular forums convened to enlighten citizens on local and higher government policy. They also serve as arenas in which both collective and personal grievances may be aired and brought to the attention of local authorities. In certain conditions they are legally permitted to initiate referendums on important local matters. The referendum provision, however, is little more than a propaganda weapon in the hands of those people's committees which might be seeking public

[17] Such a claim was first made at the Sixth Party Congress. (See Rankovic's address to the Congress as printed in *Politika* [Belgrade] Nov. 7, 1952.)

acclaim for action taken, since the prior permission of the republican authorities is required before a referendum can be initiated.

Today voters' meetings are held regularly in many of the local communities throughout Yugoslavia. Even though they are almost always led by the "conscious socialist forces," they do in practice serve to lessen the gap between the governors and the governed. It is more or less standard practice for the local people's committee, or the ward committee in the larger towns and cities, to post advanced notices of meetings along with their proposed agendas. Meetings are presided over by a committee of three chairmen elected at each session from the persons assembled.[18] After all business on the agenda has been discussed, new business may be brought to the attention of the meeting by any individual present. If it weren't for the fact that the average Yugoslav citizen knows that his own best interests are better served by keeping most of his grievances to himself, the voters' meeting might bear close resemblance to the New England "town meeting." Nevertheless, Yugoslav citizens can and do use the voters' meetings to complain about such universal grievances as the lack of adequate housing, poor street development, and a variety of matters which harass the "conscious socialist forces" and the ordinary citizen alike.[19]

[18] The author attended several voters' meetings in 1955. At these meetings it was obvious that the "conscious socialist forces" had agreed among themselves beforehand as to whose names were to be suggested as chairmen for the meeting. But the list this group presented could have been beaten in the election if the rest of the persons present thought it important enough. The "conscious socialist forces" were obviously in the minority. With respect to this indirect type of minority rule, however, it is important to note that since many Yugoslavs are completely inexperienced in the type of direct participation in local affairs which the voters' meetings represent, the leadership of the "conscious socialist forces" is often necessary to make certain the meetings progress in an orderly fashion.

[19] Even though some of the rules of procedure of the meetings are obviously fixed to assure the leadership of the "conscious socialist forces," public matters were frequently discussed at the meetings the author attended in 1955. As the meetings "warmed up," more and more individuals aired their personal grievances. At one meeting in Belgrade, an army colonel (in uniform) spoke heatedly of the ward budget then under con-

The reformed system of planning, budgeting, and taxation brought into being in 1952 unquestionably made the people's committee, particularly the district committee, the most basic administrative organ of state control. The first important step in drafting the yearly federal social plan now truly begins at the local level. There each people's committee co-ordinates the production plans of the economic organizations within its jurisdiction and draws up for its own area its own over-all plan and budget. The people's committees are now legally responsible, within the framework of federal and republican social plans, for the assessment of most social contributions and taxes to be collected from the institutions and individuals in their areas. In the main, the people's committees now finance a large part of their own yearly budgets from income earned in their own areas. Economic decrees and regulations, such as those permitting local people's committees to fix wage scales, to appoint enterprise directors, to grant or to refuse permission to build new enterprises, and to supervise the disposal of surplus profits earned by local enterprises, add to the importance of the people's committee as the fundamental administrative authority within the economy of its area. Reforms in the judicial and

---

sideration. According to his reasoning, it did not include sufficient appropriations for housing. His remarks were obviously not planned for they embarrassed the group which represented the "conscious socialist forces." When the colonel finished speaking, he was immediately supported by a number of persons who were obviously not of his "stature." As a result of the housing discussion, the representatives of the ward people's committee were hard put to it to explain the size of the appropriation in the draft budget for committee employees and personnel. The final recommendations of the meeting (drawn up in secret by the three-man presidency in charge of the meeting) included a strong recommendation for a greater housing appropriation and a suggestion that the personnel and employee appropriation estimate be cut.

At another meeting, a man complained about a slaughterhouse which kept his children awake at night. The final minutes of the meeting (which always go to the people's committee of the area concerned) contained recommendations which were both practical and logical. Here it is interesting to note that in January 1956 a decree was passed which organized and regulated slaughterhouses (*SL* No. 17, Jan. 28, 1956). Among other things the decree provided that slaughterhouses could only be built outside populated areas.

social sectors have helped to round out the system of local self-government as it exists today.

From a cursory glance it might be felt that the Titoists mean their local people's committees to be semiautonomous units. Theoretically this may be the ultimate intention, but existing practical considerations require the Titoists to explain contemporary communal self-government as a synthesis of the controls required during the "transition period" and the local autonomy which is to prevail in a truly socialist society. In all of the reforms in local self-government since 1952, the district people's committee has been made the wheel horse of the system. Federal laws often fail to make this clear, but the more specific republican statutes passed to regulate the technical details of federal legislation remove any doubt. In actual practice, the district people's committee either executes or is responsible for the close supervision of all the major economic, social, and political functions assigned to the local organs of self-government. In this fashion, nation-wide unity of the system of economic and social self-government is assured, and the central authority's control is effectively guaranteed. The 1952 people's committee law provided that the members of the district committee be elected directly by the citizens and the producers concerned. However, it has been hinted that district committees would be more effective if they were composed of delegates appointed by the local committees from among their own ranks.[20] Such a method of staffing the district committees would serve to tighten the lines of authority from the central government to the lowest local levels.

The provisions of the 1952 people's committee law establishing forms of direct democracy, particularly those pertaining to the voters' meeting and the permanent and *ad hoc* citizens' committees, have brought greater realism to the Titoist system of local self-government. However, the new system has always been considered by the Titoists to be

---

[20] See Part III of Kardej's Oslo speech, "Socialist Democracy in Yugoslav Practice," *Borba*, Jan. 1, 1955, p. 1.

only a transitional arrangement. The ultimate goal was to be the creation of a system of state administration based upon a community of local units which were to resemble those which Marx claimed had been visualized by the Paris Commune of 1871.[21] This final step was taken in June 1955 with the enactment of the General Law on the Organization of Communes and Districts.[22]

In introducing the new law to the National Assembly, Kardelj said that it had been the Titoists' aim to have the "commune" represent the base of the Yugoslav socio-political structure. According to Marx, the commune was to be "that fundamentally discovered political form within which can be implemented the emancipation of labor." [23] The Titoist aim, Kardelj continued, has also been to make the Yugoslav society into an organic "national community" of communes "which is not a federation but an integrated organism within which the individual cells will live a full life and draw their strength from society as a whole and from their own initiative." The Titoist planners have endeavored, according to Kardelj, to have the whole mechanism of such a society "as close to the working masses as possible so they could participate in it as directly and as broadly as possible."

The new communes are to incorporate within themselves the territory of two or more of the local units which they supersede. Supposedly they are thereby to unify those geographical areas which are economically and culturally homogeneous. Communes are therefore expected to be more effective in linking urban areas with their rural hinterland. By so doing, they will eliminate many of the existing differences and contradictions between more developed and less developed communities and between industrial and agricultural areas.

The creation of communes has not required fundamental

[21] See footnote No. 2.
[22] For the text of this law see *SL* No. 26, 1955. A translation of parts of the text is given in *NYL*, VI:3 (July-Sept. 1955), pp. 28-33.
[23] Kardelj, "The New Organization of Municipalities and Districts," *NYL*, *op. cit.*, p. 3.

changes in existing local self-government laws and regulations. Only a statute drawn up by the people's committees
of the area to be consolidated into a single commune is required to furnish the legal foundations of the commune.[24]
The basic administrative organ of the new commune (both
local and district) is to be the same type of people's committee as before. All local communes, regardless of their size,
are called "municipal communes." The rights and duties assigned to the former local and district people's committees
by the 1952 people's committee law and by the laws and
regulations which have followed were automatically transferred to the new municipal and district commune committees.

When the campaign to form communes is completed the
number of old-type municipality, town, and city people's
committees will have been reduced from 4,121 to 1,438
municipal communes; the number of districts will have
been cut from 341 to 107.[25] Despite the Titoists' claim that
the new commune represents a higher form of socio-economic self-government, the creation of communes also has
at least two less-publicized practical purposes. First, the
geographical regrouping of the new districts has been so
arranged as to cut down the participation of the peasants in
the organs of local self-government.[26] Secondly, as the communes are consolidated and the number of basic political-

[24] A translation of portions of the Kranj (Slovenia) municipal and district
commune statutes is given in NYL, op. cit., pp. 31-39. Kranj was the first
commune, established in May 1955. It is one of the most industrialized
communities in that area of Yugoslavia which has benefited the most by
the Westernizing influences of its long sojourn under the Austrian-Hun-
garian empire. The Kranj commune serves as the guinea pig of the "com-
munization" program.

[25] Kardelj, op. cit., p. 18.

[26] Ibid., pp. 18-19. Kardelj mentioned that the new territorial reorganization of the district governments will cut down the predominance of agricultural representation in the producers' councils of the district people's
committees (see footnote No. 15). It will be recalled that representatives to
the producers' councils are elected in proportion to the percentage their
economic sector contributes to the district's "total social product." According to Kardelj, approximately 70 per cent of the new district committees will comprise areas in which more than 50 per cent of the "total
social product" comes from non-agricultural labor.

administrative units reduced, the previous lines of authority from the top to the bottom of the state administrative pyramid will be considerably simplified. In presenting the new law on communes to the National Assembly, Kardelj admitted that class antagonisms in Yugoslavia were still strong enough to represent "a danger to socialism" and to require determined vigilance from the central government.[27]

Thus, while the Titoist leaders theoretically intend the communes to represent the foundation and source of state power, the line of authority in Yugoslavia must in fact still run from the top to the bottom. Nevertheless, increased efficiency of centralized control automatically reduces federal and republican interference in local affairs. The Titoists are wont to advertise this improvement as an indication of the "withering away" of their state. However, more efficient government does not necessarily mean diminishing government power. In fact, increased efficiency means more effective administration of state power—particularly in an autocracy.

THE 1953 CONSTITUTIONAL REFORM

The Fundamental Law on the Bases of Social and Political Organization of the Federal People's Republic of Yugoslavia and of the Bodies of Government,[28] for short the Constitutional Law, was adopted by the National Assembly on January 13, 1953, and entered into force on the same day. Article 115 annulled all of Part II of the 1946 Constitution on state organization, except the two comparatively general chapters on the courts and the army, as well as all other provisions of the old Constitution or of laws and regulations which might be contrary to the provisions of the new law. Considering that the provisions of the Constitutional Law are extremely comprehensive, when it is combined with

[27] Kardelj, *op. cit.*, p. 5.
[28] The full text of this law is given in *New Fundamental Law of Yugoslavia* (Belgrade: Union of Jurists' Associations of Yugoslavia, 1953), pp. 53-99.

what remains of the 1946 Constitution it represents Yugoslavia's new Constitution. This new Constitution maintains all of the basic principles of a Marxist-type "democracy": the sovereignty of the people instead of the nation, the idea of direct democracy, the unity of powers through rule by the elected assembly, and the primacy of the economic over the political.

The Constitutional Law incorporated the principles of workers' self-management and self-government as formulated by the pertinent fundamental laws enacted since 1950. Article 2 states that all power belongs to the working people, who "exercise their power and manage social affairs through their representatives in the people's committees and the people's assemblies, in workers' councils, and in other self-governing bodies, as well as directly through election, recall, referendum, meetings of voters, citizens' committees, participation of citizens in administration and justice, and through other forms of self-government." Article 3 makes the people's committees "the basic organs of state authority" in the municipalities and districts, and limits the powers of the federal and republican governments to those rights specifically granted them by the federal and republican constitutions. These rights are, of course, extensive.

The sovereignty of the people is supposedly guaranteed by the right to vote for and to recall all elected representatives. Soon after the promulgation of the Constitutional Law, enabling legislation for the use of the recall was enacted. The people's sovereignty and, incidentally, the central government's direct contact with the local governments was further enhanced by the new provision which made the deputies to the National Assembly ex officio members of the people's committees of the areas from which they are elected. This same provision required deputies to keep their constituents informed as to the National Assembly's work and to keep the Assembly informed of the proposals and opinions of their constituents. The possibility of referendum is also provided for in the new Constitution, but as yet no enabling legislation has been introduced. A kind of referendum is envisaged by the provisions governing the dissolution and re-election of the Assembly or of its upper house in case of unresolved differences between its houses.

The National Assembly: The Constitutional Law declared that the National Assembly is the representative of the sovereignty of the people and is the highest organ of authority of the federal government. Through the principle of unity of powers, all federal rights are exercised by the Assembly directly or through the President of the Republic and/or the Federal Executive Council, or through those federal organs of administration which are supervised jointly by the Federal Executive Council and the Assembly. The extensive rights and duties of the federal government are specifically listed in the Constitutional Law. The Assembly's control over its executive organs is theoretically assured by its right to elect and to recall the President of the Republic and the members of the Federal Executive Council. Its control over the judicial system is made possible through its right to appoint and recall the judges of the Federal Supreme Court and by the right which the law grants the Federal Executive Council "to guarantee the uniformity" of the entire judicial system.

The National Assembly as created by the 1953 law is bicameral, consisting of the Federal Council and the Federal Producers' Council. However, under certain conditions, the Assembly is in practice tricameral. A Council of Nationalities existing within the Federal Council acts as a separate unit in all instances when federal "general" laws—that is, acts stating only the basic objectives of policy and leaving the details of implementation to republican statutes—or when constitutional changes, or the Federal Social Plan, or other matters which could affect relations between the republics are considered. In all other instances, the deputies of the Council of Nationalities function as regular members of the Federal Council. The reduced importance of the Council of Nationalities after 1953 reflects the diminished importance of the nationalities problem since the enactment of the 1946 Constitution. The 1946 Constitution had made the two houses of the Assembly equal in authority, but under the 1953 law the two, or in certain instances three, houses are not equal since the Federal Council takes part in all the rights and duties assigned to the National Assembly. The other house, or houses, have only limited jurisdiction.

The Federal Council represents both the unity of the country and the separate major nationality groups. It is therefore composed of deputies chosen in two different ways: those elected by all of the citizens on the basis of universal, equal, direct, and secret suffrage at the rate of one deputy for each sixty thousand inhabitants; and those elected by the upper houses of the republican and the two autonomous district parliaments from amongst their own memberships to serve as the Council of Nationalities within the Federal Council. For this latter purpose ten deputies are elected from each republic, six by the Autonomous Province of the Voivodina, and four by the Autonomous District of Kossovo-Metohija.

The Constitutional Law established producers' councils as the second chambers of the federal and republican assemblies. This act completed the policy begun by the 1952 people's committee reform. The Titoists reason that in their present transitional stage of socialist development, the only way to avoid turning the government over to the working class party—which action automatically breeds an anachronistic self-perpetuating bureaucracy—is to give the working class the opportunity to participate directly in government.[29]

---

[29] For an excellent presentation of the theory and practice of producers' councils at all levels, by a leading Yugoslav Marxist, see Geršković, "The System of Producers' Councils in Yugoslavia," *International Labor Review, op. cit.*

Although Mr. Geršković claims that the producers' councils were established to keep the Party from serving as the workers' only representatives in government, and although there are no official statistics available to prove the following assumption, it is more than probable that the largest part of the deputies to the federal and republican councils are Party members.

They explain that the institution of producers' councils is not an indispensable element of social democracy under all conditions. Nevertheless, in a relatively backward country like Yugoslavia it must exist as a method of permitting the working class to express itself in accordance with its "genuine economic and social role" rather than merely by its numerical strength. The fact that the system is undemocratic in that it gives superior representation to a minority does not disturb the Yugoslav Marxists. They claim that the method of choosing representatives to the producers' councils in proportion to the contribution their sectors of the economy make to the total social product makes the system truly democratic in the social sense, since it permits industrial workers fair representation in proportion to their superior contribution to the national income. In fact, the Titoists consider their producers' council system to be based on an entirely new democratic principle. They feel that they have replaced the classical liberal democratic principle of "one man, one vote" and gone on to a higher social democratic principle which permits the individual to be represented in his government in direct proportion to his contribution to society.[30]

Deputies to the federal and republican producers' councils are elected (indirectly, through their agencies of self-management) by their economic enterprises, agricultural co-operatives, and arts and crafts co-operatives at the rate of one deputy for every seventy thousand members of the producer population. The term "producer population" in this instance includes both the active producer and those members of his family whom he must support. Since approximately 85 per cent of the peasant population belong to general co-operatives, most of the peasants are permitted to participate in the elections. However, the rule making representation proportionate to the amount each economic

[30] See Jovan Djordjević, "New Features in the Yugoslav Political System," *RIA*, VI:142 (March 1, 1956), p. 11.

sector contributes to the total social product keeps the numerically superior agricultural group from capturing control of the federal and republican councils.[31]

The election procedure for the producers' councils at all levels is extremely complex. It is constantly being changed. It has been very difficult to find a system equitable to all groups within each branch of industry and trade which will simultaneously assure the regime the control it requires to make certain that the majority of representatives, especially at the republican and federal levels, are members of the "conscious socialist forces." For example, the earliest election regulations barred members of the technical and other leadership ranks from standing for election. But this made it too easy for the less "culturally advanced" workers to be selected. Therefore, later regulations permitted the election of directors of enterprises and other managerial personnel as well as officials of trade unions and co-operatives.[32]

The Constitutional Law arranged that the Federal Council should have numerical superiority over the Federal Producers' Council.[33] Thus, the supremacy of the Federal Council in all matters on which the two houses sit in joint session is guaranteed. The law did, however, give the producers' council one exclusive function in which the upper house plays no part: to make recommendations directly to

[31] Gerškovič, *op. cit.*, p. 47, gives the following table of membership in the federal and republican producers' councils (1954):

	Federal			Republican		
	Indust.	Agric.	Total	Indust.	Agric.	Total
Serbia	44	30	74	67	50	117
Croatia	35	14	49	74	33	107
Slovenia	18	4	22	59	13	72
B-H	25	12	37	60	22	82
Macedonia	10	5	15	45	29	74
Montenegro	3	2	5	30	22	52
Total	135	67	202			

[32] *Ibid.*, pp. 46-52, discusses in detail the problems and shortcomings of the system of choosing representatives to the producers' councils at all levels.

[33] The present Federal Council has 353 deputies and the Federal Producers' Council 202.

economic enterprises and to government agencies concerning the economy, labor, and social security. Further legislation is to define these rights and duties more thoroughly. If this legislation is enacted it is expected to give the Federal Producers' Council a type of special powers which will transform it into an institution resembling a Supreme Workers' and Peasants' Council of Yugoslavia. In such matters as the acceptance of the Federal Social Plan, the federal budget, and other expressly named business dealing mainly with the economic rights and duties of the federal government, the Constitutional Law provides that both houses of the Assembly have equal jurisdiction and that the full consent of both is required for final approval. All business not specifically listed by the law as belonging to the jurisdiction of both houses, or to the producers' council alone, is considered the exclusive right of the Federal Council. Thus, most purely political and cultural matters are the jurisdiction of the Federal Council alone.

The National Assembly and each of its houses have their own permanent and *ad hoc* committees.[34] The Assembly does not sit in permanent session. However, its committees and those of its houses meet much more frequently than the Assembly itself. The Assembly's Commission for the Interpretation of the Law is an invention of the 1953 reform. It has been given the right to issue binding interpretations of all federal law and is also required to consider the constitutionality of proposed laws. Thus, through the work of this commission, the National Assembly in effect exercises the highest judicial function of interpreting the constitutionality of its own laws. The courts are not permitted to exercise this function.

The Executive Organs: According to official propaganda, much of the over-bureaucratization before 1953 sprang from the duality of the executive branches of the federal and republican governments as created by the 1946 Constitution.

---

[34] See Jovan Djordjević, "The Committees of the Federal People's Assembly," *RIA,* VI (Jan. 1, 1956), pp. 14-17.

This duality had made it possible for the executive organs to evade proper control by the federal and republican assemblies. To re-establish the theoretical unity of the state within the duly elected representative National Assembly, the 1953 constitutional reform abolished the Presidium and all federal ministries. However, since there was no effective method of having the entire Assembly perform the executive function, the Constitutional Law established the President of the Republic and the Federal Executive Council as the responsible executive organs of the Assembly.

The President of the Republic is elected by the National Assembly from amongst its members. He is legally responsible to the Assembly for his work, and serves for the same four-year term for which the Assembly is elected. He may be removed by the Assembly before the expiration of his normal mandate. He remains in office if the Assembly dissolves itself or if it is dissolved because of disagreement between its two houses, until a new Assembly and president are elected. He is president of the Federal Executive Council and the supreme commander of the armed forces. In his latter capacity, he appoints and dismisses all generals, admirals, and other officers so designated by law. He presides over the Council for National Defense whose members are appointed by the Federal Executive Council upon his suggestion. He represents the state both within the country and in its international affairs.

Titoist theorists reason that the institution of the President of the Republic does not change the collective nature of the executive organs of the National Assembly nor does it introduce a presidential system as it exists, for example, in the United States. Furthermore, the Yugoslav President is not the "head of state" in the traditional sense since many of the duties and functions of the traditional head of state are given by the 1953 Constitutional Law to the Federal Executive Council. Rather, the President of the Republic is permitted to exercise only those specifically granted powers which "are thereby realized in a more rational and better way." [35]

The Federal Executive Council as created by the 1953 reform is the Government of present-day Yugoslavia both in theory and in practice. In effect, it combines the Presidium and the Government (the Cabinet) as they were created by the 1946 Constitution, although the Titoists argue that this is not so. They base their argument upon the somewhat tendentious reasoning that the Federal Executive Council exercises only the "political" side of the executive function while the newly created organs of administration alone are responsible for the carrying out of the purely "administrative" side. This distinction between the "political executive" and the "administrative executive" exists more in theory than in practice. It all but disappears when it is recognized that the Constitutional Law makes the Federal Executive Council primarily responsible for the supervision of all the administrative agencies.

The Federal Executive Council is elected by the National Assembly from amongst the members of the Federal Council. It serves for the four-year period for which the Assembly is elected, but legally it may be recalled in part or *in toto* by the Assembly before the expiration of its term. The Constitutional Law lists in detail the specific rights and duties of the Federal Executive Council. The list covers practically every facet of state administration. Restrictions upon the Council's activities theoretically exist in the provision of the Constitutional Law which permits the Assembly to request random reports from the Council on the status of the individual tasks it is carrying out. The law also states that the Assembly may invalidate any act of the Council found not to be in conformity with existing law. In actual practice the first of these rights has been used by the com-

---

[35] See Kardelj in *New Fundamentaal Law of Yugoslavia, op. cit.*, pp. 37-38, and Jovan Djordjević, "Producers' Councils," *RIA*, V (Oct. 1, 1954), pp. 234-35.

mittees of the Assembly and of its houses in their examination of economic and other non-political legislation. However, the invalidation by the Assembly of any act of the Council is unthinkable, unless the Council itself should decide that such action might serve its own best interests.

The Federal Executive Council supposedly functions by the principle of collective responsibility. This method of reaching decisions is considered to be more in keeping with the nature of the Council's political-executive functions and is expected to prevent the Council from being converted into an organ of administration, usurping the independence of the purely administrative organs. The Council is permitted by the Constitutional Law to establish permanent and *ad hoc* committees and commissions composed of its own members. These committees and commissions are responsible for the drafting of legislation and of decrees and regulations required in the Council's fulfillment of its executive duties. The Council's committees and commissions are broken down into secretariats composed of the administrative and technical personnel charged with the carrying out of the day-to-day executive tasks within their competence.

Like the first President of the Republic, the first Federal Executive Council was elected by the old National Assembly in January 1953. It was composed of forty-nine members in compliance with the provisions of the Constitutional Law which required the Council to consist of from thirty to forty-five deputies from the Assembly's upper house, the President of the Republic, and the chiefs of the six republican governments. In January 1954, the total membership of the Federal Executive Council was cut to thirty. In the spring of 1955, it was raised to thirty-four.

The Administrative Organs: In the belief that administrative independence and bureaucracy naturally occur "when the political and administrative elements of the executive function are united in a single body in the Government or in its ministries," [36] the Titoists invented their theoretical

---

[36] Kardelj, *op. cit.*, p. 40.

separation of the "political executive" and the "administrative executive" functions. To achieve this distinction, the Constitutional Law abolished all ministries and replaced them with State Secretariats and various types of so-called independent administrative agencies and institutions. The law also prescribed very general operational rules for all administrative organs. Legally they were to be separate from the Federal Executive Council. The Council was only to issue general directives for the organization and work of each administrative unit. It was to be responsible for supervising the legality of the work of each unit. In practice, however, the Council has taken its rights of supervision so literally that the administrative organs turned out to be little more than branches of the Council.

The 1953 Constitutional Law created five State Secretariats: Foreign Affairs, Internal Affairs, Defense, National Economy, and General Administration and Budget. The number of other administrative agencies has changed constantly to meet the requirements of the time. According to the 1953 law, State Secretariats could be created and dissolved only by the National Assembly. The Federal Executive Council, with the consent of the Assembly, could create or dissolve all other agencies whenever the Council might consider such action necessary.

The heads of State Secretariats are relatively more independent of Federal Executive Council supervision than are the chiefs of the other administrative agencies. They are the highest civil servants of the government. Except for the State Secretaries of Foreign Affairs and National Defense, who in view of the importance of their functions are appointed from amongst the membership of the Federal Executive Council, the 1953 law provided that State Secretaries and all other heads of administrative agencies were not to be deputies of the National Assembly. State Secretaries and all other administrative chiefs are appointed by the Federal Executive Council.

In the spring of 1955, it was admitted that the "political

executive" bodies of both the federal and republican governments were still performing too many of the old "administrative executive" tasks.[37] A joint Federal Executive Council-National Assembly commission was formed to study the problem and to make proposals for its solution. In March 1956, the National Assembly adopted two new laws: The Law on the Organization of the State Administration,[38] and the Law on State Administration.[39] The first law reorganized the administrative-executive apparatus as established by the 1953 Constitution, and the second set forth in detail the rules and regulations outlining the rights and responsibilities of the separate units of the entire federal administrative apparatus. Immediately following the passage of these two federal statutes, similar laws were passed reorganizing the administrative apparatus of the republican, district, and municipal governments to bring them into accord with the changes made at the federal level.

The 1956 administrative reorganization established four main categories of administrative agencies: (1) State Secretariats, (2) Federal Committees, (3) Secretariats of the Federal Executive Council, and (4) administrations, boards, inspectorates, and administrative institutions. As created by the 1953 Constitution, State Secretariats are to control those functions so comprehensive in nature as to demand the existence of a strong and independent federal organ of administration. The State Secretariats for National Economy and General Administration and the Budget were abolished by the 1956 reorganization. In their place were created the State Secretariats for Finance and for Commodity Trade.

The Federal Committee is a new creation. It is also concerned with the handling of matters considered to be

[37] Kardelj in an address to the National Assembly, *Borba*, March 10, 1955, p. 2.

[38] The text of this law appears in *SL* No. 13, March 28, 1956. A translation of important sections of the law is given in *NYL*, VII:2 (April-June 1956), pp. 21-25.

[39] The text of this law appears in *SL, op. cit.* A translation of pertinent sections of the law is given in *NYL, op. cit.*, pp. 37-55.

of national interest. However, unlike the State Secretariats where the State Secretary has relative autonomy in carrying out the functions of his department, the Federal Committee must make collective decisions and assume collective responsibility. Its members are the representatives of those administrative units and authorized social organizations whose work the Committee is expected to co-ordinate. The only Federal Committee created by the 1956 law was that of Foreign Trade.

The third category, the Secretariats of the Federal Executive Council, existed prior to the 1956 reorganization. In their former practice they were purely the inner, specialized organs of the Council. As such, they theoretically bore no responsibility for the execution of policy. The 1956 reorganization provided them with legal instruments which converted them into actual administrative-executive organs. Such secretariats are set up only in those fields where federal administrative jurisdiction is relatively small, that is, in fields where most of the federal responsibilities have been shifted to the lower echelons of state administration or to the agencies of workers' self-management. These secretariats are supposed to operate strictly within the framework of powers granted them by the Federal Executive Council. Their primary responsibilities are: to supervise the legality of the work of the lower organs of administration within their spheres of competence, to furnish expert advice and assistance to these lower organs, and to furnish the Federal Executive Council with suggestions for new laws and regulations. The 1956 law created twelve such secretariats covering, in the final analysis, the entire spectrum of Yugoslav economic, social, and political life.

The fourth category of administrative agencies mentioned by the 1956 law, the administrations, boards, inspectorates, and administrative institutions, have greater or lesser independent powers and responsibilities according to their importance. Within this category little has been done to change the organizational pattern that existed before 1956.

Most of these agencies are either directly or indirectly connected with the State Secretariats or the Secretariats of the Federal Executive Council.

Under the 1953 Constitution, State Secretariats may be created or abolished only by the National Assembly. The 1956 law placed Federal Committees under the same injunction. As under the 1953 Constitution, the Federal Executive Council appoints and releases all State Secretaries, with the approval of the Assembly. The Council also appoints and recalls Federal Commissioners, with the approval of the Assembly. As in the past, all other chiefs of administrative agencies can be appointed and recalled at will by the Council. The 1956 law did, however, make an important change in the 1953 Constitution with respect to the chiefs of administrative agencies. The new law provided that deputies to the Assembly *may* now hold the appointment of State Secretaries or chief of the Secretariats of the Federal Executive Council. Formerly, only the State Secretaries of Foreign Affairs and Defense could be deputies of the Assembly. This new regulation permits the Titoists to bring their legislators directly into administration. If the Yugoslav leaders so desire, they can therefore organize a parliamentary type of government.

The legal expansion of the powers of the twelve Secretariats of the Federal Executive Council represents an admission that the Titoists' previous efforts to differentiate between the "political executive" and the "administrative executive" were only figments of their imagination. Their Federal Executive Council has now dropped all pretense. In the 1956 administrative reorganization, the Council clearly showed itself to be what it has been in practice since its creation in 1953: both the executive and the administrative branches of the contemporary Titoist government.

The Republican Governments: The six constituent republics were ordered by the 1953 Constitutional Law to enact their own constitutional reforms to reorganize their government structures after the pattern of the new federal organs of authority. The republican assemblies were made bicameral, with the republican council as the upper house having the same broad general expanse of powers as its federal counterpart, and the republican producers' council as the lower house. The old republican Presidium and Government were replaced by an Executive Council elected by the entire assembly from the membership of its upper house. There is no president of each republic since the republics are not permitted to perform any of those functions requiring the existence of a chief of state. The highest republican official is the president of the republican Executive Council. Republican ministries were dissolved and replaced by administrative organs similar to those in the federal government. However, the content of these republican administrative agencies often differs from that of their federal counterparts since some of the republican units, for example those in the fields of education, health, and social security, are the principal instead of the secondary administrative bodies in their areas of competence. In such instances, the federal agencies are merely co-ordinating and supervisory organs composed mainly of experts whose advice and counsel is available to the republican administrators.

The 1946 Constitution listed the specific rights and duties belonging exclusively to the federal government and explicitly left all others to the republican governments. The 1953 Constitutional Law made no attempt to differentiate between the rights and duties of the two branches. Instead, it listed in broad general terms the all-encompassing rights and duties of the federal government and made no mention of those belonging to the republican governments other than to say that "federal laws are directly executed by the people's committees or by the respective republican organs of state authority." [40] Furthermore, the 1953 reform law, unlike the 1946 Constitution, made no mention of the sovereignty of the republics.

[40] See Article 9 of the 1953 Constitutional Law.

The continued existence of the republics is still both a psychological and a practical administrative necessity. But if the word "independence" is used today in connection with the republics, it is more correctly read as "interdependence." Kardelj, in an article written at the end of 1953, made clear the regime's opinion concerning the real role of the republics within the federation. He wrote of the federation and the republics as the third determinant factor of Yugoslav social life, and admitted that he spoke of them "as one and the same factor because, in reality, they fulfill the same functions," namely, "the functions common to society and which cannot, consequently, be exercised except by the central organs." [41] The de-emphasis of the independent role of the republics both by the 1953 Constitutional Law and by Kardelj seem to illustrate that the Titoist leaders have decided that Yugoslav intra-national sensibilities have diminished to the point where they no longer require the careful coddling given them at the time the 1946 Constitution was drafted. In fact, to continue to stress republican "independence" would probably only serve at this stage to aggravate that very ailment of separatism which the Titoists are so determined to cure.

The reformed political-administrative apparatus requires constant adjustment to bring it into smoother working order. Nevertheless, the state administrative machinery created by the 1953 Constitutional Law has been in existence long enough to prove that, when it is compared with the one it replaced, it represents a far more efficient and democratic apparatus through which the Titoist regime may exercise its rule.

The fact that the Federal Executive Council, with a single exception,[42] is made up of the top leaders of the Yugoslav

---

[41] Kardelj, "Le Role du Citoyen dans Notre Système Politique et Economique," QAS, No. 22 (Jan.-Feb. 1954), p. 130.

[42] Sava Kosanović, a member of one of the pre-war leftist parties in Yugoslavia. He was the first Titoist Ambassador to Washington. (Mr. Kosanović died Nov. 1956.)

Communist party has both in theory and practice removed much of the ambiguity which existed in the state apparatus prior to 1953. The reform welded the "shadow" and "substance" governments into a single, practical working unit at the head of both structures. The ruling cadre is therefore composed entirely of men singularly devoted to their cause and certain of its correctness of purpose. They are constantly searching for a working compromise between the democratic principles they now see as essential and the dictatorship they must maintain if their futuristic system is to be achieved in Yugoslavia. Their purpose would be frustrated by complete dependence upon the use of force alone.

The Titoist leaders are undoubtedly aware that the democracy they preach—even the formal amount envisaged by their basic reform laws such as the 1953 Constitution— is impractical at this stage of Yugoslav development. The Yugoslav people have seldom, if ever, had a chance to develop the mutual confidence and respect for their fellow man that must lie at the roots of any truly democratic system. Titoist social democracy is supposed to represent an even higher form of democracy than the "bourgeois" variety. But the Yugoslav people—including many of the "conscious socialist forces" as well—have yet to absorb even the most fundamental lessons of "bourgeois" democracy. It is, therefore, necessary for the Yugoslav improvisers to supervise closely the practice of their more liberalized political-administrative apparatus. This supervision often demands actions which are denials of the essential spirit of the constitutional and administrative reforms. Nevertheless, the spirit of the 1953 Constitutional Law, though often violated in practice, serves at least to accustom the untrained Yugoslav mind to the nature of democratic forms.

The 1953 constitutional reform theoretically made the Titoist state a government by assembly. The National Assembly is meant to be the repository and the controlling factor of all political power. However, in practice all policy decisions and legislation are the exclusive province of the

Titoist regime, working through its institutional façade, the Federal Executive Council. The Assembly is still little more than a rubber stamp. Nevertheless, since the 1953 reform the Assembly, through its committees, has been permitted, even encouraged, to take a greater part in the formulation of legislation. For example, the committees subjected the 1954 draft Federal Social Plan to a type of scrutiny and debate which the *New York Times*'s Belgrade correspondent reported as disclosing "a range and intensity of criticism not only of specific provisions of the draft plan, but of some general attitudes." [43] Leading members of the Federal Executive Council appeared before the committees to defend their draft, with the result that substantial changes were authorized by them. Wide publicity was given to the substance of these debates. In February 1955, three draft laws were returned by Assembly committees to the Federal Executive Council for its more detailed consideration.[44] These are but two of the relatively frequent instances in which Assembly committees have employed their new prerogatives to question matters sent on to them by the Federal Executive Council. Even though it is inconceivable that committees would be permitted to take such independent action as to return a draft law to the Council for further consideration without the Council's prior permission, the fact remains that committee discussion is permitted to uncover inconsistencies or inadequacies in the drafts as first presented.

However, the amendment of draft laws is to be carried out only by the committees and not on the floor of the Assembly or its houses. Furthermore, committee examination of drafts is in no way to extend itself to criticism of their political content. Apparently some deputies confused these functions when in 1954 they drafted procedural rules for committee work. One of the Assembly's vice-presidents felt called upon to speak out against this misconception of duties.[45] He

[43] *New York Times*, Feb. 14, 1954, p. 15.
[44] See *Borba*, Feb. 6, 1955, p. 2.
[45] Vladimir Simić, "A Year's work of the Federal People's Assembly," *RIA*, V (Jan. 1, 1955), p. 15.

wanted it understood that even though the constitutional reform had made the Assembly the repository of all political power, there must be no confusion concerning political responsibility. This is to be borne exclusively by the Federal Executive Council. He explained that the primary reasoning behind the reform is to have the committees become "initiated as much as possible in the problems of the economy and basic development," and thereby to engage themselves "as much as possible in work on problems of state and social life" in an effort to help bring the fullest co-operation, experience, and unity to government policy. It was wrong "to expect that in the mechanism of legislative functions the Assembly plenary meetings would be much livelier, provide more scope for discussion, amendments, and even outvoting." Contemporary Titoist theory demands that amendment and debate be restricted to the committees so that there will be little or no need for either in the plenary meetings.

THE 1953 ELECTIONS

The Law on the Rights and Duties, the Election and Recall of Federal People's Deputies[46] was enacted on September 10, 1953, to bring the reformed National Assembly into being. Republican laws of a similar nature were passed immediately thereafter to provide for election of deputies to the new republican assemblies. These laws contained all of the major principles of truly democratic election procedure. But, like the constitutional reform from which these laws sprang, their liberal theory was meant to be practiced only insofar as such practice did not challenge the Titoist regime's total power. An American scholar who visited Yugoslavia at the time of the 1953 federal elections found that "the chief problem of the government in running the elections under the new system was to make them as

---

[46] The text of this law is given in *SL* No. 35, Sept. 10, 1954. Translation of text in *NYL*, V:2 (1954), pp. 51-82.

free and as democratic as possible in form, while at the same time insuring that the 'right' results were obtained." [47]

The 1953 law provided two methods of nominating candidates to stand for election to the National Assembly: by voters' meetings and by petitions signed by two hundred voters. As for candidates nominated by voters' meetings, the regulations covering nomination procedure made it practically impossible for anyone not sponsored by the "conscious socialist forces" to be nominated. Nominations for the all-important Nominating Committee of each voters' meeting had to be proposed by at least ten people and each proposal had to contain enough names to form a complete committee ranging from seven to fifteen members. Obviously, any opposition to the "conscious socialist forces" seldom had, or did not dare to indicate that it had, sufficient organization to fulfill this requirement. Once selected, the Nominating Committee had extraordinary powers in arranging and submitting the slate for final acceptance. Futhermore, to be accepted by a single voters' meeting did not make a man a candidate. He had to be proposed in meetings representing at least one-fourth of the total electorate of his constituency.

Although there were only eight candidates to the National Assembly named by petitions of two hundred voters, the number so named to stand for election to the republican assemblies was much larger. [48] Communists who permitted themselves to be nominated without the approval of the local Socialist Alliance or Party committees were usually openly denounced by these two groups. While no trouble of this kind was encountered in the federal elections, there were several instances on the republican level. In some cases, "non-official" Communist candidates were even elected to the republican assemblies.

The nominating process turned out to be by far the most

[47] See Thomas Tyler Hammond, "Yugoslav Elections: Democracy in Small Doses," *Political Science Quarterly* (March 1955), p. 52.

[48] *Ibid.*, p. 62.

important part of the election. Of the 484 elective National Assembly seats, including the producers' council but excluding the Council of Nationalities whose members are appointed not elected, only thirty-four were contested. This means that for the other 450 vacancies, nomination was tantamount to election. The number of contested seats on the republican level was somewhat greater, but in all amounted to a little less than one-fourth of the total.[49]

Campaigning on a personal basis was not permitted. It was even suggested that when two or more members of the Socialist Alliance were nominated for the same office, they must not criticize one another. On the contrary, they were advised to try to assist each other as much as possible.[50] The voting procedure created by the new law represented a decided improvement over the old laws, however. For the first time in Yugoslav history, printed paper ballots were used. The law also called for voting booths. In practice these "booths" were often little more than a low cardboard screen on the table where ballots were to be marked. Less pressure was exerted on voters to get out and vote in 1953 than had been the case in previous Titoist elections. Nevertheless, only 10.6 per cent of the entire electorate failed to exercise its prerogative.[51]

The Titoists would, of course, like to have freer elections, but only if they could be sure of obtaining a sweeping majority. Since this is at present a practical impossibility, they liberalize the election procedure only in those ways which will not materially affect the results. The democratic tendencies which the 1953 elections were allowed to exhibit undoubtedly stemmed from the regime's certainty that there was no danger of any organized opposition taking advantage of these relaxations of control. Where there was a contest for a seat it was usually between two Communists. However, even this situation works to the regime's advan-

[49] *Ibid.*, p. 61.
[50] *Borba*, Aug. 24, 1953.
[51] Hammond, *op. cit.*, p. 68.

tage. It can now threaten any errant local Party leader with the possibility of permitting the electorate to vote him out of office in the next election.

The 1953 election law also prescribed the method by means of which the people might recall their deputies. The right to recall representatives is essential to the type of commune praised by Marx.[52] According to the law, Yugoslav voters are allowed to recall their deputy if he no longer enjoys their confidence. The procedure is not simple, however. The right to call the electors' meeting to institute recall proceedings is given to the upper chambers of the district and municipal people's committees of the pertinent constituency or to one-third of the electorate itself. No group except the Socialist Alliance or the Party is sufficiently organized, or would dare show sufficient strength, to muster one-third of the electorate of a constituency. On the other hand, when the democratic recall process is of use to the regime, it is easily put into motion. For example, after Milovan Djilas, then a prominent member of the Titoist leadership, disgraced himself in January 1954, the voters of his Montenegrin district immediately "recalled" him without any apparent difficulty. This occurred despite the fact that he was tremendously popular in a district which had elected him slightly less than two months earlier with a higher majority than even that of Tito himself.[53]

[52] See the quotation from Marx given in footnote No. 2.
[53] *New York Times,* Jan. 26, 1954, p. 6. Djilas had received 98.8 per cent of the votes in his district. Tito had received only 97.7 per cent of his.

CHAPTER VIII

Major Social Reforms

In social welfare services the Titoists have managed to achieve a form of administration which comes closest to reconciling their theory of self-government with their actual practice. The role played by the central authority in this instance is essentially one of providing expert advice and counsel to the lower, relatively self-governing agencies of the social welfare system. The regime can safely permit this comparative independence, since social services of this type are not too directly concerned with major political and economic goals. Independence in this sector represents no real threat to Titoist control. Furthermore, if the independent management of social services is successful, it can only bring credit both to the regime and to the basic political philosophy it proclaims.

The educational system is another matter. The regime must make certain that the younger Yugoslav generations are properly indoctrinated. Hence, social self-management in education has not been permitted the same degree of independence given to the social security system. Serious decentralization reforms were not begun within the educational system until 1954. But the reforms then started have made a very real advance in freeing Yugoslav educational and cultural institutions from the earlier tightly centralized system of control. These reforms presage an equivalent improvement in the standard of scientific, educational, and cultural activities within the country.

The Titoists' ultimate goals in the improvement and expansion of their social security and educational systems are still far from realized. Nevertheless, the improvements already achieved and those for which the Titoists claim to be striving are the aspects of Titoism most genuinely appreciated by the average Yugoslav.

The desire of the Titoist leaders to permit greater freedom of individual action in the non-political areas of Yugoslav social life led to still other reforms which have bolstered the average Yugoslav's feeling of personal security. Most significant is the decision that the individual's desire to own the house in which he lives is in no way incompatible with socialism. In reaching this decision the Titoists have brought an entirely new "socialist" interpretation to the fundamental Marxist concept of private property.

SOCIAL SECURITY

A comprehensive system of social security is one of the fundamentals of socialism. In Titoist Yugoslavia social security has come to resemble closely those systems sponsored by social democrats in western European countries. It provides services to the individual from the time he is born to the time he is buried. It is limited only by the country's capacity to execute and support such a program. By 1955, total social insurance and health benefits accounted for approximately 13 per cent of the Yugoslav national income.[1] At the present time, this coverage extends to almost every worker and employee within the country.[2] However, until 1955, a large segment of Yugoslav society, the peasantry, was almost entirely excluded from the system; steps were then first taken to bring the peasants within the scope of the scheme. The Titoists hope eventually to give full cover-

[1] Todor Vouiachévich "La Sécurité social en Yougoslavie," QAS, No. 31-32 (July-Oct. 1955), p. 83.

[2] At the end of 1955, the number of members of the social security system was 2,478,998. This figure does not include the members' families, who are automatically included within the health service programs and many of the other benefits received by members. See Table 26-8, *Statistički Godišnjak FRNJ 1956* (Belgrade, July 1956), p. 344.

Vouiachévich, *op. cit.*, p. 84, mentions that a total of 7,000,000 persons were covered in 1955 by the social security program in one way or another.

age to all Yugoslav citizens. Ultimately the liberal social security program will be a potent factor in wooing the peasants and other self-employed individuals to accept socialization.

Prewar Yugoslavia had a comparatively modern system of social security which protected a large part of its wage earners and salaried workers. The system was sponsored either by the government, although government employees were generally excluded, or by individual private concerns. Coverage, range of benefits, and amounts of premiums paid differed according to the sponsor and often according to the group covered. During the period of reconstruction immediately following liberation from the Nazis, the Titoists permitted the old scattered system to continue under the administrative supervision of a federal social security agency. The only changes then made were those which tended to equalize benefits and premiums throughout the existing system.

In January 1947, a unified state system of social security was introduced. It covered all non-agricultural workers and employees, giving them accident, health, unemployment, old-age, and burial insurance. The system was administered by the central government through a newly established Federal Institute for Social Security, which had its own branches at the republican and local levels. The Institute assumed all obligations of the social insurance programs of the former private and public agencies. The funds of these agencies were liquidated. Since social security was now considered a state expense, these funds were integrated into the federal budget. However, the 1947 system was not considered sufficiently socialist in content. It had maintained such hangovers of the old system as having the insured pay part of the premium himself, and it still linked the amount of benefits to the number of years the insured had been paying premiums. Therefore, on January 21, 1950, a new and more comprehensive law known as the Law on

Social Insurance of Workers and Employees and Their Families[3] was enacted. It reorganized the entire social security system, filled in the "unsocialist" gaps left by the previous regulations, and expanded the coverage of the system. The system created by the law of 1950 still serves as the framework for the Titoists' contemporary social security program.

The 1950 law gave equal rights to all persons belonging to the social security system. It provided that the insured was no longer to pay any of the costs from his own salary. It abandoned the principle of linking benefits to the number of years the insured had been paying social security premiums and made most benefits depend solely upon the number of years the worker or employee had spent in worthwhile employment. Coverage was extended to include persons elected to representative bodies, the employees of certain social institutions, members of the arts and crafts co-operatives, students doing practical work as part of their studies, and persons temporarily employed either with or without pay in public works. Eventually artists, writers, doctors, lawyers, and others whose work is considered socially useful and who have become members of their respective professional associations were brought within the scope of the system. Even those members of the clergy who have joined the government-sponsored priests' associations now receive full social security coverage.

The 1950 law guarantees to those insured:

(1) The right to health protection, including all forms of treatment and medical care. All health services available to the insured are, without reservation, available to all members of his family.

(2) The right to compensation for temporary absence from work through sickness or accident.

(3) The right to assistance during pregnancy and childbirth.

[3] For the text of this law, see SL Jan. 21, 1950. A résumé of the text is given in NYL, I:1 (1950), pp. 19-27.

(4) The right to children's allowances.

The children's allowance has received special emphasis in Yugoslavia. The Titoists look upon the allowance as an important contribution to family income which should help to make it financially possible for parents to permit their children to continue their education. A fixed monthly sum is paid to parents for each child up to fourteen years of age if the child is not then still in school, and up to twenty-four years of age if the child continues with higher education. These allowances are paid to all workers and employees, and to all members of peasant working co-operatives, arts and crafts co-operatives, social organizations, and economic enterprises; to all persons serving in elected bodies, either political-administrative or social; to active officers of the armed forces; to persons living on pensions; and to many types of invalids. However, the right to the allowance is in some instances determined by the economic situation of the family. It is not given, for example, to employed persons who also receive "substantial" revenue from agricultural property. Thus, almost all part-time peasant workers in industry are excluded.[4]

(5) The right to compensation in case of diminished ability to work.

(6) The right of invalids to be trained for and transferred to work which is within their capacity to perform.

(7) The right to invalid pensions regardless of whether inability to work is the result of accident at the place of employment or accident outside employment.

(8) The right to old-age pension. Men fifty-five years of age who have completed thirty-five years of work and women of fifty years of age who have completed thirty years of work are entitled to 100 per cent of the pension rate fixed by law. Men over sixty-five and women over sixty who have not worked the full qualifying period but who

---

[4] By the end of 1955 there were 798,740 recipients of children's allowances covering 1,638,239 children. From Table 26-10, *Statistički Godišnjak, op. cit.*, p. 344.

have worked for at least fifteen years are entitled to not less than 50 per cent of the full rate depending upon the number of years they have worked. Present practice permits the full pension rate to be as high as 90 per cent of pre-retirement wages and salaries. Rates are based upon regular wages plus permanent allowances during the last year of work, or during the last five years if that should be more favorable to the insured. The employment period includes the entire time the insured has worked regardless of whether he previously had social insurance. The employment period also includes time spent in the armed forces, in prisoner of war camps, and in military exercises from 1914 to 1941. A recipient of an old-age pension may continue to work and receive the full pension to which he is entitled. His pension is added to by each extra year's service he gives until it reaches 10 per cent more than the amount to which he was entitled at retirement age.

(9) The right to pensions for the family in case of death, provided that: in general, the deceased had had at least five years of employment before his demise, or that he was a pensioner because of partial or total disability, or that his death had resulted from accident or illness connected with his work.

(10) The right to funeral expenses.

The 1950 social security reform marked one of the Titoists' earliest acts of administrative decentralization. In many ways it set the pattern for the first attempts at decentralization in other spheres. The reform abolished the Federal Institute for Social Security and created in its place a Committee for Social Welfare whose task it was to advise and co-ordinate the activities of the six republican ministries of social welfare. The republican ministries in turn supervised the work of the social welfare officers attached to the district, city, town, and municipality people's committees. The right to decide upon the validity of minor claims and to make short-term and single payments was turned over by the 1950 law to the management of the enterprise, co-operative, or institution at which the insured worked. Larger claims were to be settled by the municipality, town, city, district, or republican social welfare agencies, depending upon the type and importance of the claim being adjusted.

Prior to the enactment of the 1950 law, appeals by the insured against the rulings of the Institute for Social Security and its branches could only be made to special social security tribunals. The 1950 law made it possible for the insured to appeal first to the next higher social welfare agency, and then to the regular courts if satisfaction was not received. The law also prescribed the punishment of those who attempted to keep the insured from realizing his social security rights, and of any insured person who attempted to abuse these rights.

In April 1952, steps were taken to provide for the eventual administration of the social security system more or less by the insured themselves. By the end of that year, independent social security agencies had been created at the municipality, town, city, district, and republican levels. Social security funds were removed from the federal budget and were distributed to the lower agencies along with instructions to work out systems whereby they would be able to finance themselves in the future from local resources. By the beginning of 1953, these social security agencies were replaced by the so-called independent social security assemblies. These independent assemblies now exist at the municipality, district, and republican levels. The lowest are elected directly by the insured, the district assemblies are elected by the local assemblies, and the republican assemblies by the district assemblies. Each assembly elects a management board and a director charged with carrying out the daily business of the agency.

According to federal regulations, the local assemblies are technically the highest organs of authority within the entire system. Their management boards legally have broad rights enabling them to settle independently almost every claim made within their areas. In practice, however, the local agencies have only had the responsibility for running the health services. The majority of the other services rendered by the social security system, with the exception of the smaller claims settled directly by individual enterprises and institutions, are managed at the district or republican levels.[5] Government organs are supposedly permitted no authority over the self-governing agencies of social security other than to make certain that the agencies operate within the framework of administrative and financial laws. Only the regular courts are technically competent to judge the legality of agency acts.

By the end of 1953, the local self-governing agencies of the entire social security system were attempting to finance their own operations by funds received from economic and other sources within their areas. But it was soon discovered that the system of self-financing at the local level was impractical in some respects. Since there was no connection between the funds of the individual local agencies, there were some areas which had large deficits and others which had large surpluses. At the beginning of 1955, a system of "reinsurance funds" was created at the republican level to establish a mutual relationship between the funds of the individual local units. At the same time this republican reinsurance fund is to furnish a source from which local agencies can obtain funds to cover legitimate deficits. Each local unit is now assessed to contribute a certain proportion of its yearly receipts to the republican reinsurance fund. The poorer districts are assessed smaller amounts. Provided that the deficits are not the result of carelessness or mismanagement, any local agency is entitled to draw from the fund to make good its losses; otherwise, it must borrow directly from the banks.

The difficulties resulting from the new self-financing meth-

[5] This information came from an interview the author had with Gustav Vlahov in the beginning of 1955. Vlahov also said that the health services carried out by the local agencies amounted to only approximately 12½ per cent of the total amount of funds expended under the entire social security program (during 1954).

ods apparently convinced the Titoists that the entire system had been over-decentralized. In April 1955, a Federal Social Security Institute was established to replace the more loosely constituted Committee for Social Welfare which had been created by the 1950 reform. The new Institute is composed of an assembly of representatives elected by each of the republican "self-managed" social security assemblies. The Institute's assembly in turn elects an Executive Council to serve as its permanent organ. In theory, the Institute is to be a body of experts available for consultation by the republican and district branches which continue to bear almost all of the administrative responsibility for the day-to-day work of the system.[6] The Institute is to serve as the clearinghouse for experiences gained at the various local levels throughout the country, so that if, for example, Croatia suddenly develops a malaria problem, the Institute will arrange for Croatian health officials to discuss their problem with Macedonian health officials who have had long experience in dealing with malaria. The Institute will attempt to see that the underdeveloped districts are given the additional assistance they require. It is not to concern itself with the collection and distribution of funds. Fund collection is left entirely to the republican and district self-governing assemblies. The Institute is to keep the Federal Executive Council supplied with draft laws and regulations aimed at the constant expansion and improvement of the social welfare service. It has the right to call the Council's atttention to any malpractice it discovers in the work of any republican or local agency. It has no authority to stop these malpractices itself, although it can suggest remedies to the offending agency.

In an article published just prior to the Institute's establishment, the Belgrade newspaper *Politika* hinted that the Institute's lowest units would eventually be the district

---

[6] This and the remainder of the information in this paragraph came from an interview the author had in 1955 with the director of the new Institute.

assemblies, with the agencies at the lowest local levels "charged only with enabling the insured to realize his rights." [7] This undoubtedly indicates that the district social security assembly is to be the lowest agency maintaining funds and making payments for all but minor claims. Present practice has proved that minor claims are most effectively handled by the enterprises and other individual institutions themselves.[8] There is, of course, no suggestion that the local, district, republican, and federal agencies are not to remain organizationally the same type of independent self-managed institutions they were originally meant to be. The whole purpose of the establishment of the federal Institute appears to be to restore to the social security system the necessary minimum of operational unity and efficiency lost in the over-atomization caused by the 1952 reform. It is interesting to note that two of the twelve Secretariats of the Federal Executive Council created by the 1956 administrative-executive reorganization are to concern themselves primarily with matters of social security and health protection.

At the end of 1954, a health insurance plan was enacted which extended this type of insurance to persons outside the regular scope of the social security system.[9] From the earliest stages of Titoist development medical treatment for contagious and other diseases considered harmful to the community, maternity treatment and childbirth, and treatment of children up to three years of age have been free to the entire population. All other health services required by persons not covered by social security must be paid for by the patient. Members of peasant working co-operatives have ordinarily paid only half price for such services. Under the

[7] *Politika,* Feb. 26, 1955, p. 3.
[8] In the interview with Vlahov he mentioned that each economic enterprise or other institution within the social security system directly pays sick and injury allowances as well as all children's allowances. The amount it pays out under these programs it deducts from the amount it must turn over to the local social security agency or to the republican reinsurance fund. He said that in 1955 all enterprises and institutions had been ordered to pay 45 per cent of their total salary funds as their contribution to social security.
[9] See Gustav Vlahov, "A New Phase in the Development of the Social Insurance System," *RIA,* V (Jan. 1, 1955), p. 16.

1954 health insurance law, peasants are permitted to sub-
scribe for health insurance, but on a limited scale related to
the capacities of the medical services in their areas and to
the financial contributions they are willing to make for protection.

The Titoists have made valiant efforts to increase the
number of doctors, hospitals, and dispensaries in Yugoslavia.
Despite the fact that admirable progress has been made,[10]
it will be some time before truly adequate facilities are provided. As the number of doctors, hospitals, and other medical services increases, the extent of coverage offered to the
peasants and urban self-employed can be proportionately
increased. Certain areas of Croatia took steps as early as
spring 1955 to include in the health insurance plan all the
peasants, both private and collectivized, who desired to pay
a modest premium for membership.[11] Yugoslav officials are
having some difficulty in working out an equitable rate to
be paid for health insurance by peasants and private individuals. Since workers pay no premiums, and since expenses
for health services to workers come out of the lump-sum payments made by their collective enterprise to a social security
fund, there is no simple way of estimating what would be
fair payment to demand of private individuals. Once a
permanent formula is worked out, however, it is expected
that old-age and other benefits will also be offered to all
peasants and to private individuals who are willing to pay
the necessary premiums.

[10] While the number of doctors has been steadily increasing, by Feb.
1955, there was still only one doctor for each 2,585 inhabitants (*Vjesnik*
[Zagreb], Feb. 22, 1955, p. 3), and there were districts where doctors
were all but non-existent. For example, even though the number of doctors
in Bosnia-Hercegovina had doubled since the war, there were districts in
that republic which in January 1955 had only one doctor to 40,000 inhabitants (Kathleen M. Stahl, "Lenient Austerity," *Manchester Guardian*,
Jan. 17, 1955, p. 6). The problem of the dearth of doctors in the rural
areas is aggravated by the fact that most doctors prefer to remain in the
urban areas.

For statistics concerning the growth of hospitals, dispensaries, clinics,
crèches, etc., see Section XXVII, *Statistički Godišnjak, op. cit.*, pp. 347-58.

[11] See *Slovenski Porocevelac* (Ljublijana), March 15, 1955, p. 3.

EDUCATION

In wartime the Titoists had appealed strongly to the military and civilian masses by their efforts to overcome illiteracy and by their promises to improve cultural opportunities after liberation. Article 38 of their 1946 Constitution stated that: "In order to raise the general cultural level of the people, the state guarantees that schools and other educational and cultural institutions are accessible to all citizens; the state accords special attention to the youth of the country and protects its rights to education; the schools belong to the state; primary schooling is obligatory and free; and the school is separated from the church." [12]

The number of all types of educational and cultural institutions has been substantially increased since the Titoists came to power. The number of students in secondary schools and higher institutions has increased proportionately. The emphasis has been upon expanding both general and vocational training at the secondary level. The increase in the number of teachers has been much less impressive. The regime had little confidence in most of the teachers who were still in Yugoslavia at the close of the war. As in so many other fields, the Titoists pioneered in Marxist-Leninist indoctrination through the schools, and most Yugoslav teachers were not sufficiently instructed in the fundamentals of Marx, Engels, Lenin, and Stalin to serve as indoctrinators to the Titoists' satisfaction. After 1950, however, the compulsory course in Marxism-Leninism was dropped in the universities. But ideological indoctrination in one form or another has continued in the intermediate schools. By the school year 1952-53, the Titoist normal schools were turning out substantial numbers of young teachers whose ideological training was more to the Titoists' liking. In that year the number

---

[12] This Article is from a part of the 1946 Constitution which was not annulled by the 1953 Constitutional Law.

of elementary school teachers—the last teaching category to do so—finally surpassed the figure for the year 1938-39.[13]

The Titoists expect their educational system to encourage young people, particularly peasants, to enter occupations other than those of their parents. The regime's emphasis upon the importance of education has created a growing appetite for schooling among the Yugoslav masses. Nevertheless, although proportionately more peasant children now attend elementary and even secondary schools, peasant enrollment in the higher schools has not increased to any worthwhile extent. In the school year 1953-54, for example, only 5 per cent of all university students were of either peasant or worker origin.[14] Since children's allowances are usually available only to members of peasant working cooperatives and not to the majority of peasants, peasant parents are effectively denied one important source of encouragement to send their children on to the university. On the other hand, workers are entitled to children's allowances. Therefore, the low percentage of working class children in the universities must be attributable to some other cause— possibly to the attitude of many Yugoslav parents, workers and peasants alike, toward higher education.[15]

At the beginning of 1955 it was reported that more than 25 per cent of all Yugoslav children still do not complete their elementary schooling (the first four grades), and that about 55 per cent finish elementary school and go no further.[16] The same source stated that of the 1,753,000 Yugo-

[13] See Table 23-1, *Statistički Godišnjak, op. cit.,* p. 305.

[14] See "Children's Allowances and Scholarships," YR, III (May 1954), p. 10.

[15] See, for example, Ruth Trouton, *Peasant Renaissance in Yugoslavia 1900-1950* (London: 1952), p. 268, where she quotes one Yugoslav educational expert who reported that: "Many parents believe that the lower gymnasium examination is sufficient for a minor official and on the other hand that it is too high a qualification for an apprentice—that it is a waste for those who take it to learn a trade or to come back to till their land in the village."

[16] See "Youth Problems Through Figures and Statistics," *Omladina* (Belgrade: Feb. 2, 1955).

slavs in the fifteen- to nineteen-year-old group, over 12 per cent are illiterate. Nevertheless, the regime eventually intends to provide facilities for at least eight years' compulsory schooling for all young Yugoslavs. The achievement of this aim has so far been possible only in limited areas where adequate facilities were available. The rural areas will be the last to be brought within the scope of this plan, partly because of the difficulties in making adequate equipment available to them and partly because these areas were the most consistently ignored by the prewar Yugoslav governments. But, as rural school buildings are provided and as more and more teachers are turned out by the normal schools, the goal of at least eight years' compulsory education for all Yugoslav children will eventually be realized. At the present time, the Titoists have presumably managed to provide the minimum facilities to permit every Yugoslav child to obtain the first four grades of elementary schooling.[17]

In addition to children's allowances, the state furnishes supplementary allowances to some students in secondary and higher schools either as permanent or as temporary scholarships and stipends. By 1950, it was discovered that many recipients of scholarships and stipends were merely loafing at government expense. Many of these students had little to recommend them other than the fact that they were the children of parents who had some claim upon the regime. The standard of education naturally suffered as a result. Therefore, during the years 1950 and 1951, the number of state scholarships and stipends was drastically reduced.

Tuition in all secondary and higher schools is free. Before 1953, students were not permitted to choose freely the faculty in which they desired to continue their university education. The FiveYear Plan of 1947 had estimated the number

[17] This supposition is supported by the fact that the preliminary figures of the 1953 census show that there were 1,440,000 children between the ages of six and ten (Table 3-3, *Statistički Godišnjak, op. cit.*, p. 52), the ages at which Yugoslav children are normally expected to be attending elementary school, and this figure differs only slightly from the one given in Table 23-1, *ibid.*, p. 304, showing that in the 1954-55 school year there were 1,456,049 students in elementary school.

of doctors, engineers, teachers, lawyers, and so forth, which
the state would presumably need by 1951. Preference for
admission to the professions deemed to have a good future,
such as medicine and engineering, was generally given to
the children of the most influential parents. Other students
often had to be satisfied with courses of study which were
of no real interest to them. In September 1953, however, it
was announced that qualified students could freely enter
any field of study they chose. Despite protests, the Federal
Executive Council simultaneously decreed that universities
and some of the other higher schools were not to limit the
enrollment of qualified students in any way. The Medical
School of Belgrade University, for example, planned for 260
new students for the 1953-54 school year, but 2,032 had to
be registered.[18]

To some extent the government can indirectly influence
the number of students entering the different university
faculties. It can do this by judiciously manipulating the
scholarships and stipends it offers. It can also influence the
number of scholarships offered by industrial and social organizations to promising students who, like those receiving
government aid, are expected to pledge a certain number of
years' service after graduation. In the long run, however, the
government's control has often been thwarted by the students themselves. Many linger on as long as they possibly
can without taking their final exams. In order to avoid being
sent off into the hinterland where their services are most
needed, many graduates take jobs outside their planned
profession and reimburse the government in cash for the
amounts spent on their education. Furthermore, since the
need for trained minds in industry is constantly increasing,
business concerns have been known to pay off a student's
obligations to the government in return for a contract entitling the enterprise to his services. Government agencies
as well as economic enterprises often post notices on university bulletin boards making attractive offers for person-

[18] See *Politika,* Oct. 2, 1953, p. 3.

nel. It has not been unusual to have one enterprise bidding against others for the services of a likely candidate even though he may have a scholarship "contract" with a totally different organization. The federal government tried to put a stop to this type of trading in scholarships in the Basic Law on Scholarships enacted in July 1955.[19]

Until 1950, the Titoist educational and cultural systems were highly centralized. They were under the direct control of the Federal Ministry of Science and Culture, which along with the six equivalent republican ministries made all the pertinent decisions and closely supervised their execution. By 1950, the Titoist leaders had decided that state interference was undesirable in educational and cultural activities, and that steps must be taken to enable broader participation by the citizens in the administration of educational and cultural affairs.

Early in 1950, the Federal Ministry of Science and Culture was abolished and replaced by the more loosely conceived Federal Council of Science and Culture. The Council functioned as the supervisory head of the educational and cultural administrative hierarchy until it was abolished by the general decentralization reforms of 1953. In the 1953 reforms the Council and the republican ministries were replaced by still more loosely formed councils of education, science, and culture. Representatives of the highest scientific, educational, and cultural institutions as well as a number of individuals distinguished in educational and cultural affairs were included in these councils. The 1952 people's committee reform had created similarly constituted organs at the district and local levels. The chairman of each of the new councils was a state official, but the Titoists regarded the inclusion of members who were not government employees and who were responsible only to their own individual educational and cultural institutions as marking a break with the old practice of control by civil servants alone.

However, the first truly decisive break with centralized

[19] The text of this law appears in SL No. 32, 1955.

control came at the end of 1953. The government announced
that all scientific institutes were to be eliminated from the
state budget. Henceforth, they would have to obtain their
financial support from economic enterprises, universities, or
the Academy of Science. If a worthwhile research project
found no outside backers, the government would then consider granting assistance—not in the form of a subsidy but
rather in the form of a contract. Apparently, however, this
decentralization of control over scientific research institutes
did not work out as well as had been anticipated. One of the
joint Federal Executive Council-National Assembly *ad hoc*
commissions formed in March 1955 to make intensive studies
of different state policy problems was charged with investigating the whole matter of scientific research institutes. The
joint commission was to pay particular attention to finding
ways to "stimulate the community's interest in scientific research activity" and to "solve the problems related to the
matter of financing such work." [20]

The Titoist improvisers had a difficult time finding a new
system for the social self-management of educational and
cultural institutions which would neither stifle the initiative
required by progressive educators nor permit educators so
free a hand that they might build their institutions into cita-
dels of reaction or criticism against the regime. After a long
struggle within the inner circles of the regime a formula was
finally worked out, first for the universities and then for the
remainder of the educational system. Staff members of universities naturally held that proper self-management meant
management by themselves alone, whereas non-educational
leaders insisted that self-management meant that universities
were to be managed entirely by society or its representatives.
The fourth draft of the General Law on Universities[21] was
finally enacted by the National Assembly in June 1954. Titoist theorists looked upon this law as a suitable compromise

[20] *Borba*, March 19, 1955, p. 1.
[21] A partial text of this law can be found in *Le Nouveau Droit Yougoslave*,
V:3-4 (Belgrade: 1954), pp. 12-24.

which eliminated the danger that a form of self-management beyond the realm of direct "social" control might be created.

The university law brought a uniform type of self-management to Yugoslavia's five universities,[22] making each university a "community" of semiautonomous constituent faculties. Each university and each of its constituent faculties draws up its own separate statutes to state its respective aims and ambitions and to outline in detail the methods to be used in achieving these goals. The university serves primarily as a unifying administrative organization for its community of faculties. Each faculty is to decide more or less independently upon its own organization, curriculum, and teaching methods, within the general limits set by the university statute and by the republican and federal university laws. Only the Executive Council of the republican government can supervise the legality of the university and its faculties. The university's budget is an integral part of the republican budget.

The federal university law established the organizational machinery of the universities as well as the fundamental principles to prevail in the statutes developed by the individual universities and faculties. It prescribed such things as the methods of engaging and dismissing the teaching staffs and the officials and research assistants of institutes and of other scientific organizations attached to the universities and faculties. It fixed the general principles underlying the kind and quality of services the universities and faculties are expected to render to the students and to the social community. Furthermore, it outlined the rights and duties of students.

According to the university law, each university is administered by three separate but interlocking agencies: the University Council, the University Administration, and the Rector of the University. The Council is composed of a fixed number of members elected by the republican national assembly from specialist groups outside the university, the Rector of the University, one member of each constituent

[22] The universities of Belgrade, Zagreb, Ljubljana, Sarajevo, and Skoplje.

faculty elected by each Faculty Administration from among its own membership, one member elected from the ranks of its educational councilors by the people's committee of the city in which the university is located, and one student member elected by the student body. The Council performs all functions considered by the federal and republican laws to concern both the university and the social community. The University Administration is composed of the Rector, the Vice-Rector, and the deans of each of the constituent faculties. It performs those functions considered by the federal and republican laws to be purely university business. Under certain conditions, student delegates are permitted to attend Administration meetings and to make their views known during the meeting. The Rector and Vice-Rector are elected every two years by the University Assembly (made up of all regular teaching personnel and a fixed number of assistants and collaborators from university and faculty scientific institutes and organizations). The Rector represents the university, presides over the meetings of the University Administration, and is generally responsible for the execution of the decisions of the Council and the Administration.

Each faculty is administered by a Faculty Council, a Faculty Administration, and a dean. The Council is composed of a fixed number of outside specialists named by the republican national assembly, a fixed number of faculty members named by the Faculty Administration, one student elected by the student body, and the faculty dean and assistant dean. The Council deals with that business specified by the federal and republican university laws to concern both the faculty and the social community. The Faculty Administration is composed of all faculty teachers and a stated number of assistants and experts attached to faculty institutes. It performs those legally defined functions considered to be purely faculty matters. Delegates of the student body have the right to attend Administration meetings when questions of teaching methods and of the application of study regulations are being discussed, and to make known their ideas and suggestions. The dean is elected yearly by the Administration from among its members. He represents the faculty, carries out the decisions of the Faculty Council and the Faculty Administration, names the members of the faculty administrative secretariat, and supervises the secretariat's daily work.

By this somewhat complicated and cumbersome arrangement, the Titoists have managed to achieve a compromise which permits them to claim that their universities manage their own affairs and yet are controlled by society. Each university and each faculty is now run by two dovetailed but separate bodies: a Council and an Administration. The Council represents both the social community and the university or faculty. Appointments to the Council are easily controlled by the ruling Titoist hierarchy. The Administration is composed entirely of teaching staff members and their collaborators. The new system, especially when it is compared with the former highly centralized control exercised by the federal government, is a compromise which produces relative independence for the universities and for their individual faculties. The election of senior university officials is now legally in the hands of the teaching staffs themselves. Presumably more competent candidates less dependent upon Party status will now be elected.[23] Naturally, no one known to be anti-Titoist could possibly be elected, but a person overtly against the regime is quite unlikely to be a member of a university or faculty staff.

As long as university officials stay within the bounds of

[23] In May 1955, a new dean of the General Arts Faculty of Belgrade University was elected. He was not a Party member. His election was reportedly carried out in strict accord with the new federal and Serbian republican university laws. The election was purely a faculty performance with no interference from the regime. However, in this instance, the regime can easily afford to permit free elections. All "reactionary" and anti-regime elements have long since been disassociated from all Yugoslav universities and faculties. It is not likely, however, that someone who is not a Party member would be elected Rector of a university.

The fact that anti-regime elements have been thrown out of the universities does not mean that all members of the remaining teaching staffs are pro-regime. It means, rather, that the large majority of these staffs are apolitical, or have managed to convince the regime that they are so.

propriety in exercising their independence, the administrative system as established by the 1954 law should serve to raise the level of teaching as well as the general standard of university education and scientific development in Yugoslavia. However, the development of a better university system will depend in these formative years upon the intelligence and tact of the new managers of the universities and faculties. The Titoists have every right to be apprehensive of too much independence on the part of their universities. Eastern European universities and their student bodies have in the past frequently been hotbeds of opposition to the government. Even when the Yugoslav universities were under the strictest Titoist control there were student riots containing traces of resistance to the regime.[24]

Soon after the promulgation of the General Law on Universities, attention was turned to the matter of self-management in the lower branches of education. The 1953 policy of administering the educational system by means of republican councils of science, education, and culture, assisted at the district and local levels by citizens' committees of "experts," had admittedly produced a certain amount of disunity in education throughout the country.[25] Concepts applied by one local organ of authority often differed widely from those

[24] There were two demonstrations at Zagreb University in 1951. The first was organized against one of the professors, and the second was more spontaneous. It developed as the result of Croatia's winning a soccer match. In their enthusiasm, the students began to yell, "Off with your hats," which in Serbo-Croatian sounds very similar to "Down with the K. P. (the Communist party)." Masses of students, caught by the full meaning of what they had originated in innocence, marched to a statue of one of the early Croatian kings and began a pro-Croat demonstration which was only broken up by the militia and mass arrests. Neither of these demonstrations received anything more than superficial coverage in the Yugoslav press at the time.
Still another student demonstration took place in 1954 in Belgrade University dormitories when it was announced that fees for student mess halls, lodgings, and transport facilities would be increased. The demonstration turned into a riot which was only put down by the militia after a physical clash in which both sides suffered injuries and about fifty students were reportedly arrested. (See *New York Times*, Nov. 16, 1954, p. 13.)
[25] See Mirko Tepavac, "La Gestion Social des Écoles," *QAS*, No. 27 (Nov.-Dec. 1954), p. 98.

applied in other areas. The Federal Bureau for the Study of Educational and School Problems was therefore created in February 1955 to counter this disunity and to act as a coordinator for the entire educational system. The board is a body of experts available to advise all lower educational and cultural agencies. It replaced in many respects the old Federal Council of Science and Culture which had been abandoned in 1953. Hence the new board acts to restore to the educational and cultural systems a degree of unity lost in the excessive decentralization resulting from the 1953 reform.

In March 1955, the government passed the Law on Social Management of Schools.[26] This law, unlike the university law, did not attempt to define the basic educational principles to be observed by elementary, secondary, and higher general and professional schools. More general unifying legislation is expected to do that later. The new law called for a system of school management modeled on the General Law on Universities. Each school is to have a School Council composed of representatives from the local people's committee, important local citizens from all walks of life appointed by the people's committee, and, in the secondary and higher schools, a representative of the student body. The Teachers' Council of each school is to be elected by the full teaching staff from among its own membership. The School Council is to handle all matters in which the social community is involved, and the Teachers' Council is to carry out those functions considered to be purely scholastic.

By the beginning of 1956, a federal commission had been appointed to examine the whole problem of reform of the elementary and secondary schools.[27] The commission is charged with formulating uniform standards and requirements for elementary and secondary education throughout the country.

[26] The text of this law is in *SL* No. 11, March 16, 1955.
[27] See J. Lukatela, "The Reason for School Reform," *RIA*, VI:141 (Feb. 16, 1956), p. 4.

Thus, the Titoist educational, scientific, and cultural systems have now been reorganized, or are in the process of being reorganized, to permit them self-management to the extent considered by the regime to be safe. The reforms already in practice have given greater independence to the staffs of educational and cultural institutions. At the same time, the reforms have been so devised that "society" can control the direction of educational and cultural development. By this "division of powers" the Yugoslav Marxists undoubtedly feel that they are within sight of resolving the conflict between the liberty required by the educational system if it is to be of maximum social utility to Titoism and the authority the regime must maintain if educational and cultural institutions are not to become rallying points of reaction against Titoism.

THE RIGHT TO OWN REAL ESTATE

No survey of the development of Titoism is complete without some account of the relatively liberal attitude the Yugoslav Marxists have developed toward the right to own real estate. They had never legally nationalized all dwelling houses per se. Ordinances had been passed limiting the amount of space an individual and his family could occupy in a house. Even the land reforms did not confiscate all an individual's land—in most instances they merely limited the amount of arable land a man could own. Plots upon which private dwellings stand were never nationalized or sequestered unless they belonged to enemies or absentees or were considered especially useful to state or local authorities.

In June 1954, the National Assembly enacted a law generally regulating the ownership of land and houses regardless of whether these were privately or "socially" owned.[28] This new statute declared that nationalized arable land could only

---

[28] See Jovan Djordjević, "Regulations Governing Real Estate in Yugoslavia," *RIA*, V (Feb. 16, 1956), p. 4.

be transferred to private ownership under the exceptional conditions which the law specifically listed. It provided that nationalized land could not be sold to private individuals for building sites on any condition, but that all individuals could acquire "rights of utilization" for such land. Nationalized buildings are, in principle, marketable under conditions prescribed by the new law. The person who buys such a building automatically acquires a lasting "right of utilization" of the building site as long as the building remains on it. The law also permitted the free sale of privately owned lands and buildings to other private individuals. It abolished the former right of the local people's committee to examine the transfer of such property and to regularize such transactions by special permit. However, business premises could still be bought and sold only with the permission of the local people's committee. A special provision of the law allowed the free purchase and sale of component parts of buildings for use as dwellings by private individuals.

The law authorized farmers freely to sell and to purchase private land provided that they at no time owned more than a total of ten hectares of arable land. A special provision was made for those inheriting land which brought their total ownership to more than ten hectares: the inheritor could retain the surplus, not as his own property, but for temporary use.

There are no legal restrictions on the number of houses an individual may own. But existing laws place all buildings of more than two flats under a system of social management which makes it possible for owners to sell such property only with the permission of local authorities. Since a flat is considered to be as much space as the authorities decide to be necessary for an individual or a family, a smell dwelling of five rooms, for example, may be considered a building of three, or even four, flats. Private owners of more than one house or of buildings with more than two flats—even though they are considered to be the legal owners of such property

—are entitled to only 10 per cent of the rental collected. The remainder goes to the local authorities. Hence a private owner usually receives insufficient money to pay for upkeep and repairs. Therefore, because the local Housing Commission is only responsible for the maintenance and repair of socially owned buildings, most of the privately owned houses in Yugoslavia rapidly reached an advanced state of dilapidation.

The Titoists are convinced that this new property law does not affect the essential premise of socialism on the right to own property, especially since this free exchange of land and buildings can only be carried out within limits which do not encourage "capitalist tendencies" or the "establishment of exploitation and enrichment of individuals at the expense of others of the community." [29] They further insist that, in a socialist society, once land becomes communal property it cannot ordinarily become an object of free transaction. Communal ownership of the land gradually transforms land into the concern of everybody in general and of nobody in particular—into a general national property. The new "right of utilization" theory is a compromise between the right of the community to own the land and the right of the individual to use it. This compromise does not lead to state ownership of the land. Rather it makes land general national property upon which economic organizations and individuals may have definite rights of utilization for both social and personal purposes. Insofar as buildings are concerned, the Titoists have decided that "the nationalization of buildings is neither a necessity nor a logical premise of socialism." On the contrary, "socialism must insure the right of a person to happiness, to a comfortable, pleasant, and independent personal and family life; hence the right of citizens to have a dwelling house or flat in a definite building is not alien to socialism." [30]

[29] *Ibid.,* p. 12.
[30] *Ibid.*

By the end of 1954, the number of "housing co-operatives" had grown considerably.[31] There are two main types of such co-operatives. The first organize the planning and construction of new apartment buildings by selling shares to prospective residents. Such organizations may, if they are equipped to do so, carry out all operations necessary to the establishment of the co-operative and to the construction of its buildings without consultation with government authorities. Housing co-operatives of the second type are formed by owner-residents to manage their building and to attend to its upkeep. If the building concerned is socially owned, it may be purchased from the local authorities either by the co-operative as a whole or by the individual residents who receive title to their separate flats. All housing co-operatives have basic statutes which serve as a contract between the different members. Housing co-operatives must join the General Co-operatives Union, and their members are therefore entitled to such privileges as tax exemptions and other concessions granted only to the socialized sector of society.

Housing has been a serious problem in Yugoslavia, constantly aggravated by rural migration to the towns. In the earlier days of Titoist rule no one would think of building a house. Even the owners of small individual dwellings had little incentive to keep their homes in good repair. Not only were the costs of building and repair materials prohibitive, but no one could be certain whether his home was his own property or the property of the state. When by the end of 1954 the regime had clearly stated that the individual had a right to own his own home, the ordinary Yugoslav citizen was given new incentive to build himself a home or otherwise to improve his own housing conditions. This revival of private building has been spurred on by the government's own determination to do its part in improving housing. By 1956, the government had added to the yearly levies made upon all economic enterprises a special assessment to be turned

[31] See "Housing Co-operatives in Yugoslavia," *Bulletin*, III:4 (Belgrade: Glavni Zadružni Savez, 1954), pp. 9-10.

over to the Housing Construction Fund. The money so obtained is distributed by the banks at modest interest rates to private and corporate individuals alike as loans to build or to improve dwelling houses.

CHAPTER IX

Major Legal Reforms

By the middle of 1951, the Yugoslav Communist leaders had mustered sufficient confidence in the new political philosophy they were preaching to consider reforms for their totally degenerate legal system. Until that time, in every practical sense, only might made right in their country. As they progressed from intimidation to persuasion, from the Stalinist-type autocracy they had first fashioned for their state to what they now called social democracy, the need for an objective legal system became clear. Economic, political, and social decentralization had outmoded the old police-state power structure.

To make certain that the decentralization reforms succeeded and yet did not automatically challenge the ruling minority's control, the leaders shifted the power emphasis from the controlling bureaucracy to the legal system. The fundamental laws establishing the Stalinist-type state, the courts, the judiciary, and the other organs of legal administration were reformed to permit these agencies to take over many of the supervisory duties previously executed entirely by the bureaucracy and its police forces. This task was officially begun with the enactment of the revised Criminal Code in February 1951.[1] Like its Soviet prototype, the earlier Titoist Criminal Code did not recognize due process of the law. It permitted the police to arrest, detain, and punish individuals at random under a procedure known as "administrative punishment." The new code attempted to transfer criminal judicial powers exclusively to the courts and to curb the almost limitless powers of the public prose-

[1] The text of the Criminal Code appears in *SL* No. 13, March 9, 1951. A translation of the text is in *NYL* II:2-3 (1951), pp. 39-114.

cutors and the police. In brief, it attempted to restore democratic practice to Yugoslav jurisprudence and it thereby inspired a serious re-examination of the entire Titoist judicial structure. This re-examination in turn led to the codification, recodification, or adjustment of many basic civil laws so that they might reflect more accurately the fundamentals of the new Titoist philosophy.

In June 1951, the Fourth Plenum of the Central Committee of the Yugoslav Communist party was convened for the purpose of informing party members of the changes the regime intended to make throughout the entire Yugoslav legal system. The Plenum was addressed by Alexander Ranković, the all-powerful hatchet man of the internal security forces. In his talk he presented some startlingly frank facts and figures on malpractices and inadequacies in the judicial system as it then existed.[2] He suggested a series of basic reforms, all duly adopted by the Plenum, which prepared the way for the establishment of legality as a fundamental pillar of the Titoists' new administrative control system.

The Titoists' shift in emphasis from the police to the judicial system as the principal social control factor has brought Yugoslavia a more efficient state apparatus. Legislation is now more carefully planned and drafted to permit the courts to handle systematically a wider and wider range of complaints. There is a steadily growing respect for the technique of ruling by law and a constant growth in the legal-mindedness of those in whose hands the country's immediate destiny resides. But the most revolutionary result of the rebirth of legality in Titoist Yugoslavia is the right now accorded ordinary citizens to challenge many administrative acts in the regular courts. Arbitrary action by the administrators has decreased considerably.

The new emphasis upon legality does not, however, mean that the federal lawmakers, that is, the Federal Executive

[2] See Alexander Ranković, "For the Future Consolidation of the Judiciary and Legality," *NYL*, II:4 (1951), pp. 3-34.

Council, are in any way restricted by judicial review. The courts have no direct authority to question the constitutionality of federal laws or decrees. The function of the judiciary is limited to the interpretation of the laws and to the examination of their application. The fundamental Titoist principle of the unity of powers precludes any separate status for the judiciary. The Titoist theorists have tried to create a certain equality for the judiciary within the unified structure representing the "people's sovereignty," the National Assembly, by ruling that the courts are independent of all outside interference in the rendering of legal decisions. Nevertheless, the judiciary, bereft of the power to declare federal laws unconstitutional, and having no legislative or executive responsibilities while the legislative and executive branches do have judicial responsibilities, is not equal in status to the other two branches. Rather, it is a primary, quasi-independent arm of the supposedly unified and mutually interdependent executive and legislative branches to which it is responsible for its work.

Even though the judiciary is not permitted to interfere with the basic lawmaking process, a dispassionate judicial system can serve the Titoists well by bringing a greater feeling of security to the ordinary Yugoslav. The more he becomes accustomed to receive justice from the courts the greater will be his respect for the laws, even though most of these are fashioned without his approval or consent. As respect for the law per se increases, the necessity for the regime to take arbitrary action to protect itself and its ideas decreases. Thus, as the respect for law increases, the regime's own security can depend more and more upon the nature and scope of the laws it enacts rather than upon its police powers. A growth in the dependence upon law can, in turn, encourage the Titoists to expand the careful use of those democratic concepts which they already recognize as essential to their own welfare and to the welfare of their socialist system.

THE POLICE

In the period prior to the introduction of social democracy, the Titoist police forces were clearly the regime's third major administrative instrument, the first being the Federal Cabinet and the second the army. Upon seizing control of Yugoslavia in 1945, the Communists disbanded what remained of the existing police forces and organized their own police divided into two main categories: the uniformed militia, serving mainly in the cities, towns, and villages as more or less ordinary civil police, and the secret police.

The exact number of organizations within the secret police category is not generally known. However, the main body is the organization first known as OZNA (the Department for the Protection of the People) and after 1948 as UDB (the State Security Administration). It had originated during the war. It was then, and still is, a nation-wide organization of political police, staffed mainly by reliable Communists. Supplementing UDB was an organization known as KOS (the Counter-Intelligence Service), a body of plain-clothes agents (until mid-1952 UDB police wore uniforms) who circulated freely among the public, often posing as anti-Communists or reactionaries in order to trap suspects. Like their UDB colleagues, KOS agents had the right to make arrests on the spot.

Within the armed forces there existed a secret police organization known as KNOJ (the National Defense Corps). Modeled after the Soviet NKVD, it consisted of a relatively large force of political police in military uniform. In December 1952, it was announced that KNOJ was to be dissolved and reorganized as a group restricted to the military protection of the Yugoslav frontiers.[3] Approximately six months later the political commisariats within the armed forces were likewise abolished and regular staff

[3] See *New York Times,* Dec. 27, 1952, p. 1.

officers were given the responsibility for seeing to the "political awareness" of the ranks.[4]

All of the secret police organizations worked closely together through a fine-meshed network of espionage which reached into every phase of daily existence throughout the entire country. No ordinary Yugoslav citizen ever knew the strength of the secret police or the size of their budget or any other important detail concerning them. He only knew that their agents were able to observe every conceivable facet of his life, and that the secret police were above and beyond the law—that, in fact, they *were* the law. They made arrests on the spot, whisked people off to jail, and sentenced them at leisure without even being required to tell the apprehended individual why he was being arrested and punished. It was not at all unusual for an individual to be snatched from his home or office at any hour of the day or night and kept incommunicado in an unknown place for months on end.

With that amazing guilelessness which Communist officials are so often apt to display, Ranković pointed out to the June 1951 Plenum of the Party's Central Committee that "certain UDB organs" had in the past failed to grasp the fact "that a sound knowledge of and strict adherence to all the laws and prescriptions is called for in their action and activities." [5] He then admitted that of the total number of arrests made by UDB in 1949, 47 per cent had been illegal. Twenty-three per cent had concerned crimes of a minor nature which should have been handled by the militia or by local political-administrative organs.

The revised Criminal Code of 1951 began to reduce the powers of the secret police by outlawing arbitrary arrests and punishment in criminal cases. At the end of June 1952, it was announced that UDB was to be transformed from its semimilitary, uniformed status into a plain-clothes civilian agency.[6] Its members were to be placed on the same civil

[4] See *East Europe and Soviet Russia,* IX (London: June 18, 1953), p. 24.
[5] Ranković, *op. cit.,* pp. 15-16.
[6] *New York Times,* July 1, 1952, p. 10.

service basis as the members of other state administrative organs and paid according to the general classifications then being worked out for the entire civil service.

The civil police, or militia, had been constituted by a 1946 law, which, as amended in 1949, laid the groundwork for its contemporary organizational pattern.[7] Members of the militia are appointed by the people's committee of the area in which they serve. The local militia forces are linked vertically through the district people's committee to the republican Secretariat of the Interior, and through it to the federal Secretariat of the Interior. It has been reported that since 1950 the strength of the militia has been pared down and that by the end of 1953 it contained only 28,076 members compared with 41,247 at the end of 1950.[8]

There is no way of knowing whether or not UDB forces have been reduced proportionately. But in view of the curtailment of their independence since 1951, and of the very real decrease in their overt activities since that time, it would seem logical to assume that the organization's ranks have been reduced in number. It is claimed that UDB is no longer an organ of power but only an administrative branch of the federal Secretariat of the Interior.[9] This claim is partially substantiated by the fact that one no longer hears of brashly arbitrary UDB activity. The procedure which the militia and the secret police supposedly follow today requires them to do no more than report a suspected criminal act to the public prosecutor. If the prosecutor decides that grounds for legal action exist, he turns the report over to the appropriate court for investigation. The court, if it chooses, may use the militia or UDB to help it complete its investigation. Of course, if the suspected criminal act involved the security of the regime, or something of equal importance, there is no doubt that the secret police would pay little or

---

[7] The text of the 1946 law can be found in SL No. 107, 1949. The text of the amendment is in *ibid.*, No. 106, 1949.

[8] YR, III (Jan.-Feb. 1954), p. 12.

[9] This claim was made by Dr. Milan Brkić, an Assistant Federal Prosecutor with whom the author talked in May 1955.

no attention to legal procedure but would act independently.

In brief, once the Titoists had been expelled from the Cominform, their all-powerful secret police had to be "decentralized" as a result of the regime's need to establish an equitable, dispassionate, and trusted legal system to replace the bureaucratic legal structure of a police state. However, because the ranks of the "conscious socialist forces" have not yet been swelled to the proportions where they outnumber the possible reactionaries, the secret police are still maintained as an instrument of control. Nevertheless, today the police must make some effort to exhaust all legal means before resorting to purely arbitrary measures in their task of defending the Titoist regime and its system of government. The average Yugoslav today therefore feels freer and acts more freely than he has at any time since the Yugoslav Communists came to power.

THE PUBLIC PROSECUTOR

The institution of public prosecutor first appeared in Yugoslavia during the last war. The Partisans, borrowing directly from Soviet legal practice, appointed a public prosecutor to represent the omnipotence of "the people" in all legal cases, though he was not necessarily a part of the judicial system nor was he a party in cases being heard by the courts. In February 1945, the wartime institution of the public prosecutor was formalized by a decree of the Presidium of the Anti-Fascist Council of National Liberation (AVNOJ).[10] The essential provisions of this decree were incorporated into the 1946 Constitution, which established the Public Prosecutor's Office as a permanent agency of the National Assembly, operating independently of republican and local government organs. The final organizational details and the rights and duties of the agency were defined by a federal law enacted in August 1946.[11]

[10] See Josip Hrnčević, "The Public Prosecutor's Office of the FPRY," *NYL*, I:4 (1950), pp. 17-19.

[11] The text of this law appears in *SL* No. 60, 1946. A résumé of the law is given in *NYL*, I:4 (1950), pp. 46-49.

By the legal definition of its duties and responsibilities the Public Prosecutor's Office was technically intended to represent both the government and the individual citizen to prevent either from trespassing on the other's rights. In practice, however, until the reforms which began in 1951 substantially curbed its arbitrary powers, the Office acted in every instance as a watchdog over the regime's best interests, whether these interests were legal or not. The courts existed only to formalize the prosecutor's personal legal decisions. Though the Public Prosecutor's Office was legally to have no purely judicial powers, the supervisory responsibilities given to it by the 1946 enacting law were so extensive that it easily became the primary judicial agency of Yugoslavia. Public prosecutors gave directives to the courts as to who was to be tried, for what he was to be tried, how he was to be tried, and in many instances even what sentence the court was to hand down.

The 1946 Constitution provided that the Federal Public Prosecutor and his two deputies should be elected by the National Assembly. The prosecutors of the six constituent republics were to be appointed by the Federal Public Prosecutor with the approval of the respective republican assemblies. All public prosecutors at the local levels were appointed by the republican prosecutors with the consent of the Federal Public Prosecutor. The principle of "democratic centralism" was the primary administrative rule of procedure within the hierarchy; under this rule higher public prosecutors could order lower prosecutors to do their bidding. All prosecutors were independent of all local organs of state administration and were subordinate only to the higher echelons of the Public Prosecutor's Office.

Soon after the June 1951 plenum of the Party's Central Committee, the powers of the Public Prosecutor's Office began gradually to be whittled down. In the spring of 1952, a nation-wide network of "public attorneys" was organized, headed by a Federal Attorney General named by the Presidium of the National Assembly and after 1953 by the

Federal Executive Council. Lesser public attorneys were named at their respective levels by the Executive Councils of the republican governments and by the district and local people's committees. At the time of its creation the public attorney system was assigned many of the tasks previously carried out by the public prosecutors. But, by the end of 1953, when the system of public prosecutors had been effectively reorganized and its powers suitably reduced, many of those responsibilities given to the public attorneys in 1952 were returned to the public prosecutors. Today the major function of the public attorney is to serve as legal adviser to the government agencies which appoint him. The large majority of his work is concerned with the handling of property matters and economic disputes which involve foreign countries or firms.

A substantial inroad into the power of the public prosecutors was made by the Code of Criminal Procedure passed in September 1953.[12] This new Code removed the prosecutors' former right to carry out investigations in criminal cases. The new Code provided that such investigations are to be carried out exclusively by the judges of the appropriate court with the assistance of the authorized agencies (the police) of the Secretariat of the Interior. Prosecutors now have only the right to request the courts to make criminal investigations. They are no longer entitled to decree imprisonment during the investigation, this right being left entirely to the discretion of the investigating judge. As a result of this provision, the proportion of people arrested before prosecution in comparison with the total number of individuals prosecuted for criminal offenses dropped from 21.6 per cent in the first half of 1952 to 5.4 per cent for the same period of 1954.[13] The 1953 Code also ended the public prosecutors' right to interfere in proceedings dealing solely

[12] The text of the Code appears in SL No. 40, 1953. A translation of the text is in *NYL*, IV:3-4 (1953), pp. 25-76, and *ibid.*, V:1-2 (1954), pp. 27-50.

[13] See *Report of the Federal Executive Council for 1954*, Joint Translation Service Supplement (Belgrade: April 25, 1955), p. 11.

with private charges. Furthermore, the public prosecutors must now appear in court in the capacity of a contending party and not as a representative of abstract "public interest" or "society." They are no longer above and beyond the court.

In November 1954, a new Law on the Public Prosecutor's Office[14] was promulgated. It consolidated the changes which had gradually taken place since 1951 in the organization and function of the agency. The new law, significantly differing from the 1946 law, emphasized the judicial character of the Public Prosecutor's Office and declared that agency to be a component part of the state machinery, not a semidetached organization as it had previously been. The public prosecutors were now confined to the use of purely legal instruments and the courts for the execution of any remedy deemed expedient. As defined by the 1954 law, the essential duty of the hierarchy of public prosecutors is to sue persons who commit criminal acts or economic offenses.

The new law did not alter the principle of strict "democratic centralism" within the public prosecutor hierarchy. However, the law did provide that, with the exception of the Federal Public Prosecutor, all prosecutors and their deputies must be persons who have passed the state examinations for lawyers and judges and who have had fixed periods of legal experience, the length of these periods depending upon the importance of the post concerned. The law prescribed the amount of legal training and experience required of staff personnel in prosecutors' offices. Provisions were also made for special courts to try cases of disciplinary violations committed by public prosecutors or members of their staffs.

In March 1955, a law was passed which reformed the system of military prosecutors.[15] Since the founding of the Titoist

[14] For the text of this law, see *SL* No. 51, Dec. 8, 1954. For a résumé of the important changes made by this law, see Jovan Djordjević, "New Code on Criminal Procedure," *YR*, III (Jan.-Feb. 1954), p. 13.

[15] The text of this law appears in *SL* No. 11, March 16, 1955.

state the armed forces have had their own separate system of judicial procedure. The rights and duties of the military prosecutor were first briefly set forth in a special law passed in 1946 which made him responsible for the proper implementation of all laws within the armed forces. The 1955 reform was an attempt to bring the rights and responsibilities of the Military Prosecutor's Office into harmony with the new juridical principles formulated since 1951. Under the new law, the Military Prosecutor's Office was divested of its role as the general legal supervisory organ of the armed forces. It was now to occupy itself mainly with the prosecution of offenses against regular criminal law committed by military personnel. When allowance is made for the special sphere of competence within which the military prosecutor must work, his duties and responsibilities since the 1955 reform closely parallel those of the new public prosecutor.

Thus, by 1955, the Titoist public prosecutor, once the all-powerful protector of the regime's arbitrary whims, had been largely transformed into a government attorney practicing in criminal, economic, and administrative courts. He is now forced to organize his cases carefully and according to the law since he is no longer above and beyond the courts and must plead all but the most political of cases in public trials[16] where the defending lawyer is now given relative freedom. It is unquestionably true that, until it was decided to reform the legal system, the major requirement for the post of public prosecutor was to be a trusted member of the Communist movement. Not too many of the country's professional legal corps could meet this qualification in the earliest years of Titoist rule. The standing of the legal system quite naturally suffered from arbitrary prosecutors who were judges in their own and the state's cause. The provisions of the 1954 Law on the Public Prosecutor's

---

[16] The author visited courts in Belgrade and Zagreb in 1955. In every instance he was given a list of cases being tried and was permitted to wander at random from one courtroom to another listening to the different proceedings.

Office requiring all public prosecutors to be trained jurists should serve to raise the standard of the agency.

There is no reason to doubt that if the general trend toward the creation of a more equitable and dispassionate legal system continues, the aura of extra-legality which still clings to the public prosecutor's reputation and person should eventually disappear. When this stage is reached, the role of the Titoist public prosecutor will take on a closer resemblance to that of the American state attorney general. In fact, if the stage is ever reached where the large majority of Yugoslavs move into the ranks of the "conscious socialist forces," the Titoist public prosecutor will probably disappear and all of his functions will be given over to the public attorney introduced in 1952.

THE COURTS

Upon taking to the field in 1941, the Yugoslav Communists disavowed the existing legal order and its machinery and set up their own system of courts and legal procedure. The first courts were purely military in character. But as the Partisans began to liberate more and more of the country, judicial committees developed within the communal and territorial Liberation Committee governments. Out of the judicial committee there grew the institution known as the "people's court" whose officials meted out "local justice" as they conceived it.

The Law on the Organization of People's Courts was one of the first statutes adopted by the provisional National Assembly in 1945. The fundamental characteristics of the court system established by this law were incorporated into the 1946 Constitution. In June 1946, the Presidium of the National Assembly issued a decree also entitled the Law on the People's Courts[17] which, until the general court reforms

[17] For the text of this decree, see *SL* No. 51, 1946. For a résumé of the decree (including amendments made in 1948 and 1949), see *NYL*, I:4 (1950), pp. 41-46.

of 1954, served as the basis of the Titoist system of courts.

The new attitude of the emancipated Yugoslav Communists toward their legal system was first reflected in the Basic Law on Contraventions adopted by the National Assembly in September 1951.[18] The 1946 Law on the People's Courts had made no reference to the various magistracies attached to local political and administrative organs for dealing with administrative and other petty offenses and misdemeanors. Such petty cases had been left more or less to chance handling. The new Law on Contraventions attempted to bring order to the method of dealing with petty offenses and misdemeanors. It set out to restrict as much as possible the autocratic and inept arbitrariness previously displayed in these tribunals. It also provided that local magistracies be staffed by persons with legal training and experience and not, as had heretofore been the case, by random favorites of the agency responsible for the appointment.

In April 1952, the Law on Administrative Complaints[19] was enacted. This reform probably marks the practical turning point in Titoist legal history. It was the first substantial indication of the regime's honest intention to make justice a tangible reality rather than the subjective chimera it had previously been. The prewar system of administrative courts had been disbanded by the Titoists soon after they came to power. The ordinary Titoist citizen seeking redress for administrative abuse before 1952 could file an appeal with the agency against which he desired to complain, or he could ask the public prosecutor for protection. The individual who used either of these two legal resorts, however, probably received nothing more than a stay in prison for

---

[18] For the text of this law, see SL No. 40, Oct. 17, 1951. For a résumé of the text, see NYL, II:4 (1951), pp. 62-67.

[19] The text of this law is given in SL No. 23, April 23, 1952. A detailed discussion of the law is contained in an article by N. Styepanovitch, "La Loi Yougoslave sur le Contentieux Administratif," Revue Internationale des Science Administratives, XVIII (Brussels: 1952), pp. 819-26.

his audacity. The 1952 Law on Administrative Complaints was the first recorded instance of a Communist state breaking with the Soviet tradition of permitting the administration itself to settle all complaints against its own acts. In other words, the Titoist law of 1952 broke with the Soviet tradition of the infallibility (and irresponsibility) of state administrative organs.

The administrative court law of 1952 gave the Yugoslav citizen the right to appeal to the republican supreme courts for redress against unlawful administrative acts of republican and local agencies. The Federal Supreme Court is to serve as a court of appeal for administrative cases decided in the republican supreme courts; it also serves as the court of first instance in all complaints against illegal administrative acts of federal agencies. The law specifically declares that citizens cannot contest the constitutionality of laws and regulations passed by the National Assembly, by the republican assemblies, or by their respective executive councils. Citizens can contest the legality of rules and instructions issued by administrative bodies of the federal, republican, and local governments, and cases can be brought against the legality of laws made by people's committees. By the beginning of 1955, the number of administrative cases in the courts was so great that consideration was being given to the creation of administrative courts at a level lower than the republican supreme courts, and a thorough examination of the organization and procedure of the existing system of administrative law had been ordered.[20]

Until the appearance of the general court reform legislation of 1954, there was a single hierarchy of non-military criminal and civil courts, each higher court having the right to supervise the work of the courts below. The hierarchy began with the Federal Supreme Court; then came the

[20] From conversations the author had in 1955 with members of the Belgrade University law faculty.

supreme courts of the six constituent republics and of the Autonomous Province of the Voivodina (Kossovo-Metohija's highest court is the Serbian Supreme Court); then the regional courts; and, at the bottom, the district courts. The territorial areas of the regional and district courts are fixed by the federal and republican governments and do not necessarily coincide with those of the political-administrative units.

The 1954 court legislation reorganized the Titoist judicial structure by creating three separate groups of courts: the "general" courts, the "economic" courts, and the military courts. The Law on the Courts[21] enacted in July 1954, the Law on Economic Courts,[22] and the Law on Military Courts[23] passed soon thereafter, together constituted a codification of all structural legislation pertaining to the Yugoslav criminal, civil, and military court systems. Part I of the Law on the Courts is considered to be a constitutional law.[24] It annuls the whole of Chapter XIII of the 1946 Constitution, which had set forth the general principles under which the judicial system was supposed to work prior to 1954.

The Titoists do not consider the economic and military courts as extraordinary courts. Rather, they look upon them as ordinary courts forming branches of a single, unified judicial system. All three branches are constituted upon the same fundamental principles, namely, that courts act in accordance with the law and are independent in their re- sponsibilities to mete out justice; as a rule, they hold hear-

[21] For the text of this law see *Bilten Narodna Skupština FRNJ* (Bulletin of the National Assembly of the FPRY), No. 5, July 24, 1954. For a translation of parts of the text see *Le Nouveau Droit Yougoslave,* V:3-4 (Belgrade: 1954), pp. 39-48.

[22] For the text of this law, see *SL* No. 31, July 28, 1954. For translation of text, see *Le Nouveau Droit Yougoslave, op. cit.,* pp. 55-60.

[23] For the text of this law, see *Bilten Narodna Skupština FRNJ,* No. 7, Dec. 31, 1954.

[24] For a discussion of this point and of the fact that constitutional laws do not necessarily have to be appended to the Constitution itself, see Vladimir Simić, "New Juridical Laws," *RIA,* V (July 1, 1954), p. 17.

ings in councils composed of more than one judge, each of whom enjoys equal rights in the proceedings; appeal is allowed against all decisions of lower courts; and, all citizens are equal before the law and before the courts.[25]

The internal organization of the courts within the three branches may differ slightly according to the nature of the different cases coming within their respective competence and jurisdiction. The unity of the tripartite system is assured by the role assigned to the Federal Supreme Court. It must review all decisions made in the second or third instance by the Federal Supreme Economic Court and by the Supreme Military Court. It is the final court of appeal for all three branches within the judicial system. It also settles all disputes of competence and jurisdiction amongst the three branches.

The hierarchy of general courts remains the same as that created by the 1946 Law on the Organization of People's Courts. The Law on Economic Courts established a ladder of economic tribunals beginning at the regional level, passing through a supreme economic court in each of the republics and in the Voivodina, and ending with the Federal Supreme Economic Court.

Economic courts are arbitration tribunals rather than judicial courts. Generally, they do not deal with cases involving legal penalties. If a case being examined by an economic court is discovered to contain elements of a criminal nature, it must be referred to the general courts. In view of the nature of Titoist socialism, in which the interests of "society" per se are so closely involved in the country's economy, it is logical to assume that more and more economic offenses will come to be classified as criminal as time goes on. As this happens, the need for a separate branch of economic courts will gradually diminish. There are already some Titoist theorists who believe that it will

[25] See Jovan Djordjević, "The New Judiciature Acts," *RIA*, V (Dec. 16, 1954), p. 11.

not be long before the work of the economic courts will be entirely absorbed by the general courts.[26]

Under the 1954 court reforms, military courts, since they apply the same laws as regular courts, are considered by the Titoists to be in most instances ordinary courts. The Law on Military Courts established a two-step ladder of military tribunals: a military court of the first instance, and a Military Supreme Court which serves both as a court of first instance in specified cases and a court of appeal for cases tried by the lower military courts. Both are criminal courts whose normal jurisdiction covers criminal offenses committed by military personnel. They may also try certain specified crimes committed by non-military persons, but only if such crimes directly affect the security of the armed forces.

Since the creation of the first wartime civilian tribunals, all Titoist courts have been collegial. The jury was completely discarded. Instead, each court was made up of a council of judges. At first all court councils consisted of three judges. Reforms in 1953 and 1954 provided for councils of five judges in certain cases of the gravest importance and of a single judge in cases of minor significance. The role of "the people" in the courts received recognition in the fact that in certain instances two of the members of the three-judge court councils are "judge-jurors" chosen from among the civilian population. In the regular court system, judge-jurors serve only in cases of the first instance tried by district and regional courts. The court councils in all higher courts are composed of professional judges. The councils of the economic and military courts of both the first and second instance consist of one professional judge and two judge-jurors.[27] Judge-jurors therefore serve in all seven republican

[26] Several Yugoslav law faculty members expressed this point of view in discussions with the author in spring 1955. Also, see *Borba*, Jan. 19, 1955, p. 2, which reports on a special session of the Federal Supreme Court which examined pressing problems of the judicial system.

[27] See Nikola Srzentić, "L'Organization de la Justice en Yougoslavie," *Le Nouveau Droit Yougoslave, op. cit.*, pp. 28-29, for a short explanation of the competencies of the different post-1954 courts and of the composition of their councils.

and provincial economic supreme courts and in the Military Supreme Court.

The judges and judge-jurors of the military courts are all named and relieved by the supreme commander of the armed forces (the President of the Republic). The judges of the general and economic federal supreme courts are, as were Federal Supreme Court judges before the 1954 court reform, elected and recalled by the National Assembly. As in the past, the judges of the republican and Voivodina supreme courts (in both the general and the economic court systems after 1954) are elected and recalled by their respective national assemblies. Under the 1946 system, both the professional judges and the judge-jurors of the regional and district courts were elected in most instances by the people's committees involved. However, since 1954, the professional judges of the general and economic regional courts are elected by the republican and provincial national assemblies. The judge-jurors of the regional courts and the judges and judge-jurors of the district courts are elected by the local people's committees concerned. The republican and provincial Secretariats for Judicial Affairs draw up the lists from which the local people's committees may choose judges and judge-jurors. The regime is in this way able to assure its control over the important personnel in the lowest branches of the judicial system.

The lack of independence and initiative of judges and judge-jurors in the courts before 1951 was rightly considered one of the most serious weaknesses of the entire judicial system. The 1954 Law on the Courts set out to raise the professional standards of judges and judge-jurors and to assure them the independence of action and security formerly denied them. It provided that anyone who wished to become a judge had to be able to fulfill all regular civil service requirements, to have a law degree, and to have passed the state examination for lawyers and judges. To be elected to the panel of judge-jurors, a citizen must "show an aptitude for exercising the judicial function." [28] The law specifically provided for the freedom of expression and conscience of judges and judge-jurors in the courts. Anyone who attempts to exert illegal pressure upon judges or judge-jurors is liable to punishment. The law also provided that judges were to have tenure in the courts to which they were elected and could not be transferred to other courts except with their own consent. The law placed judges within the regular civil service salary classifications and gave them the same social security and other privileges as other government officials. Judge-jurors, however, receive no payment for their services other than reimbursement of contingent expenses. The law also made the judges and judge-jurors liable to the state for damages caused by their illegal acts. The state was made responsible for damages which judges and judge-jurors might cause a citizen, intentionally or otherwise. Further, the law specifically prescribed methods for removing all judges and judge-jurors for incompetence or on grounds of moral disqualification.

The 1954 court reforms made the internal administration of each court the responsibility of the president of the court. It gave supervisory responsibility to the Federal Executive Council's Secretariat for Judicial Affairs and to the same secretariats of the executive councils of the republican and provincial governments. The hierarchy of secretariats makes certain that court administrative personnel are chosen according to government regulations, that courts have the necessary operational funds, that the statistical services of the courts function properly, and so on. It is obvious that the hierarchy of secretariats also maintains constant watch over the courts to make certain they do not become over-impressed with their new freedom. A further political-administrative check on the regional and district courts is provided through the periodical work reports which these courts are required to submit to the people's committees in their areas.

The decline of Party influence in the courts has resulted

[28] Article 47 of the 1954 Law on the Courts.

not so much from the 1954 court reforms themselves as from the regime's desire to have the legal system work in as democratic a manner as possible. In the words of a leading Titoist official: the law court is now to safeguard "the fundamental unity of our socialist order. . . . The organic solidarity between the development of the courts and social democracy is the characteristic trait of our social and general development today." [29] The liberalized official attitude toward the courts has given the people greater confidence in the legal system, and has led to a corresponding increase in the amount of court business. The increase in Serbia has been so great, for example, that the Serbian Secretary of State for Judicial Affairs has referred to it as the "suing passion." [30]

The Titoists' growing respect for legality has produced a corresponding change in the position of the professional lawyer in Yugoslavia. The Titoists, suffering from the usual Communist mistrust of the legal profession, badgered most Yugoslav lawyers out of practice during the period from 1945 to 1952. Since 1952, however, respect for the lawyer has grown steadily and his position has considerably improved as legal procedure has been liberalized under the 1951 Criminal Code, the 1953 Code of Criminal Procedure, and the various subsequent court and judicial reforms. A lawyer can now freely argue any civil or criminal case. If he loses his case, he has a reasonable chance of getting a minimum sentence for his client. However, since most practicing lawyers in Yugoslavia received their training before the last war and are therefore still somewhat suspect by the regime, the average lawyer hesitates to accept clients whose crimes are of an important political nature. [31] The regime has been

---

[29] Ranković, "Sur les Tribuneaux Judiciares," *Le Nouveau Droit Yougoslave, op. cit.,* p. 7.

[30] See his letter to the editor, *Borba,* Feb. 8, 1955, p. 2.

[31] The Yugoslav lawyers with whom the author talked during his 1955 visit admitted that in all but the most political of cases, a defending lawyer is given every facility to enable him to prove the innocence of his client.

During 1955, there were several cases in the courts of "crimes against the state" stemming from the Djilas-Dedijer controversy which had reached a climax in January 1955. The lawyers with whom the author discussed

anxious to increase the number of lawyers trained since the
war in order to make legal counsel and advice available to all
citizens. But progress in this respect has been slow. By the
end of 1955, there were still only 2,553 private lawyers practicing in the country.[32]

Private legal practice has now become one of the most
lucrative professions in Yugoslavia. A good lawyer earns
amounts well beyond the salary of even the highest paid government official. This incentive and the regime's more liberal
attitude toward the legal profession should attract more and
more young Yugoslavs. With the gradual replacement of
judges and lawyers by younger "cadres" whose training has
been carried out in Titoist schools, much of the Yugoslav
Communists' mistrust of professional jurists should disappear. As the Titoists' confidence in the personnel of their
judicial system grows, the administration of justice in Yugoslav courts should improve proportionately.

The Redrafting and Codification
of Basic Criminal and Civil Law

The redrafting of fundamental laws and the formulation
of new fundamental law where it is needed to furnish a
consistent legal foundation for Titoist social democracy have
made rapid progress since 1951. The most important organizational laws, such as those on the courts, on the public
prosecutors, on redress for administrative wrongs, and on
the handling of petty offenses and misdemeanors, have been
described earlier. By 1956, the basic criminal law and criminal procedure had undergone extensive codification. How-

---

some of these cases claimed that they did not necessarily shy away from
the cases, but that they did not seek them out. If they took one, however,
they usually found that even here the new trend toward legality was present and of a certain validity if only that it caused the public prosecutors
to seek valid legal reasons to prove their accusations in most cases. Defending lawyers have little chance of winning such cases, however. The
best they can hope for is to obtain a minimum sentence for their client.

[32] Table 28-3, *Statistički Godišnjak FRNJ* 1956 (Belgrade: July 1956),
p. 361.

ever, the failure to produce a civil code and a code of civil procedure has worked considerable hardship upon the courts, especially since much of the increase in court business in the freer atmosphere of contemporary Titoist judicial practice has been in the realm of civil law.

The Criminal Code of February 1951 [33] began the process of diverting basic Titoist law from its Soviet orientation. Henceforth, the Titoists' fundamental law attempted to strike a working compromise between the judicial principles of the West and the special needs of the type of socialist community the Yugoslav Marxists are trying to build. But the Titoist improvisers were inexperienced in any but Stalinist methods. Furthermore, by 1951, they had only begun to feel themselves at ease with the new, revolutionary philosophy they were in the process of devising to suit Yugoslav conditions. It is therefore understandable that the Code of Criminal Procedure[34] should have been enacted in September 1953 to put right some of the shortcomings that had become increasingly obvious in the 1951 Criminal Code.

The 1953 Code of Criminal Procedure transformed Yugoslav criminal procedure into a body of law sufficiently progressive to make it theoretically acceptable to the most liberal of Western jurists. Its drafters claimed to have taken into account the most progressive legal and political attitudes of the time, and to have given broad application to the basic principles of the United Nations' Universal Declaration of Human Rights.[35] The Code is based upon the following generally recognized legal principles: legality in the conduct of criminal proceedings; the innocence of the accused until proved guilty; legal indictment as opposed to any form of inquisitory proceedings; legality in the institution of criminal proceedings by the authorities as opposed to arbitrary prosecution; the right of the accused to defend himself in public proceedings; the guarantee of *habeas corpus;* direct

[33] See footnote No. 1.
[34] See footnote No. 12.
[35] See Jovan Djordjević, "New Code of Criminal Procedure," *YR,* III (Jan.-Feb. 1954), p. 10.

and oral proceedings; and the admission of free confession
as evidence only if it is corroborated by the legally established facts.

Soon after they came to power the Yugoslav Communists
decided that the special importance of the institution of the
family to a socialist society made it necessary to free the laws
on the family from the "property rights" flavor "bourgeois
practice" had given them. The 1946 Constitution promised
that the state would protect marriage and the family, and
set forth the fundamental Titoist philosophy concerning
these two institutions.[36] The basic "family legislation" which
followed soon after the enactment of the Constitution was
designed as an elaboration of the fundamental principles
outlined in the Constitution.

This special "family legislation" consists of the following
four laws: the Basic Marriage Law of 1946;[37] the Basic
Guardianship Law of 1947;[38] the Basic Law on Adoption of
1947;[39] and the Basic Law on Parents' and Children's Relationships of 1947.[40] The Titoist legal theorists reasoned
that these laws had been developed "with the clear perspec-
tive that the norms governing family legislation are not of a
civil-juridical type but that they pursue the specific object of
regulating the new progressive and humane matrimonial and
family relationships in a people's state," and that "owing
to the momentous significance of matrimony and family in
their bearing on the life and development of our citizens
and our youth, the family legislation in the new Yugoslavia

[36] Article 26 of the 1946 Constitution.
[37] For a résumé of the text of this law, see NYL, II:1 (1951), pp. 22-26.
For a discussion of the law (and of its 1948 amendment) and of the fundamental concepts it attempted to encompass, see ibid., pp. 4-10.
[38] The text of this law appears in SL No. 30, April 11, 1947. A résumé of
the text is in NYL, op. cit., pp. 31-32. For a discussion of the law and its
theoretical concepts, see ibid., pp. 18-21.
[39] The text of this law is in SL No. 30, April 11, 1947. A résumé of the
text is in NYL, op. cit., pp. 27-30. For a discussion of the law and its
theoretical concept see ibid., pp. 15-17.
[40] The text of this law is in SL No. 104, Dec. 6, 1947. A résumé of the
text is in NYL, op. cit., pp. 26-28. A review of the law and its theoretical
concepts appears in ibid., pp. 10-15.

has emerged as a separate branch of our general positive legal system." [41]

Regardless of the philosophical or legal justifications for the Titoists' insistence upon the separate nature of family legislation, the four basic family laws also had an undeniably practical purpose. They formed a nation-wide codification replacing the disjointed and scattered laws formerly found in the "family law" branch of Yugoslav civil jurisprudence. This heterogeneity arose from the varied historical and religious customs of the many national groups that comprised the Yugoslav state. Since most of the cases on marriage and the family fall within the jurisdiction of civil courts, the codification of Titoist "family law" constitutes a first major step toward an eventual comprehensive codification of the labyrinthine collection of civil laws inherited by the Titoists from their predecessors.

The codification of Yugoslav criminal and family law met comparatively little resistance. These two fields involved no major revolutionary principles over which the new ruling group could haggle amongst itself. However, efforts to codify the remaining branches of civil law, particularly economic law, have not fared so well. These branches are too closely concerned with a problem which lies at the very roots of the fundamental creed of the ruling minority. They deal essentially with the problem of property and property relationships. Almost all Yugoslav Marxists felt that social ownership and social management of the means of production in Yugoslavia have not yet operated long enough for permanent legal concepts and categories based upon them to be formulated. Formulation would jeopardize the fluidity of thought and practice which is still vital to these totally new sociopolitical concepts. Among Yugoslav theorists, views on the new concepts of social ownership and management have ranged from the total elimination of the concept of ownership from the legal system and the substitution in its place of the so-called right of management, to the total identifica-

[41] See "Editorial Note," *ibid.*, p. 2.

tion of the concept of social ownership with the classical
concept of private ownership.[42]

In June 1954, the National Assembly passed a law regulating some of the problems of property in real estate.[43] For
Marxists this was a revolutionary step which recognized the
individual's right to own real estate. The right of the individual in the socialist society to own private property in
general was defined in the Law on Inheritance[44] passed by
the Titoists in May 1955. This law is based upon the clearly
stated premise that Yugoslav social democracy recognizes
both private and social ownership of property.[45] Such things
as the "major means of production," all agricultural land
above the limits prescribed by law, and all businesses requiring the use of hired labor are, of course, clearly defined
as social rather than private property. As such they cannot
be inherited. However, the inheritance law explicitly provides for the routine transfer, either by statute or by testa-
ment, of all legal types of private property from the deceased
to his heirs.

Many of the difficulties encountered in completing the
codification of the uncodified sections of Yugoslav civil law
stem purely from the basic ideological problems which such
a task presents to the ruling group. But many difficulties also
result from the more mundane influences exerted on the
minds of the leaders by the different customs, traditions, and
historical development of the various parts of the country
from which they come. In prewar Yugoslavia there were
six different judicial territorial areas in which the customs
and traditions of common law were recognized in the civil
courts.[46] Often these six areas were subdivided to permit the

[42] See Radomir Lukić, "Codification of the Yugoslav Laws," RIA, V (Jan.
15, 1955), p. 13.
[43] See Chapter VIII, and Jovan Djordjević, "Regulations Governing Real
Estate," RIA, V (June 16, 1954), pp. 11-12.
[44] The text of this law is given in SL No. 2, May 11, 1955.
[45] See Nikola Srzentić, "Notes on the Law on Inheritance," NYL, VI:4
(Oct.-Dec. 1955), p. 20.
[46] See Vladimir Simić, "The Yugoslav Law on Inheritance," RIA, V (Feb.
1, 1955), pp. 5-6.

recognition of some of the most important customs and traditions of the larger non-Yugoslav minority groups. For this reason alone, codification of Yugoslav civil law represents a herculean task. And when these complications are added to the ideological problems which face a group of Marxist-Leninist-Titoists attempting to codify civil law, the job might appear well-nigh impossible. Nevertheless, the Titoists are making valiant efforts and there is no reason to believe they will not eventually succeed. Furthermore, their new civil code or codes will undoubtedly reflect the same compromise between standard liberal democratic principles and the Titoists' own conception of socialism as may be found in the codes and other fundamental laws they have already completed.

PART IV

"VERTICAL INTEGRATION" THE REMEDY FOR EXCESSIVE DECENTRALIZATION

CHAPTER X

Decentralization as Re-centralization

The decentralization reforms in Titoist Yugoslavia sharply contrasted with the arbitrary and bureaucratic form of state management which they replaced. They had been implemented with the thoroughness and rapidity characteristic of totalitarianism. By the end of 1953, however, there were signs that decentralization had sometimes been over-hasty. Often a certain amount of efficiency had been unnecessarily lost. For example, the expanded powers granted to local political-administrative units all too frequently inspired officious interference with the running of local economic enterprises, and such interference caused needless losses. But by far the most distressing ailment fostered by decentralization was "localism," the tendency of individuals or local communities to spend their resources upon their own pleasures rather than upon those endeavors which the regime considered to be the needs of the total community. The Titoists had never intended decentralization to challenge the idea of socialist unity, and by 1954 they were strengthening the "ladders of vertically linked self-governing associations" to be used as a major weapon to combat "localistic anarchism." By 1955, Kardelj listed these vertical associations as one of the three basic organizational factors of Yugoslav social democracy.[1]

The social security system represented the outstanding instance of excessive decentralization.[2] By 1953, it had become a nation-wide net of loosely knit, self-governing, self-financing agencies which were impractical in operation since there was no connection between the funds maintained by

---

[1] Kardelj, "Contemporary Yugoslavia," *RIA*, V (Jan. 1, 1955), p. 2.
[2] See Chapter VIII.

each local unit. Therefore, some local units ended their fiscal years with huge deficits and others with huge surpluses. The creation of the "reinsurance funds" at the republican level restored some of the lost unity. Each local unit now had to pay a fixed contribution to the fund and could call upon it for loans to cover legitimate deficits. However, the most important step in reunification was taken in 1955 with the re-establishment of the Federal Social Security Institute which had been abolished in 1950. While this last reform did not change the basic principle of self-management at each rung in the ladder of vertically linked social security agencies, it did restore much of the dissipated unity by conferring supervisory and co-ordinating duties and responsibilities upon the re-created Federal Institute.

One of the important reasons for the transformation of the units of local self-government into "communes" in 1955[3] was certainly the fact that this reorganization strengthened the central authority's control over local administration. Most of the new local communes have replaced and consolidated old local territorial units. Thus, the number of local self-governing political-administrative organizations has been considerably reduced. The number of district communes has likewise been substantially reduced. By reducing the number of local and district organs of administration, the lines of communication between the periphery and the hub of the Titoist state administrative system are markedly simplified.

The Federation of Yugoslav Trade Unions[4] is one ladder of vertically linked associations which has existed since the earliest formation of the Titoist state. Its success as an effective means of communication between the central authority and the working masses undoubtedly inspired the drive to create such ladders in other sectors of Yugoslav life. The regime's main problem with the Federation has been to reduce the semi-independent power it once exercised throughout the economy without ruining the organization's

---

[3] See Chapter VII.
[4] See Chapter V.

usefulness as an important network of communications and control. By making certain that the Federation's highest official echelon is staffed by persons of secondary importance and by transferring the emphasis of the Federation's operations from the federal to the local branches, the Yugoslav leaders unquestionably hope to deflate the organization's importance. It is to be no more powerful than any of the other ladders connecting the hub of the Titoist wheel of authority with its rim.

The General Co-operatives Union, the federal organization meant to unify the self-governing agricultural, arts and crafts, and housing co-operatives,[5] had never been as powerful an agency as the Federation of Trade Unions. This was so mainly because the large majority of the co-operatives it represented were composed of sullen peasants who wanted nothing to do with the organization or with anything for which it stood. The 1953 agricultural co-operatives reform served to reduce the power of the General Co-operatives Union even further. The regime's main preoccupation with the Union today is to make certain that it does not fail entirely as an important means of communications and control within the agricultural sector. To obtain greater control within this sector a loosely formed Federation of Agricultural Chambers was established in 1954. This Federation was transformed into the more compact Federal Chamber of Agriculture in April 1955.[6] The Chamber has branches in each republic and at the district and local levels wherever practical. Membership is now obligatory for all organizations, institutions, and enterprises engaged in processing agricultural products. Purely agricultural co-operatives are not themselves to be members, but the branches of the Co-operatives Union to which such co-operatives must belong are expected to appoint representatives to the equivalent echelons of the Federal Chamber of Agriculture.

[5] See Chapter VI.
[6] See *Politika* (Belgrade), April 29, 1955, p. 1.

The pyramids of "higher economic associations"[7] envisaged by the 1950 Workers' Council Law as an integral part of the workers' self-management system had proved too impractical to be achieved. In all but the most homogeneous branches of the economy "higher economic associations" were never formed. In place of such associations there were formed, wherever practical, loosely knit voluntary industrial chambers. In 1954, these chambers were unified by federal decree into the Federal Industrial Chamber. By 1955, this Chamber was officially entrusted with important general supervisory powers which permitted it to perform "the role of social co-ordinator, harmonizing the relations between individual branches of the economy and between economic organizations and society."[8] Membership in the Chamber is obligatory for all industrial and trade enterprises.

In March 1954, a Federal Chamber of Foreign Commerce was established.[9] With branches at the republican level, it is composed of all economic enterprises which export or import goods. Its primary responsibility is to bring a greater unity to the foreign trade system and to supervise import-export trade so that efficiency and standards are improved.

Most professional groups have their separate associations and societies. Individual membership is considered voluntary. However, since individuals who do not join are usually not eligible for social security, tax, and other such benefits enjoyed in the socialized sector of society, all but the most die-hard of professional men are members. Lawyers, doctors, educators, artists, even the clergy, all have their own professional societies consisting of at least federal and republican branches. There are also local branch associations wherever practical. Each organization represents a ladder of self-governing institutions ascending from its lowest level to the appropriate federal unifying body.

These are but a few of the most important ladders of ver-

[7] See Chapter V.
[8] See *Borba*, March 28, 1955, p. 1.
[9] See Chapter V.

tically linked self-governing associations. Other ladders are being created in every possible field of Yugoslav endeavor where they are thought to be of use in bringing greater unity and control to the Yugoslav social and political system. The emphasis is upon the economic and trade sectors since unity and efficiency in these areas are the most vital to the regime. The ladders are often interrelated; for example, representatives from the Co-operatives Union serve as members of the Chamber of Agriculture. Individual enterprises are generally represented in more than one vertical association. Some associations, such as the trade unions, have a double vertical structure. Almost every trade union has its own local, republican, and federal branches and is also a member of the local, republican, and federal branches of the Federation of Yugoslav Trade Unions.

The ladders of vertically linked self-governing associations are composed of members elected directly or indirectly by the large masses at the base of each ladder. The workers, usually through their workers' councils, the co-operatives, the professional associations and societies, and so on, directly elect their representatives at the lowest rung of their respective ladders. Each higher rung in the ladder consists of representatives elected by the next lower unit. Thus, it is possible to be certain that only representatives with the highest degree of "socialist consciousness" serve at the republican and federal levels. It is because their authority theoretically comes from the masses which they technically represent that the Titoists fondly refer to the ladders as "self-governing" associations. And, because the regime has turned over to these "self-governing" associations some of the responsibilities of supervision and co-ordination formerly exercised by state organs, the ladders are touted as another example of "the withering away of the Titoist state—as a further fusion of the interests of the individual citizen and those of society as a whole." [10]

The powers and official responsibilities of the vertically

[10] See Kardelj's address as printed in *Borba*, March 10, 1955, p. 2.

linked self-governing economic associations are to be defined in more detail by a General Law on Associations in the Economy which is presently being drafted by a joint *ad hoc* commission of the Federal Executive Council and the National Assembly. More specific laws on association will be passed for each separate branch within the economy once the basic law has been enacted.

Legislation of this sort begins to have a familiar ring. However much the Yugoslav Communists would scorn the imputation, the theoretical as well as the practical intent of their vertically linked self-managed economic associations bears the mark of Mussolini's prewar corporate state. The Titoists of course argue that theirs are "self-managed" associations of industrial and social institutions owned by society and not by the state or by private individuals. Nevertheless, in an economy ruled by a powerful Federal Industrial Chamber broken down into a number of individual branches—each with its own quasi-governmental association whose rules and regulations are explicitly fixed by law—the comparison is inevitable. The observer is reminded of the economic organization that flourished before the last war just across the Adriatic from Tito's promised land.

The Titoists stoutly deny that their efforts to strengthen the role of vertically linked self-governing associations is recentralization. Instead, they insist that the attainment of an even greater degree of decentralization lies in the fact that the associations perform functions which were once the responsibility of the state bureaucracy. But much of the validity of their argument depends upon which side of the Titoist coin is being examined.

It is true that in the Titoist sense of the word the associations are essentially "self-governing" since their officials are either directly or indirectly elected by the masses they represent. But in practice the electoral procedure is so rigged that only those candidates considered sufficiently enlightened by the regime could possibly work their way up to the controlling federal branches of each ladder of associations. It is true that the associations are beginning to exercise authority formerly wielded by the state and that this shift does, when taken out of context, represent a kind of decentralization. However, each of the ladders of associations operates under the direct supervision of the Federal Executive Council. Therefore, authority has merely been transferred from a full-time state agency to a technically "self-managed" agency which is at least a part-time member of the government apparatus.

In the spring of 1956, Kardelj himself removed all doubt concerning the amount of freedom of action to be enjoyed by the so-called self-managed associations. He spoke particularly of the economic associations. In stressing their importance to Titoist social democracy, he stated that experience had shown that they could be entrusted with broad responsibilities, "provided always" that strong control over their actions was "simultaneously and suitably secured" for the Federal Executive Council and the federal administrative organs to supervise all decisions "with a wider social significance." [11] What Kardelj did not say was that the ladders of self-managed associations were useful to the regime only as the executors of policy handed down to them from above. Any attempt on the part of the associations to initiate policies not acceptable to the regime would not be tolerated.

The policy of strengthening the vertically linked self-governing associations is clearly a measure of re-centralization. The Titoists themselves admit that one of the primary objectives of the policy is to put a stop to "localism," that is, to restore some of the unity and efficiency of the over-all system which was lost when decentralization gave freer rein to selfish impulses. The ladders of vertically linked associations provide the comparatively small group of men who exercise total authority in Yugoslavia with a most effective communications network from the central authority down to the

---

[11] Kardelj, "Our State Administration Under the New Conditions," *NYL*, VII:2 (April-June 1956), p. 19.

grass roots. The ladders have therefore increased the efficiency of the central controlling agency.

However, it would be unfair to assume that the ladders of vertical associations are being strengthened solely to make control more simple for the regime. The ladders also serve the regime's honest desire to make its system as unoppressive as possible. Not only do they serve to transmit information from the center of the Titoist system to its periphery, but they also facilitate the transmission of important information from the periphery to the center. Thus, legislation and administrative policy can more closely reflect the real needs and demands of the society which the Titoists rule.

The Yugoslav leaders fear the word "re-centralization" because to them it intimates that their decentralization has been a failure and is being abandoned. Their fear is partially justified. The decentralization they have so far carried out has neither been a failure nor is it about to be abandoned. "Re-centralization" as the word has been used here to describe the policy of strengthening the vertically linked self-governing associations refers only to the policy of restoring some of the unity and efficiency lost through excessive decentralization. "Re-centralization" in this instance is the creation of a more effective mechanism to prevent decentralization from being carried to the point where it impedes rather than enhances the cause the Titoists claim to serve.

"Adjusting the imbalances resulting from over-decentralization" is the kind of phrase the devoted Titoist would prefer to substitute for "re-centralization." Nevertheless, a rose by another name is still a rose.

PART V

MAJOR IDEOLOGICAL DEVELOPMENTS

INTRODUCTION TO PART V

The Titoists describe their phase of development since 1950 as "social democracy." Both in theory and in practice Titoist social democracy is the most recent chapter of Marxist-Leninist doctrine on the state, the Party, and the individual in the period of transition from capitalism to socialism. Only history itself can decide whether the Titoist chapter is apocrypha or gospel.

Stripped of its theory, Titoist social democracy represents a somewhat confused combination of those Western liberal concepts of democracy, now recognized by the Yugoslav rulers as essential to socialist progress, and those centralized controls required if socialization is to be forced by a small, zealous minority upon an ignorant and often unwilling majority. It is difficult to know precisely what the Titoists mean when they refer to "democratic" concepts. Each of their "democratic" concepts is restricted in application to those limited areas in which it can safely be permitted to operate without weakening the regime's total control. Titoists speak openly of the importance of democracy to socialism. They say that socialism can only develop "through democratic forms." [1] They look to democracy as a means through which "to achieve the main goal, to achieve socialism, which intrinsically contains the most democratic form of government." [2] They also maintain that under specific conditions, "certain elements of democracy can be restricted for the sake of socialism and socialist development." [3] Yet, in public at least, they never really come to grips with the

[1] See, for example, Kardelj, "The Role and Tasks of the Socialist Alliance," *YR, II* (March-April 1953), p. 15.
[2] From Tito's statement to the Central Committee of the CPY concerning the Djilas case, *YR, III* (Jan.-Feb. 1954), p. 18.
[3] Jovan Djordjević, "About Socialist Democracy," *RIA, IV* (Jan. 1, 1953), p. 18.

problem of defining their use of these terms or of differentiating between what is democratic and what is socialist in their theory of social democracy. The one man (Milovan Djilas) who did give serious public consideration to the role of democracy per se in the Titoist system was promptly expelled from the ruling hierarchy for his pains.[4]

The Titoists make one thing clear, however. They are opposed to some of the most essential concepts of democracy as they are accepted in the West. For example, in all but the most exceptional of cases, present Yugoslav practice permits the nomination and election of only those individuals personally acceptable to the regime, yet Titoist laws of self-government are based upon the right of the individual citizen freely to nominate and to elect his own political representatives. Again, the concept of majority rule is allowed to function only in those instances where it cannot threaten the regime's over-all control. Finally, democracy to the Titoists in no way includes the right of any form of organized opposition to exist.

At the highest level of generalization it may be presumed that when, either in theory or in practice, the Titoists use the word "democracy" apart from its socialist context, they are equating it with that amount of freedom for the individual which does not threaten their plans for continued socialization.

While the Titoists have not felt required to explain what is distinctly democratic and what is distinctly socialist in their political system, they do have a relatively concise theoretical rationale for social democracy as such.[5] As good Marxists they insist that all governments—even their own social democracy—are little more than the reflection of the organization of a specific class society at a fixed stage in its development. Each government is given its form and its substance by the class relationships which prevail within

[4] See Chapter XII.
[5] For the most complete development of this theoretical rationale to date, see Kardelj's Oslo speech "Socialist Democracy in Yugoslav Practice," *Borba*, Jan. 1, 1955, p. 1.

the society it represents—and to Marxists all class relationships are primarily those existing between the individual and the means of production. Therefore, "bourgeois" democracy, as the Titoists refer to Western democracy, is purely a political democracy. The real power within it, according to the Yugoslav Marxists, belongs only to those whom the Titoists erroneously insist upon seeing as the constantly dwindling number of private owners of the means of production. They likewise insist that majority rule is permitted to operate freely in a bourgeois democracy only if it does not endanger the basic premise of bourgeoise society, namely, private ownership of the means of production.

The Titoists did, however, in their consideration of bourgeois democracy, depart from standard Leninist-Stalinist theory. They discovered that there is no final, unchanging form of political democracy. They admitted that social relationships in bourgeois democracies are constantly undergoing the process of change brought about by the political victories of the working class and other progressives. Thus, the Titoists came to reason that the peaceful transition from bourgeois political democracy to the larger form of social, or economic, democracy is often possible even in bourgeois societies.

The Titoist theorists claim that in classical bourgeois democracy the rights of the individual in the economic sphere are merely an incidental appendage to his political rights. Only indirectly, through the exercise of his political rights, can the individual in a bourgeois society possibly influence his material destiny. In social democracy, the Titoists maintain, the emphasis is less upon the individual's political rights and more upon his economic rights. Economic rights are essentially the individual's right to manage the socially owned means of production and his right to decide upon the distribution of the profits resulting from that part of his labor which he donates to society. The Titoist theorists conclude that if the individual can be given his full economic rights, he has then achieved a higher form of democracy which automatically transcends the basic bourgeois concept of political democracy. Therefore Titoists are not preoccupied with such purely political democratic rights as free elections, majority rule, and organized opposition.

To Marxists all democratic forms of government are but a reflection of the relationships between man and the means of production. Consequently Yugoslav social democracy must by definition represent a higher political form than bourgeois democracy, because social democracy presupposes the nationalization of the means of production. However, nationalization is only a preliminary requirement and not an essential component of social democracy. Nationalization, as in the Soviet Union, can all too readily lead to state ownership and from that to state capitalism. In state capitalism the exercise of economic and social power becomes concentrated in the hands of the ruling bureaucracy, which in a Marxist state is synonymous with the Communist party. Social democracy, on the other hand, is founded upon the premise that nationalization has been superseded by "social ownership" of the means of production. Social ownership is reached when the producers have moved on from being mere wage laborers to become the managers of the means of production. To the Titoist the right of the workers to manage the means of production is a "new democratic and political right" through which those who create material value by their labor also dispose of it.

The Titoists do not mean that their social democracy rests solely upon the principle of producer self-management. They intend self-management to turn the "passive principle" of people's sovereignty, frustrated in its pure political form by economic and class limitations, into an "active principle" by direct participation of working people in the representative bodies which govern the political and social life of the country. The producers' councils, as the second chambers of the local, district, republican, and federal government structures, were created to secure the direct participation of workers in government.

Titoist theorists claim that their social democracy, as a fuller type of democracy which represents wherever practical a synthesis of economic and political democracy, gradually changes the role of the state as an instrument of class consciousness. They believe that the rights of producer self-management and producer self-government, both of which are supposedly exercised outside the sphere of state power, guarantee this reformation in the role of the state. Their social democracy therefore demands the constant withering away of the state and the continuous extension of democratic privileges. Entire fields of social endeavor in Yugoslavia are more and more to be governed solely by free associations of citizens or administered socially through self-governing institutions like those already established for social welfare and education. The Titoist theorists believe that they have also created a form of direct democracy in which political parties, which for Marxists are purely the creatures of class interests, become less and less necessary. In brief, the Titoists theorists are satisfied that by their reforms they have emancipated the individual from exploitation, inequality, and coercion. To them, there has been achieved in Yugoslavia "the birth of a new humanism which alone can be the basis for the real enjoyment of human rights and human dignity." [6]

[6] Djordjević, *op. cit.*, p. 18.

CHAPTER XI

The Role of the State

Marxist theory contains no thorough and precise analysis of the role of the state in the period of transition from capitalism to socialism. Marx and Engels wrote only of the need for the state to "wither away" once the proletariat had taken over the ownership of the means of production. The vagueness of their doctrine allowed the Yugoslav leaders a comfortable latitude in purging their system of the debilitating weaknesses of Stalinism. The contemporary Titoist state is a dictatorship, but now relatively decentralized. It freely dispenses democratic privileges wherever these encourage socialization without endangering the regime's new remote control of the entire administration.

The inefficiency and impracticality of the centralized state as it existed prior to 1950—when it attempted to oversee every possible facet of Yugoslav life—became apparent to the Titoist leaders once they had given up all hope of reconciliation with Stalin. The Titoists had to seek a new theory for their state if they were to survive without relapsing into the most ordinary kind of military dictatorship and thereby precluding every hope of achieving socialism. This new theory had to serve both ideological and practical needs. The Yugoslav leaders, like Lenin in his time, found no difficulty in fitting the cloth to the suit. The concept of the withering away of the state—so conveniently ignored by Stalin—became the "scientific" explanation for the decentralization demanded by Titoist social democracy.

After their expulsion from the Cominform the Titoist leaders discovered that their state was over-centralized. In consequence it had become over-bureaucratized and socialist development had been retarded rather than hastened. Therefore, from the practical point of view, decentralization was to loosen the death grip which the Stalinist-type bureaucracy held on Yugoslav administration. Simultaneously decentralization could broaden the popular foundations of Titoist power. It should bring greater efficiency to state administration. It should permit the relaxation of the tensions which had resulted from the exercise of a monopoly of bureaucratic power through police-state methods. In brief, decentralization was to shift as much as possible of the responsibility for administration to the ordinary Yugoslav citizen. Decentralization, the Titoists hoped, would restore the waning vigor of their revolution.

By the end of 1949, the Titoists had completed a searching analysis of the Stalinist-type state.[1] They now publicly declared that the Soviet state was the total negation of Marxism-Leninism. Instead of socialism, the Soviet system had given birth to the highest and most reprehensible form of capitalism, the very same economic and social system it was meant to destroy. It had created "state capitalism" in which the state, as the owner of the means of production and the sole distributor of the surplus labor it milked from the toiling masses, had replaced the old bourgeois exploiting class. The Russian proletariat was still the same downtrodden, unwilling, brutally exploited mass of wage slaves that Marx and Lenin had sworn to emancipate. The Soviet state had become nothing more than a privileged, self-perpetuating bureaucracy which had transformed itself into a force above society. Therefore, the Soviet state was playing a role diametrically opposed to that role planned for the state by Marx and Engels. At worst, Lenin had meant the Stalinist-type state to exist only for the most difficult portion of the first revolutionary period in which the interests of the proletariat had to be vigilantly protected from bourgeois attempts

---

[1] The first published report of this searching analysis was an article by Makso Bače, "On Criticism and Auto-Criticism in the U.S.S.R.," *Komunist*, No. 6 (Belgrade: Nov. 1949). The article has been reprinted in *QAS*, No. 5-6 (July-Sept. 1951), pp. 61-143.

to regain power. The Titoists now ridiculed the Stalinist argument that the Soviet state could not begin to wither away so long as Russia was surrounded by capitalist states. This argument, the Titoists scoffed, had even less validity now that the Soviet Union was encircled almost entirely by socialist countries. The Yugoslavs then set out to prove that the state could at least start the withering away process even while it still had capitalist neighbors.

The Titoists reasoned that, once the first stages of the revolutionary struggle had been completed and the transition to socialism begun, the state had two equally important obligations. The first was to fight those remnants of capitalism still within itself. The second was to fight the monopolistic tendencies which naturally resulted from the controlling bureaucracy's exercise of total power. In other words, once the revolutionary state had solidified its hold over the economy, there was no excuse for its resistance to the withering away process anticipated by both Marx and Engels for the period of transition from capitalism to socialism. Thus, the Titoists looked upon their decentralization reforms begun in the last days of 1949 as both a theoretical and a practical return to the "correct" Marxist-Leninist path.

In assisting their state to wither away, the Titoists first took steps to decentralize control over the economy by shifting many supervisory and control functions from the federal to the republican administrative levels, and from the republican to the local levels. But these were only temporary measures. They merely shifted the center of responsibility and control to the lower levels of the solidly knit state administrative structure. The Workers' Council Law of June 1950 was the first truly revolutionary act of decentralization. It changed not only the form but the content of state administration as well. This act technically transferred the right to manage the means of production from the state to the workers' collective of each individual enterprise. Ownership of the means of production was in theory transferred from the state to the socialist society as a whole.

Tito, in introducing the Workers' Council Law to the National Assembly, pointed out that Marxist theory expected socialism to be possible only in a society whose productive forces were highly developed.[2] Nevertheless, he continued, even in an underdeveloped transitional society the state cannot possibly keep all functions in its hands until all of the material and other conditions for socialism have been completed. Marx and Engels taught that the state begins to wither away at the moment when the proletariat comes to power. But, said Tito, "of course, this means when the proletariat should really be in power in every respect." In the meantime, the state can prepare for its own dissolution by gradually transferring its economic functions from the state to the working collectives. Tito warned, however, that workers' self-management must not be looked upon as a cure for all the ills of the Stalinist revisionist tactics which the regime had hitherto mistakenly adopted. Self-management was but one step back in the right direction. "State functions in the management of the economy are not yet able to cease completely, but they are no longer the exclusive factor." [3] The new system of workers' self-management would only reach its fullest meaning when the workers own "cultural advancement" had improved to the extent where they could assume their new responsibilities in their entirety. As the workers' cultural development progressed, state ownership of the means of production would gradually be replaced by the higher form of "social" ownership. State ownership, said Tito, is the lowest form of socialist ownership, and not the highest as the leaders of the U.S.S.R. considered it to be.[4]

In September 1951, Kardelj presented a concise summary of the new Titoist theory of the state. Quoting extensively from Marx, Engels, and Lenin, he summed up those tenets of Marxism-Leninism which the Titoists consider valid:[5]

[2] See Tito, *Workers Manage Factories in Yugoslavia* (Belgrade: 1950), pp. 22-32.

[3] *Ibid.*, p. 32.

[4] *Ibid.*, p. 41.

[5] See Kardelj, "Dix Ans de Révolution Populaire à la Lumière de l'Histoire," *QAS, op. cit.*, p. 11 ff.

"1. The capitalist state is a parasitical excrescence upon society and it retards social development. For the proletariat, the state is a necessary evil which it must suffer temporarily; but if this state acts in such as way as to serve as a brake upon the free movement of society, then it becomes an obstacle to the ultimate aims of society;

"2. The proletariat requires the state to protect the revolution, to liquidate the reactionary resistance of the remnants of capitalism, and to create the necessary conditions for the free development of socialism;

"3. The proletariat cannot make use of the old state apparatus; it must destroy this and replace it by its own 'truly democratic' state apparatus;

"4. The proletariat must free itself from the superstition that all common affairs concerning the total society can only be handled by the state. As a result, the functions of the state must gradually wither away immediately following the triumph of the revolution;

"5. In order to put a stop to the tendencies toward transforming the state machinery from the role of the servant of society, which it ought to be, into being the master, we must fight both against the remainder of the capitalist system in our economic life and against the bureaucratic tendencies in our state machinery. These tendencies have until now been unavoidable in all states, but the new generations, growing up in conditions of social democracy will gradually liquidate them along with all of the bric-a-brac of the state."

In speaking of the process of the withering away of the state, Kardelj wanted to make clear that the Titoists had "never cultivated anarchist or utopian theories concerning the state." They had never talked of the abolition of the state or claimed that in the period of transition it must no longer play an important role. On the contrary, the Titoists never doubted, for example, the need to strengthen the country's armed forces in order to protect the interests of the working class from both internal and external enemies of socialism. Nevertheless, Kardelj warned, one must not forget that Marx and Engels always saw the state as, by its very nature, contrary to "abstract liberty," to liberty for all and for each. It always serves one part of society against the other. Kardelj admitted that in this respect the socialist state is no different from other states. It is a reflection of the interests of the working class. But since the socialist state works to rid its society of all remnants of systems and ideologies based upon the exploitation of man by man, it is in the final analysis working to assure real liberty for all. Therefore, to fail to use the state in the period of struggle for socialist development would, "in reality, be renouncing the revolution and socialism as well."

Kardelj insisted that the constantly increasing participation of the working masses in the administration of state affairs and of social functions in general, and of economic affairs in particular, is the indispensable element of social democracy. It is "the essence of the withering away of the state." The representatives of the people at the communal level ought eventually to decide almost all questions. Their own apparatus of well-qualified men ought to execute these decisions. Here Kardelj presented his description of the type of state the Titoists hoped eventually to create in order to attain the fullest possible social democracy: "In the center, a small apparatus, highly qualified and subordinate to the central *representative* organs, with its rights and duties strictly defined. At the bottom, the real basis of social activity—in the sense of the 'commune' of Marx[6]—with the social organs of the districts, localities, factories, institutions, etc., and, as the center of gravity, a qualified apparatus of professionals responsible to these organs, fulfilling its tasks

[6] Here Kardelj is referring to Marx's exposé of the role of the local "commune" as envisaged by the leaders of the Paris Commune of 1871. See Karl Marx, "The Civil War in France, 1871," *Selected Works*, II (New York: 1933), pp. 475-525. For the portion of this address most frequently cited by the Titoists as the source of inspiration for the type of state they hope to construct under social democracy, see footnote No. 1 of Chapter VII.

within the framework of strictly determined rights and duties." [7]

The Titoists have attempted to reorganize their state to fit Kardelj's pattern wherever this has been practical. The initial preparations for shifting the "real basis of social activity" to the local levels was contained in the people's committee reform law of April 1952. It reorganized and reconstituted the local and district political-administrative organs to permit them to perform the economic and social functions which the regime intended to pass on down to them. To emphasize the pre-eminence of the working class in this system of self-government, the new law established the producers' council as the second house of all but the smallest of people's committees. The move made in 1955 to convert all local units of self-government into "communes" was theoretically meant to strengthen direct democracy at the local level.

In presenting the 1952 people's committee reform to the National Assembly, the Titoists for the first time publicly outlined an altogether new development in Marxist-Leninist theory concerning the role of the state. Here Kardelj discussed the fact that in the Soviet Union the Party and the reigning bureaucracy had become one and the same thing.[8] He pointed out that when the Party exercises bureaucratic powers it loses its identity with the working class and sets itself up as a self-perpetuating ruling caste. To correct this unfortunate development in Yugoslavia, the Titoists decided there must be separate functions for the Party and for the state bureaucracy. The Party must, instead of exercising power directly, act only politically, as the guiding élite within all social organizations. Kardelj did not explain how this separation of function was to be made when only Party members could be trusted with positions of importance in the government and in the economic and social life of the country. Nevertheless, at its Sixth Congress held in Novem-

[7] Kardelj, *op. cit.*, p. 22.
[8] See Kardelj's address to the National Assembly, *NYL*, III:1-2 (1952), p. 15.

ber 1952, the Party was instructed in its new and less powerful role as the "salesman" of social democracy and not its arbitrary executor.[9]

The year 1952 also witnessed the decentralization of the social security system as a kind of trial balloon for the projected self-management of other social functions then being controlled exclusively by the state. This was the year in which other reforms gave greater authority in planning, and in budgetary and other important fiscal responsibilities to the district and local people's committees and to the self-managed economic enterprises. The constitutional reform at the beginning of 1953 reorganized the federal and republican governments to bring them into closer accord with the new theoretical and practical demands of economic, political, and social decentralization.

Soon after the promulgation of the constitutional reform, Kardelj publicly mentioned that state capitalism constituted the greatest natural danger to the process of socialization during the period of transition from capitalism to socialism. Pointing out that the bureaucratic tendencies inherited from the former Stalinist-type state system were still a powerful factor, he then listed the following principles which he claimed underlay all Titoist efforts to discourage bureaucratism in Yugoslavia:[10]

1. To restrict gradually the functions of the state and of the state apparatus to the tasks of internal and external security and to the political protection of the socialist order, viz., to the protection of the free society from the violent anti-democratic and counter-revolutionary interventions of anti-socialist forces;

2. To guarantee conditions for the free movement and development of social forces, on the basis of the social ownership of the means of production through democratic organizational forms of social self-government;

[9] See Chapter XII.
[10] See Kardelj, "The Role and Task of the Socialist Alliance," *YR*, II (March-April 1953), p. 14.

3. To shift the center of gravity of state operations to the basic state and self-governing social organs, guaranteeing conditions for the development of the broadest initiative of those organs, and to entrust to the highest state and social organs only those functions which are of common interest and which can be performed, owing to the very nature of things, only on the highest level;

4. To guarantee democratic operational methods in all state and social organs.

The implementation of these principles, Kardelj said, is tantamount to the withering away of the state, that is, to the process which Marx considered to be essential to the struggle for socialist relationships.

The year 1954 was spent in consolidating and extending the new state theory. Numerous secondary economic and social reforms were formulated and implemented to increase the scope and practice of decentralization. The transformation of the local political-administrative units into the expanded type of "commune" came in 1955. Local self-government was thereby theoretically brought one step closer to the realization of that form of the state in which the local community serves as the "real basis of social activity."

In the summer of 1955, Tito summed up for a group of visiting Americans what he considered to be the ultimate role of the state in social democracy. The state, he said, will continue to wither away until all that remains socialized is "the conscience of the people, so that they consider the existence of the community as a necessity and do not become anarchists." [11] Tito admitted that this stage was far off. Therefore, there were still certain important functions, such as "co-ordination, control, the army, and foreign policy," which must remain the responsibility of the central authority of the Yugoslav state.

---

[11] *President Tito Interviews the Sherwood Eddy Seminar* (New York: Yugoslav Information Center, July 1955), p. 13.

Briefly summarized, the state, in the present stage of Titoist theory and practice, is to be both the activator and the passive instrument of the working class. In every possible way it is to foster the achievement of economic democracy. Yet, it has a duty to suppress those aspects of political democracy which might encourage its subjects to challenge the objectivity of its aims and methods.

The "level of socialist consciousness" is still too low among the Yugoslav population to permit the regime to relax its monopoly of political control. Therefore, the state apparatus alone must protect the Titoist system from internal and external threats and furnish as well the inspiration to drive the system further down the uncharted path of socialism. On the other hand, the Titoist leaders are convinced of the inevitability of Marxist historical materialism which provides that the state must begin to wither away as soon as the material forces of society pass into the hands of the working class. An obligation is therefore imposed on the leaders to continue to relax the monopolistic control their state had developed during its purely Stalinist period. Decentralization was the most practical method of reconciling these apparently incompatible demands of relaxation and control. Worker self-management and self-government could democratize the state both in theory and in practice and begin to merge the state with society. The Yugoslav Marxists choose to regard this merger as synonymous with the withering away of their state.

As Marxists, the Titoists see each state as the superstructural reflection of the relationships existing between the members of a society and its means of production. They claim that Yugoslav social democracy automatically represents a new and higher form of the state since it is the reflection of a system in which, for the first time in history, the means of production have been turned over to society as a whole to be managed by the workers themselves. At the same time, the Titoists believe that the new worker-ownership relationships of social democracy, being dynamic and not static, will constantly be acting upon the super-structure and will cause it to grow less powerful as the working class gains ever-greater experience in self-manage-ment and self-government. As Kardelj explained in Oslo in 1954, "with the strengthening of the material forces of socialism . . . the role of the state in economic and political life will gradually be converted into an organizational mechanism which will no longer rest upon power but on the common social interest and the voluntary observance of a social discipline corresponding to common interests." [12]

Thus, the Titoists assert that, by having changed the basic worker-ownership relationships underlying the structure of their state, they have found the way back to the true path of Marxist-Leninist dialectical materialism. To Marxists, dialectical materialism is the inevitable forward process of history which leads to that final socialist society in which the state as such disappears entirely and the matter of authority becomes nothing more than the "social administra-tion of things." The Stalinists lost this path but the Titoists believe that they have found it again. The Soviet leaders had attempted to defy the historical process of the withering away of the state. They had pursued the most unnatural— and hence un-Marxian—practice of establishing the bureau-cratic state as the essential component of socialism. The Titoists like to imagine that by severing their system from the Stalinist abnormality, they have once again released the "scientific" forces which irresistibly impel the working masses toward stateless, selfless socialism. Thus, the Tito-ist state by autocratically decreeing and jealously nurturing social democracy is, in theory at least, simultaneously pre-paring for its own demise. This explanation is always offered as a rationalization for the undemocratic methods by which Yugoslav social democracy must often proceed in its practical efforts to bring about its "totally demo-

[12] From Part I of Kardelj's "Socialist Democracy in Yugoslav Practice," *Borba*, Jan. 1, 1955, p. 1.

cratic" aim. As Leninists, the Yugoslav leaders have not the slightest doubt that the end in this instance fully justifies the means.

However, the Titoists are well aware that the truly socialist stage of development lies in the dim and distant future. They therefore admit that their state will have to remain indefinitely as a reflection of working class interests. In theory they are urging their social democracy on to that stage where the Yugoslav state, as such, will perform only the most essential duties for a society not yet arrived at the final socialist condition of grace in which its citizens willingly live by the Communist principle "from each according to his ability, to each according to his needs." In the truly social democratic stage all but "the most essential duties concerned with the total community" are to be performed by the lowest organs of self-management and self-government. The Yugoslav theorists do not bother to explain how the advanced social democratic state is to be kept from unduly interfering in the processes of self-management and self-government unless the ordinary citizen has the political right to challenge the state's authority. Their only allusions to this problem are couched in the customary Marxist mystical references to that utopian stage where man attains that selfless quality which Christ vainly exhorted him to practice.

The Titoists foresee their future state, in all measures except those affecting security and the development of socialism, as a body of experts who act as the wise and benign servants of the self-managed and self-governed communities. This process has already been started with the formation of such agencies as the Federal Social Security Institute and the Federal Bureau for the Study of Educational and School Problems. Both of these organizations were created in 1955 as groups of experts who would serve as specialist-councilors to the self-governing social security and educational systems and to the Federal Executive Council. Similarly, the role assigned by the regime to the

working committees of the National Assembly is an attempt
to bring groups of experts to work on the non-political aspects of federal legislation.

To date, however, no more than token gestures have been
made by the Titoist state in the direction of its final
metamorphosis into that form theoretically ideal for social
democracy, where the state becomes the servant and protector rather than the master of the people. The most objective of Titoist theorists might argue that their state has
progressed so little because in its contemporary form, as a
reflection of the material relationships of its present society,
it must await the awakening of a higher socialist consciousness in the majority of Yugoslav producers before self-management and self-government can reach full maturity and
thereby furnish the required material relationships for the
truly social democratic state. The more emotional, less
rational Titoist would take issue with the initial observation.
He would claim that the decentralization reforms are all
irrefutable illustrations that the process leading to the
eventual dissolution of the Titoist state has begun. To an
observer of another faith, however, these reforms have
quite a different meaning. They represent valid decentralization of control when the new system is compared with the
senseless centralization that preceded it. But they have also
had the very practical effect of ending the bureaucratic
chaos which resulted from the earlier attempt to control
by force from the center absolutely every aspect of the
country's life.

The organization of the contemporary Titoist state has
achieved a greater unity of purpose and hence a greater
centralization of authority, if not of control, than it ever
had before. This authority has been won precisely because
of the decentralization reforms. The policy of strength
through decentralization has reduced the amount of sheer
guesswork formerly required to keep the state functioning.
The Yugoslav leaders now attempt to rule by laws and
regulations rather than by security forces alone. The Titoist

social democratic state may therefore be considered more democratic than the Stalinist system it replaced, and hence it represents a swing in the direction of the "bourgeois" state. On the other hand, since the Titoist state tolerates no organized opposition, it can never be regarded as a truly democratic state in the Western sense.

The Titoist state reflects the schizophrenia of the Yugoslav rulers' theory and practice concerning it. Their state is to be both the activator and the passive instrument of society. It is to be the protector of internal and external security and yet the servant of the people as the provider of freely sought expert advice and assistance. However, the single fact that the social democratic state is responsible for foreign policy means that it cannot ever be further decentralized to any worthwhile extent. The defense of the country from outside interference demands a constant and a strongly unified organization of its total resources. The Titoists' abandonment in May 1955 of the policy of "splendid isolation" for the more standard role of a small power playing off two great powers against each other in itself represents a major setback to the effective withering away of the existing Yugoslav state.

The Titoists must, therefore, look upon their social democratic state as one which will grant the ever-increasing working class every practical form of freedom in purely economic and social matters. However, even these freedoms will be strictly limited in case they should thwart the Yugoslav Marxists in ruling as they alone see fit. The existence of these restricted freedoms makes it possible for the Titoists to claim that their state has begun to wither away, since each economic and social freedom granted represents the relinquishment by the state of some of the direct responsibilities it previously exercised. In the long run, however, this claim has little validity. The freedom to manage the means of production and to govern the local community, even if such freedoms are fairly genuine, are only of incidental value if they are not accompanied by freedom to decide who shall govern the state which dispenses these limited freedoms and what should be the guiding principles of this state. The Titoists would prefer to have everyone believe that the Yugoslav citizen entrusts these decisions to his representatives in the National Assembly. But this is true only in theory. The method of electing representatives precludes the Assembly's being truly representative in character. At best the Assembly is nothing more than a hand-picked research group sometimes used by the regime to aid in the drafting of non-political legislation.

In the final analysis, then, the Titoist state is neither Stalinist state capitalist nor "bourgeois" democratic. Instead, it is the unique creature of a comparatively small group of men who claim to have created it as a suitable instrument to foster the eventual emergence of a system wherein no form of centralized state authority will be needed. It is neither fair nor worthwhile to doubt the Yugoslav rulers' motives in this respect. Nevertheless, the Titoists are the first to admit that the stateless stage of historical development is a very long way off. They cannot even prepare for the complete withering away of their state in the foreseeable future. Since in international relationships there are still no signs of the advent of a peaceful world brotherhood, the Titoist state has little prospect of ever being decentralized into a mere clinic of experts at the beck and call of the self-managed and self-governed constituent communities. The observer's only alternative therefore is to describe the present Titoist social democratic state as an autocracy of Marxist Jesuits who hope someday to convert the entire Yugoslav people to their creed and thereby to wash away the most glaring sin in their system of government—the complete lack of the essential political rights of the individual.

It does not matter whether the state or society is the owner of the means of production. Until the Yugoslav people have the political freedom to elect their own representatives to their own government and to challenge this government's behavior, the Titoist state remains the sub-jective creation of that small group of men who are able to wield sufficient power to assure their continued control. Unless the Titoists can find a safe way to match economic democracy with political democracy, their state is doomed to remain, at best, a benevolent dictatorship—a way station between the totally state-dominated society and individual freedom. However, there is an essential difference between Marxist-Leninist-Titoist thought and Western liberal thought about such a dictatorship. The Titoists fully be-lieve that their state is not a dictatorship in the same sense that the Western liberal would use the word, simply because their final goal is the direct antithesis of all forms of state power. To such partisans, this goal automatically removes all stigma from the dictatorial means their state must necessarily use to achieve the desired utopia. To the Western liberal, this is sophistry, pure and simple. But to Marxist-Leninist-Titoist, it remains an objective truth.

CHAPTER XII

The Role of the Party and of the Popular Front Organization

Once they had assumed complete control of their country, the Titoists banned all but two political organizations. The first of these was the Yugoslav Communist party, officially called the League of Communists of Yugoslavia after the Sixth Party Congress held in November 1952. The second was the People's Front Organization known since its Fourth Congress held in March 1953 as the Socialist Alliance of the Working People of Yugoslavia.[1]

Party regulations make the Party Congress the organization's supreme agency of authority. The Congress is composed of representatives elected by the lowest units of the Party. It should be convened once every four years[2] to elect a Central Committee and to pass upon those reports which the Central Committee may submit to it. Between congresses the Central Committee serves as the Party's governing agency. It elects from among its own membership an Executive Council (before 1952 known as the Politburo), the Secretary-General of the Party, and the Central Control Commission. The latter body has jurisdiction over Party members in cases involving violations of Party rules and programs. The Central Committee also elects a Secretariat

---

[1] *Note*: Although "the Party" is always referred to officially as "the League," in ordinary conversation it is still almost always called "the Party." It will be referred to as "the Party" in this chapter except where the meaning may be more precise to call it "the League." The People's Front is always referred to as such when speaking of the pre-1953 organization. Likewise, it is always called the Socialist Alliance or the Alliance after 1953.

[2] The Seventh Party Congress was originally scheduled to convene in November 1956. However, the anti-Communist revolution in Hungary caused the Titoist leaders to postpone their Seventh Congress until sometime in 1957.

from among the members of the Executive Committee. The Secretariat is responsible for carrying out the Party's day-to-day administrative business.

Although the Party structure is meant to appear as though its lowest organs have the greatest power, the reverse is actually true. The Executive Committee is the real center of the Party's political and administrative power. Its members hold the top positions throughout the state administrative structure. Although the Executive Committee is in theory elected by the Central Committee, which is in turn elected by the Party Congress, there is no doubt that in practice the Executive Committee actually names the individuals to be "elected" both to the Central Committee and to the Executive Committee. Before the Fifth Party Congress in July 1948, there were only five members of the Politburo.[3] Four new members were added at the Fifth Congress.[4] One of these was dropped in 1952 for pro-Cominform sympathies.[5] Five more members were added at the Sixth Party Congress in 1952.[6] Since that time one member has died and one has been dropped for disciplinary reasons.[7] The Party's present Executive Committee consists of eleven members.

Each of the major national groups in Yugoslavia is represented in the Executive Council. The president of the exccutive council of each of the six constituent republics is a member. The Committee members function both collectively and as individuals in accordance with a division of duties by which each member is responsible for a particular area of Party activity. As Secretary-General, Tito is responsible for the entire scope of Party activity. The six republican presidents are responsible for Party activities in their respective republics. The remaining four Executive

[3] Tito, Kardelj, Ranković, Djilas, and Franjo Leskošek.
[4] Kidrić, Pijade, General Ivan Gošnjak, and Blagoje Nešković.
[5] Nešković.
[6] Vukmanović-Tempo, Djuro Salaj, Djuro Stari-Pucar, Lazar Kolaševski, and Bakarić.
[7] Kidrić died in 1953. Djilas was dropped in January 1954.

Committee members are respectively responsible for organization, instructions, propaganda, and discipline. Party
procedure permits Executive Committee members to act
almost independently in their individual assignments. However, each member is obliged to consult the others before
taking action which he feels may represent a departure
from standard Party theory and practice.[8]

At the time of the Kremlin-Belgrade correspondence
which led to Yugoslavia's expulsion from the Cominform,
the Yugoslav party's Central Committee had only twenty-
six members—a surprisingly small number for a Communist
party in power. The Soviet leaders made use of this fact to
support their accusation that the Yugoslav party was "undemocratic," "illegal," and "un-Marxist." The situation was
remedied at the Fifth Party Congress, and by 1952 the
Sixth Party Congress was electing 109 members to the
Central Committee.[9]

The governing agencies of the Party already described
above are duplicated, except for the office of Secretary-
General, in each of the six constituent republics. Regional,
district, and local Party units make up the republican
organizations. The territorial areas of the local Party units
do not necessarily correspond to those of the local political-
administrative units. The national organization formulates
all general policy. The entire Party structure is expected to
operate under the principle of "democratic centralism." In
theory this principle is meant to curb the autocratic power
of the Party rulers by giving the lower echelons the right
to criticize orders handed down to them from above. In
practice, however, "democratic centralism" usually means
that each lower echelon is to receive and to execute without
question or hesitation all orders received from above.

Before November 1952, there were basic "cells" of the
Yugoslav party in each economic, social, and government

---

[8] See "Statement of Milovan Djilas," *The Case of Milovan Djilas* (New
York: Yugoslav Information Center, 1954), p. 8.

[9] See *New York Times*, Nov. 18, 1952, p. 3.

organization and in each village. The 1952 Party Congress disbanded the "cells" in order to curb their all too frequent interference with the implementation of workers' self-management and self-government. Territorial wardlike units were formed in the place of the "cells" as the basic Party organizations. However, these ward units have not been entirely satisfactory. Many individual members who had shown an interest in Party work at their places of employment have failed to show a similar interest in the work of their ward units. For one thing, the ward frequently brings together an uncomfortable diversity of membership ranging from university professors to simple manual laborers. The Titoists admit that the ward system has proved extremely detrimental to Party work in such institutions as professional societies and editing and publishing concerns, where individual "cells" were a necessary asset in maintaining doctrinal purity. Steps were taken in 1954 to reinstitute "cells" in such organizations.[10]

The structure and basic organization of village Party units was not greatly disturbed by the institution of wards. The reorganization, however, weakened the emphasis previously placed upon the individual agricultural collectives as separate basic "cells." Party activities in the villages had steadily deteriorated as the regime decreed such unpopular policies as the forced delivery to the state of agricultural produce and the drive to make peasants join collective farms. Party activity reached its lowest ebb in the countryside when the new agrarian land reform followed fast on the 1953 decree permitting the dissolution of collective farms.

By June 1956, total Party membership was 635,984[11] or approximately 5.8 per cent of all Yugoslav citizens of eighteen years of age, the legal voting age, and over, or 4 per cent of the total population.[12] Of this total membership, 31.36 per

---

[10] See Ranković, "La Ligue des Comunistes," *QAS*, No. 23 (March-April 1954), pp. 14 ff.

[11] *Komunist*, No. 11-12 (Belgrade: 1956), p. 14.

[12] See Table 3-3, *Statistički Godišnjak FRNY 1956* (Belgrade: July 1956), p. 52.

cent were workers, 32.06 per cent were employees, 17.66 per cent were peasants, and the remaining 18.92 per cent listed as "miscellaneous" which undoubtedly means primarily "intellectuals" and professional men.[13] These statistics show a considerable change in the class content of the Party since the 1948 Congress when 29.53 per cent of the total membership were workers, 49.14 per cent peasants, 14.38 per cent intellectuals, and 6.68 per cent from other classes.[14] The 1956 figures indicate that the emphasis has been upon decreasing the proportion of peasant membership. They also indicate that the middle class or white-collar workers, as represented by the "employee" and "miscellaneous" classifications, had by that time come to represent the largest single class group within the Party.

There had originally been two youth organizations in Yugoslavia, one attached to the Party and one to the People's Front. After the Fifth Party Congress (1948) these two groups were amalgamated and re-formed under the name of the People's Youth Organization of Yugoslavia. The People's Youth, as it is commonly called, is led by young Party members. Although it is technically separate from the two major political organizations, the People's Youth, in its duties and responsibilities, is more closely allied to the Socialist Alliance than to the Party. All members of individual sports, higher education, and cultural clubs and societies are required to be members of the People's Youth. Nevertheless, in March 1954, total membership included only approximately 35 per cent of the country's youth aged fourteen to twenty-five.[15] The Titoist leaders are worried about this poor showing. The plenum of the Party's Central Committee which met in March 1956 had been convened primarily to discuss "the estrangement between the country's youth and the Communist party." [16]

The People's Youth Organization is headed by a Central

[13] *Komunist, op. cit.*
[14] See Josef Korbol, *Tito's Communism* (Denver: 1951), p. 67.
[15] Ranković, *op. cit.*, p. 39.
[16] See *New York Times,* March 15, 1956.

Committee elected at a periodically convened national congress. It has republican and regional branches. Originally it was made up of the separate youth groups known as "actives" which existed in schools, universities, economic and social organizations, and villages, or anywhere that young people wanted to form a group. After 1952, an attempt was made to copy the ward-type reorganization then being carried out within the Party. The People's Youth found, however, that, like the Party, many members who were active in school or work place groups became passive in the impersonal ward units. But the lack of interest in the People's Youth cannot be attributed solely to its reorganization. The primary cause is the widespread political apathy among Yugoslav youth. Having accepted the country's socialist orientation, young Yugoslavs admittedly pay no further attention to politics.[17]

[17] See *ibid.*, April 23, 1956, p. 9.

While in Yugoslavia in 1955, the author was told a story illustrating the point that the Yugoslav youth are just as materialistically inclined as any of their more "bourgeois" counterparts in Western countries.

A professor in one of Yugoslavia's universities had earlier in 1955 been discussing the mis-calculations of the 1954 federal budget with his class of forty students of which four were members of the Party. Exasperated by the students' seeming lack of interest in miscalculations amounting to more than one million dollars, the professor asked his listeners if they realized how large a sum this was. Getting no general response, he asked one student from a comparatively poor family what he would do if he suddenly had one million dollars dropped into his lap. The student replied that he would first buy himself a complete wardrobe, then he would buy a car, then a villa on the sea, then some land, and the rest of the money he would invest, part locally and part abroad.

The professor expected a protest from the Party members. None was forthcoming. He then asked a girl of bourgeois origin what she would do with such a sum of money. He was relieved when the girl said that she would first of all give half of the money to her mother. At least this was not pure selfishness. But the professor's relief was short-lived. The girl explained that she would give her mother the money so as to be rid of her. The remaining half of the money the girl decided she would spend more or less as would the first student. Still no outcry from the Party members.

The professor then asked whether any other student had any further suggestions as to how they would spend such a windfall. None did, not even the Party members.

Disturbed by his experience, the professor told the story at the next faculty meeting. He deplored the apparent lack of imagination of his stu-

The Socialist Alliance of the Working People of Yugoslavia is the only mass political organization allowed. It
was originally set up by the Titoist leaders, under the title
of People's Front, as an alleged coalition of the prewar
political parties. Perhaps during the war when several prewar parties supported the Partisan movement the legend
of a coalition was justified. But by 1945, the People's Front
was purely a propaganda device to counteract Western
charges that the old political parties had been ruthlessly
suppressed. The present Socialist Alliance equally lacks
any effective corporate individuality. It has little life or
few protagonists of its own. Most of its active leaders are
Party members or affiliates who since 1952 have been instructed to use the Alliance to propagandize and to extend
the programs of the Party and of the regime. The Alliance
as such exerts little or no influence upon the determination
of government policy.

The Alliance has a dues-paying membership of approximately 80 per cent of adult Yugoslavs, some 8,000,000
strong.[18] Most people join merely to escape the disfavor of
local officials. The Alliance has branches in every city and
town and in almost every hamlet throughout the country.
The hierarchy of Alliance units ascends from the local
branches through regional and republican levels to the
federal level. Members of all social organizations are expected to join the Alliance. All activist organizations such
as the People's Youth, the Federation of Yugoslav Trade
Unions, and the various associations for veterans, the professions, education, and so on, are expected to work through

---

dents and pointed out that their answers to his question indicated that the
coming Yugoslav generation, if his students were in any way typical, was
nothing more than a group of vulgar materialists. He persuaded other
professors to try the experiment in their own classes. One by one those
who did try it returned with results more or less the same as those received
by the first professor.

[18] Table 25-1, *Statistički Godišnjak, op. cit.*, p. 336, shows that at the
end of 1952 there were 7,775,000 members of the Socialist Alliance. An
additional quarter of a million members are supposed to have joined since
that time.

or at least closely alongside the local branch of the Socialist Alliance in carrying out their educational and other public assignments.

The Alliance is controlled by a Presidium elected every four years by its national congress. Tito is the President of the Alliance. Kardelj is its Secretary-General. Of the twenty-seven members of its present Presidium, twenty-one are also members of the Central Committee of the Party. It is therefore not easy to deny that the Alliance exists purely as a creature of the Party. In the lowest local units of the Alliance efforts are made to see that Party members do not monopolize the leading offices; but any non-members chosen are handpicked by the Party. The regime would probably prefer to have the Alliance serve as the constant and vigorous agency of local self-improvement, yet the organization generally appears to be able to act only in support of official policy, and even then only after local and national issues have been decided elsewhere. The Alliance, like an empty air mattress, is useless unless inflated by Party enthusiasm.

From Rulers to Educators to the Djilas Heresy

After intensive self-analysis following their expulsion from the Cominform, the Titoists concluded that their Stalinist-type state contained the seeds of its own destruction. They found that, when the Party, regardless of its purity and devotion to Communist doctrine, becomes synonymous with the state bureaucracy, the revolution loses its fervor in proportion as the bureaucracy ossifies into Party dictatorship *over* and not *for* the working class.

The Yugoslav leaders had to learn how to bring about the very necessary separation between the Party and the state bureaucracy without simultaneously weakening their control of the state apparatus. Minority rule demanded management of the state by officials completely in the trust and confidence of the regime; only Party members could meet this requirement. To solve their dilemma the Titoists made a questionable theoretical distinction between the Party as an organization and its individual members. The Party itself was to relinquish its role as intimidator and overseer and to become the persuader and salesman. It was to concentrate its entire energy upon raising the "level of socialist consciousness" among the masses so that eventually, like the state, the Party could begin to wither away. Those individual Party members entrusted with political-administrative management were to have dual personalities. In their capacity as Party members, they were to follow Party policy. As state functionaries, however, they were to serve only as officials of the social democratic system. This duality is a luxury not to be enjoyed by the Party rank and file. Their single task is to represent the Party as an organization. Their full and unflaging energies are to be devoted to education not to command in attaining socialism.

The first practical public notification of the intention to revise the nature and scope of Party responsibilities fittingly came from Tito himself.[19] When presenting the Workers' Council Law to the National Assembly at the end of June 1950, he pointed out that Stalin had never precisely determined the theoretical role of the Party in the transitional phase of socialist development. In practice Stalin had reduced the role of the Bolshevik party to that of the administrator of the state apparatus. Eventually the Bolshevik party became the most important part of the state apparatus and so lost all contact with the masses it supposedly represented. The Yugoslav Communists, Tito claimed, had taken the necessary steps to stop this dangerous trend in their own country and meant to keep a sharp lookout for its recurrence. The Workers' Council Law theoretically reduced the Party's power within the economy by turning the factories over to the workers.

The first positive evidence that a new and less omnipotent

[19] See Tito, *Workers Manage Factories in Yugoslavia* (Belgrade: "Juroslovenska Knjiga," 1950), p. 30.

role was being imposed on the Party came in the October 1950 decree which abolished the special food and other privileges that Party officials had previously enjoyed.[20] It is true that the decree was the direct result of the severe drought the country had suffered that year. The drought meant dire privation for the Yugoslav masses and they would have heartily resented the continuation of Party privileges. Nevertheless, in this decree a ruling Communist regime for the first time took positive steps to show that the rulers' lot was to be no better than that of the ruled.

A still clearer indication of what was in store for the Party was given at the Central Committee's Forth Plenum held in June 1951. It had been called for the express purpose of informing the Party masses that henceforth there was a need to substitute legality for arbitrary rule. As spokesman for the regime at the meeting, Alexander Ranković referred both directly and indirectly to Party malpractices as the primary cause of the deplorable state of Titoist jurisprudence and justice. He left no room for doubt that the leaders were determined to reform Party behavior.

The piecemeal nature of the changes in the role of the Party and the lack of clear instructions as to the meaning of the changes caused confusion and uncertainty within the rank and file membership. The regime's increasingly friendly collaboration with the Western powers added to the confusion and uncertainty. Some Party members began to show alarming tendencies to lapse into Western "bourgeois" habits. In Slovenia and Serbia, for example, certain intellectual groups had the temerity to vote out of office officials sponsored by the Party.[21] "Unreliable intellectuals" became the target of the Party purge begun early in 1952. But the purge did not restore Party morale and discipline. Both continued to degenerate. Fortunately, however, 1952 was the year of the Sixth Party Congress. The Congress gave the Yugoslav leaders an opportunity to remodel the

---

[20] See Chapter III for more specific references to this decree.
[21] See *New York Times*, Feb. 16, 1952, p. 5.

Party structure to have the organization serve social democracy more efficiently. The sessions of the Congress were devoted to long and careful explanations of the Party's vital importance as the salesman rather than the all-powerful overseer of the new system.

The Congress convened on November 3, 1952. Tito spoke at the opening session and discussed the theoretical role of the Party, now that the earliest stages of the revolution had been successfully completed and the period of transition to socialism safely begun. The sum and substance of the Party's new duties and responsibilities Tito explained as follows: The role of the Yugoslav Communist party consists in commanding, yet "it does not interfere in anything and everything as some kind of supreme arbiter and judge who passes his judgment on various problems of social life . . . as the final and infallible judgment." Rather, its role "lies in its most important task—in ideological and educational leadership, in its vigilance toward the development of socialist society so that the latter might proceed normally and correctly. In other words, the role of the Communists consists in re-education and education of the citizens of our country in a socialist spirit." [22] Between the lines Tito was saying that while it had been necessary to concentrate all power in the hands of the Party during the struggle for power and for the consolidation of this power immediately after the war, now that the strength of the propertied classes had been successfully broken, there was no further need for this concentration. The Party must now shift its emphasis from materialistic endeavors to purely ideological and educational tasks. Without actually divesting itself of its leading role in Yugoslav society, the Party must now learn to lead by persuasion rather than by intimidation.

The Sixth Party Congress revised the Party's basic statute to make the reforms in economic and political-administrative

---

[22] Tito, "The Struggle of the Communists of Yugoslavia for Socialist Democracy," *Sixth Congress of the Communist Party of Yugoslavia,* a mimeographed transcript of the major speeches delivered at the Congress (Belgrade: 1953), p. 41.

decentralization part and parcel of the Party's own primary aims.[23] Under the new statute, Party structure and formal practice were decentralized to a certain extent. The lowest Party organizations, the institutional "cells," were reconstituted into the territorial ward units. The autocratic executive bureau of the local Party committee was abolished in order "to increase collective leadership and collective work by the whole committee . . . and to bring the committee even closer to the lower Party organizations." Basic Party units were henceforth to have greater independence in formulating the details of local Party policy in accordance with more general directives from above. The new statute provided that local Party meetings should be held in public so that the "activities of the basic Party organizations should develop as much as possible under the control of and with the participation of the masses." The old system of candidate (alternate) members was dropped on the grounds that alternates were necessary only during the former conspiratorial days to replace members who had been arrested. Basic Party units were now to be permitted to expel members, even minor government officials, without referring the matter to higher units. Article 17 of the new statute listed in detail the main responsibilities of the basic Party units. In brief, the list exhorted Communists serving at the local level to behave with a virtue and a perspicacity which combine the talents of a Boy Scout and Mephistopheles.

In March 1953, the People's Front held its Forth Congress. It changed its name to the Socialist Alliance of the Working People of Yugoslavia, and then settled down to listen to Kardelj explain its expanded role and functions.[24] "The period of direct revolutionary processes has passed," he began. "The power of the working class in alliance with the other working people has been consolidated, and a period of systematic practical socialist construction has set

[23] See Ranković, "On the Proposed New Statute of the Yugoslav Communist Party and Some Party Organizational Questions," *ibid.*, pp. 61-64.

[24] Kardelj, "The Role and Tasks of the Socialist Alliance," *YR*, II (March-April 1953), pp. 16-18.

in." The Party, he continued, "does not consider the determination of the political line of struggle for the construction of socialist relationships . . . as its monopoly
alone." This is now the concern of "all who are honestly
giving their share to the common efforts of the overwhelming
majority of our people." Hence, the political policies formulated to assist the Yugoslav struggle for socialism "will be
the result of the conscious and active cooperation of the
working masses, organized by the Socialist Alliance."

Kardelj explained that the Alliance was to become a "mass
platform." It was to be a "political foundation for all state
and social self-governing bodies" so that through extensive
discussion and criticism "these bodies will here be under
the supervision of the masses." The Alliance must be sufficiently broad in its political platform to enlist the participation "of every citizen who comports himself honorably
toward the social community and accepts the general aims
of socialism—regardless of his ideological and other differences of opinion." The Alliance through its working
methods "should function as an all-national parliament
which is constantly in session, in which every well-in-
tentioned citizen may always advance his views, his proposals, and his criticism on any question of social life."

Kardelj then listed the three primary reasons for the new
emphasis upon the role and tasks of the Alliance. First, the
expanded responsibilities of the Alliance should make it
possible to put an end to the duplication of work between
the mass organization and the Party, "that is, an end to
the practice whereby the Party organizations at their meetings simply forward their decisions to the People's Front
organizations for approval." The Party must now concentrate upon ideological questions and upon matters of
ideological leadership in the struggle for socialism, while
concrete political and social questions must be settled
directly in the organizations of the Socialist Alliance. Second,
the Alliance must furnish the means to co-ordinate the
activities of all social organizations and movements. Thirdly,

the Alliance is to serve as the primary means of contact and co-operation between the Yugoslav people and international labor and socialist movements.

Discipline and morale within Party ranks continue to deteriorate despite the seeming clarity of the instructions delivered to the Party rank and file at the Sixth Congress and the further elaboration of these instructions at the Fourth Congress of the Socialist Alliance. There was great confusion about what was democratic and what was socialist in the new policies. The role of educator did not come easily to many local Party bosses. The reforms often seemed to threaten their sinecures. Confusion reached a climax when in the spring of 1953 the regime permitted agricultural co-operatives to disband. Not only did many a minor Party member lose his soft berth as a result of this reform, but many a member who thought he understood the basic validity of social democracy had all of his previous misgivings as to its Marxist-Leninist orthodoxy amplified. Tito's hobnobbing with silk-hatted Western diplomats—he had visited London in March 1953, and was planning visits to the King and Queen of Greece and later to Turkey—only made matters worse. Most minor Party officials either ignored the instructions of the Sixth Party Congress and continued to "reign" instead of trying to win public support for their policies, or else they relaxed completely and took to "petty bourgeois" habits as ducks to water.

The situation grew so serious that in June 1953 the Second Plenum of the Central Committee of the newly constituted League of Communists[25] met at Brioni to discuss the restoration of Party unity and discipline. The result was the issuance of what is now referred to as the "Brioni letter" [26]

[25] *Note*: After the name of the Party was changed to the League of Communists, the numbers used to identify the plenums of the Central Committee were begun anew. Thus, the Fourth Plenum of the League held in March 1954 should not be confused with the Fourth Plenum of the Party held in June 1951.

[26] The text of the Brioni letter is given in *Komunist* (Belgrade: July 1953). A brief summary is given in *The Economist* (London: Oct. 17, 1953), pp. 187-88.

to all Party officials, calling for immediate improvement of the situation. The letter criticized both left- and right-wing backsliders. It complained further that in all too many cases those who had succumbed neither to left- nor right-wing influences had failed to understand the decisions of the Sixth Congress and had merely washed their hands of Party work altogether. The letter was meant to furnish instructions for the alleviation of all the unhealthy developments within Party ranks, but most of the advice it contained was negative rather than positive or was couched in too general terms to be useful. The letter was, however, backed up with an intensification of the purge begun in 1952 to remove slackers and misfits.

It is now known that one person at the Brioni conference, Milovan Djilas, then a member of the Executive Committee and of the Secretariat of the Party, did not agree with the outcome of the discussion. He revealed at his first trial held in January 1954 that he felt that the attitude adopted by the Central Committee at Brioni was "one-sided" and that in its anxiety to curb Party deterioration the Central Committee was ignoring the simultaneous need to maintain strict vigilance against bureaucratism. Djilas insisted that democratization would suffer as a result of the drive to restore Party unity and discipline.[27]

It was partly to try to overcome the one-sidedness of the Brioni recommendations that Djilas began in October 1953 to publish a series of theoretical articles in *Borba*, the Party's official newspaper. In this series, Djilas finally brought to the surface the major paradox of Titoist social democratic theory and practice: the discrepancy between the theoretical role assigned to the Party and the actual role it must play in practice. In greater detail, Djilas pointed out the contradiction which naturally arises when the Party rank and file are told they are no longer rulers but proselytizers who must win their way solely by their powers of persuasion

---

[27] See Thomas Tyler Hammond, "The Djilas Affair and Yugoslav Communism," *Foreign Affairs*, XXXIII (Jan. 1955), p. 301.

even though the fact indisputably remains that the Party does have all the power. Its leaders are in all instances the primary decision-makers and executors of policy.

Djilas' October articles were only mildly controversial. But during November and December he perceptibly warmed to his task. His printed comments became frank and startling denials of the validity of large portions of Titoist theory and practice. For fear of making it appear that a rift had developed within the Party leadership, no move was made to stop the articles or to refute them officially. Hence, many Yugoslavs took it for granted that Djilas' remarks had official sanction. Some Yugoslav newspapers even carried out polls among the lower ranks of the Party and reported that many of Djilas' proposals had been well received.[28] Finally Djilas went too far. In the January issue of *Nova Misao* (New Thought), he published a stinging satire attacking the manners and morals of certain top Party wives who were carrying out a humiliating feud against the pretty non-Party wife of a senior Army general.[29] This was the last straw. The *Borba* articles were stopped with the announcement that the views they contained did not represent those of the Party's Executive Committee. On January 16 and 17, 1954, a special plenum of the Party's Central Committee met and tried Djilas. He was found guilty of "revisionism" and general lack of understanding of actual social conditions in Yugoslavia, and was stripped of all his Party and government titles and functions.[30]

Thomas Tyler Hammond, one of America's most astute observers of the contemporary Yugoslav scene, has conveniently summed up as follows the content of the theoretical arguments presented by Djilas in the series of articles

[28] See "Disgrace of Djilas and Its Implications," *World Today*, X (March 1954), pp. 98-99.

[29] This article is reviewed in *Life* (April 12, 1954), pp. 89-90.

[30] Besides being a member of the Party's Executive Committee, Central Committee, and Secretariat, Djilas had just previous to his expulsion been made the president of the National Assembly. He had also generally been looked upon as the most likely to succeed Tito when the time came for the latter to step down.

which led to his downfall:[31] (1) Yugoslav Communists are not willing to trust the socialist consciousness of the masses, even though, in Djilas' opinion, the majority of the Yugoslav people were ready to support the regime under more democratic conditions. (2) Communism will come about in Yugoslavia spontaneously, regardless of, or even in spite of, the Communist vanguard. (3) The class struggle in Yugoslavia has been successfully brought to an end, except that despotic officials sometimes re-create it artificially. (4) The chief enemy in Yugoslavia was not the bourgeois but the Communist bureaucrat, not capitalism but bureaucratic despotism. (5) Communist bureaucrats wield a monopoly of power, trample on the law, and prevent freedom of expression, which is essential to progress. (6) The only way to avoid developing further into Stalinist bureaucratism is by permitting greater democracy. (7) The goals for which Yugoslav Communists must strive are democracy and socialism—not communism; here Djilas expressly denied the existence of a final goal. (8) To achieve democracy the League of Communists must be completely reorganized and its discipline greatly relaxed. (9) Not only Stalinism but Leninism too contains within itself the seeds of despotism.

At the root of all Djilas' arguments was a confirmed belief that the "level of socialist consciousness" of the Yugoslav people had already reached the stage at which the Party should begin to wither away both in practice and in theory. His own thoughts on the ideal role of the Party converted it into a kind of debating society, a loosely knit league in which the important theoretical concepts required to guide the Yugoslav people ever onward to socialism could be threshed out freely and without hindrance by interested intellectuals. Those Party members who permeated society would do so as individuals qualified to lead by their own merit alone and not by the fact of their membership in an historically predestined elect.

[31] Hammond, *op. cit.*, pp. 301-2.

The embarrassing thing about Djilas' claim that Yugoslav socialization had reached the stage at which the Party no longer needed to rule was that this point now had to be denied by the regime. His critics had to argue that most of the population was not really behind the government. They also had to admit that the government depended upon coercion to maintain its rule and to carry out its programs. "People do not deprive themselves of a stick because sometimes it might strike an innocent man," said Kardelj at the Djilas trail.[32] Such admissions were a painful setback to the Titoist leaders' prior claims that their system of social democracy was a higher form of democracy than that existing in bourgeois countries.

Nevertheless, proof that at least some democratic progress had been made in Titoist Yugoslavia was apparent from the conduct of the Djilas trial. It was widely broadcast. The foreign press was permitted to be present throughout. Djilas' accusers did not revert to the usual Communist-type epithets generally reserved for such exhibitions. And Djilas was given the opportunity to answer his accusers and to make an initial and a closing statement. At the end of his trial he admitted only those of his supposed errors which he chose to recognize and denied the others. He was not ousted from the Party, even though he was deprived of all his official responsibilities. However, within a week of his trial, his Montenegrin constituency, which had elected him the preceeding November with the highest plurality in the land, even higher than Tito's,[33] recalled him from the National Assembly.

Djilas had a large following within the Party ranks, particularly among the younger members. His calm acceptance of his punishment, and his voluntary resignation from the Party in April 1954, undoubtedly discouraged many a Party affiliate who might have otherwise been ready to side

[32] See *The Case of Milovan Djilas* (New York: Yugoslav Information Center, 1954), p. 10.
[33] See *New York Times*, Jan. 26, 1954, p. 6. Djilas received 98.8 per cent of the total vote of his constituency; Tito 97.7 per cent of his.

with him. His stress upon the need to shift the emphasis of
the Titoist system toward more complete democracy seriously appealed to many a younger Yugoslav who did not,
perhaps, hate and fear socialization as his elders might, but
who at the same time yearned for greater individual freedom. Djilas' remarks, such as that in his December 20th
Borba article, seemed to hold out the first real hope for
freedom that the average Yugoslav had known since 1945.
In this article, Djilas concluded: "Today no party or group,
not even the [working] class itself, can be the exclusive
expression of the objective needs of the whole society. It
cannot assume exclusive rights to manage productive forces
without enslaving them, including the most important of
them, the men. There is, and can be, no other way out but
more democracy, more free discussion, freer elections in
social, government, and economic organs, more adherence
to the law." The Titoists were forced to reply to such dis-
turbing sentiments with the somewhat hollow claim that
the democracy which Djilas sought was devoid of socialist
content. He made socialism the outcome of democracy and
this flatly contradicted the Titoist leaders' insistence that
true democracy could only grow out of socialism; the doctrine Djilas affirmed automatically led to degenerate forms
such as a bourgeois multi-party system or outright anarchy.

The Party purge which had been intensified by the Brioni
plenum was now expanded to include incipient Djilas-ites.
The Fourth Plenum of the Communist League's Central
Committee met in March 1954 to prevent the further spread
of the idea that Yugoslavia should adopt Western democracy
as a model. The opening session of the meeting was devoted
to an attack on the concept of free political activity.[34] It
was made clear that there was to be no opposition to the
regime's pursuit of a socialist and ultimately a Communist
Yugoslavia. Tito's message to the plenum stressed the fact
that, even though the Party was now to lead by persuasion
rather than by intimidation, positive Party leadership in

[34] See *ibid.*, March 20, 1954, p. 6.

all phases of Yugoslav life was still as greatly needed as ever.

Throughout 1954, Djilas lived freely in Belgrade and openly received all foreign and local visitors who dared or cared to call upon him. In November, an Austrian newspaper published an interview which quoted Djilas as having said that the Yugoslav Communist party was becoming "reactionary" and was dominated by a Central Committee which was "conservative dictatorial." [35] By December, there were reports that he had told some of his foreign visitors that a domestic type of Stalinism had taken over in Yugoslavia.[36] On December 25, he called in the Belgrade correspondent of a Western newspaper and issued a statement in which he advocated a two-party political system for Yugoslavia and referred to communism in that country as synonymous with totalitarianism.[37]

Early in December, several of Djilas' old friends were called before a three-man control board of the Party's Central Committee to explain their continued friendship with Djilas. One of those called was Vladimir Dedijer, the only member of the Central Committee who had stood by Djilas during his trial in January 1954. Dedijer stalked out of the control board hearing before it was completed and disclosed his feelings about it to members of the foreign press. While he had been stripped of his membership in the Central Committee and of his official post as editor of *Borba* after his support of Djilas at the latter's trial, Dedijer was still a member of the Party and a deputy to the National Assembly. His behavior in discussing the control board episode with foreigners was considered a gross violation of Party discipline.

At the end of January 1955, Djilas and Dedijer were brought to trial in the regular Belgrade regional court and were sentenced for having violated Article 118 of the Yugo-

[35] See *ibid.*, Dec. 7, 1954, p. 14.
[36] *Ibid.*
[37] *Ibid.*, Dec. 26, 1954, p. 29.

slav Criminal Code which covers intent "to undermine the
authority of the working people." Djilas received an
eighteen-month suspended sentence and Dedijer received a
six-month suspended sentence.[38] The following March,
Dedijer was recalled from the National Assembly by his
constituency.[39]

Undaunted, Djilas spoke out against Tito's behavior when
the Hungarian crisis first arose. In October 1956, he issued
a statement to the official French press agency charging
the Titoist government with having abandoned "for narrow
ideological reasons" its stand against foreign interference
in the internal affairs of another country.[40] Then, in an
article written for the November 1956 issue of the American
liberal, anti-Communist magazine the *New Leader*, Djilas
hailed the Hungarian revolt as the beginning of the end of
the Communist system. In December, Djilas was once again
brought before the Belgrade court and sentenced under
Article 118 of the Criminal Code to three years in prison.
He was accused and convicted of the charge that his writ-
ings represented "a conscious slander" of Yugoslavia, and
were "intended to . . . undermine the effect of Yugoslav
foreign policies." [41]

There is no way of knowing how deeply Djilas' ideas may
have penetrated the minds of Yugoslav party members.
Therefore, it is not possible to say with any assurance that
the greater amount of liberalism represented by these ideas

[38] See *ibid.*, Jan. 25, 1955, p. 1.
[39] See *Politika* (Belgrade) March 8, 1955, which ran a short item on p. 5
announcing that Dedijer's constituency had the day before recalled him
from the National Assembly. The *New York Times*, March 9, 1955, p. 8,
reported that the recall vote had been 25,000 to 5,930. That so much time
had elapsed between Dedijer's trial and his recall is probably due to the
fact that he was a great favorite of Tito's and Tito did not return from
his visit to India and Burma until the end of February. Tito's permission
probably had to be obtained before recall could be effected. The size
of the contrary recall vote is generally attributed to the fact that, unlike
so many Party officials, Dedijer represented his own home district, where
he was very popular and where his reputation for fearlessness is deeply
appreciated.
[40] See *New York Times*, Dec. 12, 1956, p. 6.
[41] *Ibid.*, Dec. 14, 1956, IV, p. 2.

has been eclipsed along with Djilas' own official influence. There is no doubt, however, that he remains a kind of living symbol to many a Yugoslav in whose heart there glows a real yearning for the greater freedom for which Djilas has argued. The castigation and official demise of Djilas most certainly did not in themselves restore either the lost Party discipline or the waning fervor of the vital Yugoslav Communist fraternity. The continuing dissolution of the Party's organization, influence, and ideology has for some time been the freely admitted preoccupation of the Titoist leaders.[42]

THE WITHERING AWAY?

The Titoists frequently insist that their Communist party—like their state—has begun to wither away. Those who take this position argue that the Yugoslav party has relinquished the extensive powers it once wielded. They intimate that their Party has become a fraternity of devoted individuals who lead the majority by their strength of character and by their forensic abilities rather than, as in the past, by their privileged position as members of the ruling caste.

Tito had been the first to allude to the withering away of the Party—although at the time he did not use those exact words to describe its projected demotion. In his presentation of the Workers' Council Law to the National Assembly in June 1950, he referred to the Stalinist development of the role of the Party as "contrary to the teaching of Lenin" who had meant the Party to be the leader and educator and not the persecutor of society.[43] He wanted the Assembly to understand that the Stalinist-type Party was not to prevail in Yugoslavia. Four months after Tito's address to the National Assembly came the decree stopping many Party priveleges. Then, in June 1951, the Central Committee

[42] See *ibid.*, March 18, 1956, p. 10.
[43] See footnote No. 19.

plenum was called to place the Party's stamp of approval upon the leaders' decision to replace the tactics of arbitrary power with legality. In more ways than one this plenum was an act of self-emasculation. The steady decline in the discipline and morale of the Yugoslav party from that time on confirms the view that the plenum's action was more the result of "democratic centralism" than of a great revival of liberalism within Party ranks.

In the summer of 1951, Kardelj openly stated that in social democracy the Party was expected to wither away along with the state.[44] He spoke of this once again in April 1952.[45] But at the Djilas trial in January 1954, Tito himself claimed the distinction of having been "the first to speak about the withering away of the Party." [46] Just exactly when he first spoke of it in these terms is not clear. Nevertheless, his views about the withering away of the Party are made quite clear in Vladimir Dedijer's official biography of Tito, first copyrighted in 1952.

Dedijer writes of a discussion on the withering away of the Party in which Tito, Kardelj, and other senior Yugoslav Marxists explained the point to a west European socialist visitor. In this discussion, Dedijer quotes Tito as having said: "The Communist party cannot continue to function in the same old way if at the same time the state is withering away. If the state does not wither away, then the Party becomes, in a certain sense, the instrument of the state, a force outside of society. If the state really withers away, the Party necessarily withers away with it." [47] In answer to the visitor's question on the role of the Party when the management of the economy is entirely in the hands of the producers, Tito continued: "The role of the Party is historically

[44] See Kardelj, "Dix Ans de Révolution Populaire à la Lumière de l'Histoire," *QAS*, No. 5-6 (July-Sept. 1951), p. 27.

[45] See Kardelj, "On the Law on People's Committees," *NYL*, II:1-2 (1952), p. 27.

[46] "Statement of Josip Broz-Tito," *The Case of Milovan Djilas, op. cit.,* p. 3.

[47] Vladimir Dedijer, *Tito* (New York: 1953), p. 428.

limited to a certain period. How the society will then arrange its affairs remains to be determined, but [even] one party will not be necessary. The Party withers away gradually. That does not mean that a one-party system will be superseded by a multi-party system. It merely means that the one-party system, having superseded the multi-party system, will in turn vanish." [48] Kardelj here interjected, "This phase is not far away. I think we shall perhaps live to see it in our time."

Instead of being remedied by the Sixth Party Congress, the deterioration of Party discipline had been intensified. References to the withering away of the Party were therefore temporarily restrained. But the eclipse could not last for long. The withering away phenomenon had become the Titoist leaders' principal theoretical support for the actual decentralization of Party power being carried out and for their refutation of accusations from abroad that a single-party system had no right to call itself a democracy.

Foreign "reactionaries" and socialists alike constantly bring to the attention of the Yugoslav Marxists the impossibility of achieving democracy without permitting opposition groups the right to organize. At first the Titoists took refuge in the purely Marxist concept that political parties are nothing more than the representatives of selfish class interests. In a transitional socialist society like theirs, the only class interest which could be represented was automatically that of the working class. Later the Titoist improvisers evolved a more sophisticated rationale; they claimed that, since the historical progression of the Marxist dialectic doomed the Party as well as the state to wither away, Titoist social democracy was correctly assisting the process by forbidding the formation of new political parties. The moves toward workers' self-management and social self-government were presented as steps in the creation of a society in which direct democracy for each individual citizen would eventu-

[48] *Ibid.*, p. 431.

ally be assured. When direct democracy had been fully achieved there would no longer be a need for even one political party. Therefore, the Titoist theorists reasoned that any return to a multi-party system would be retrogression since the single-party system of their social democracy is assisting the development of a partyless direct democracy in Yugoslavia.[49]

Today the Titoists maintain that all references to the "classical" one-party system are irrelevant with respect to Yugoslavia. The Socialist Alliance is presented as their country's main political grouping, nevertheless they insist that the Alliance is not a political party. Instead, it is a democratic organization which unites the working class, the working peasants, the intellectuals, and all other productive sections of the population. Furthermore, the Communist party as such in Yugoslavia is no longer, in the Titoists' view, an organization monopolizing power and political life. It is no more than the "most conscious organized part of the working class" which strives within the "main political grouping" to bring the Yugoslav masses closer and closer to socialism. The Titoists contend that any reversion to a multi-party system during the advanced stage of socialization that Yugoslavia has already reached would merely force the Communist party to revert to the bureaucratic, centralistic, and monopolistic forms and methods it has already outgrown. In other words, the Titoists base their single-party position upon the thesis that, as the systems of workers' self-management and social self-government are improved and extended through practice, the need for the Party, even as the conscious organized force working to lead the masses to direct democracy, will wither away correspondingly. Thus, the contemporary Titoist explanation is that theirs is not a one-party system but rather the embryo of a partyless system.

Early in 1955, Kardelj reminded a foreign correspondent

---

[49] For a thorough exposé of the Titoists' rationale concerning political parties, see Jovan Djordjević, "A Contribution to the Discussion of Social Classes and Political Parties," *RIA*, VI (June 1, 1955), pp. 8-10.

that in the larger capitalist states the trend is toward more and more state intervention in economic affairs.[50] Therefore, he said, classical Western parliamentarianism does not necessarily represent a foolproof remedy against bureaucracy. He insisted that the only sure remedy was the one being followed by Titoist social democracy. Through the continuous expansion of worker's self-management and social self-government Titoism is producing a form of direct democracy in which all elements of political monopoly—which parties automatically represent—are being made to wither away gradually. Kardelj conceded that direct democracy does not preclude the grouping of people according to the views and attitudes they adopt on specific problems. He admitted that in the long run this is also a form of political grouping. But he pointed out that no fixed parties are needed for this type of grouping. What is required instead is the active participation of individuals in the numerous organs of self-government which replace to an increasing extent the classical government mechanism.

Kardelj's final point serves to stress the over-riding flaw in most Marxist reasoning: the complete inability to look at man as he really is and not as he might be. Here Kardelj has ignored the historical fact that many men are completely indifferent to political action, even in societies where they need but a soapbox and a public corner to become activists in the interest of their own beliefs. Marxists—and Kardelj appears to be no exception—are prone to ignore the fundamental assumption that, even if a man can be shown the truth, there is no guarantee that he will reach out and grasp it.

This seemingly congenital inability of Marxists to see man as he all too often is partially explains the great discrepancy between Titoist theory and practice with respect to Yugoslav political organizations. An outstanding case in point is the Titoists' frequent claim that their Socialist Alliance is a na-

---

[50] See Kardelj, "The Internal Political Development of Yugoslavia," *RIA*, V (Feb. 1, 1955), p. 2.

tion-wide parliament in which direct democracy is brought much closer to practical realization. They claim that the Alliance is in effect a forum of national public opinion since it is theoretically free from all ideological and political "monopolism." In reality, however, in present-day practice the Alliance is not much more than a public-address system halfheartedly diffusing the aims and ambitions of the minority group which controls Yugoslavia. In actuality it is but a façade for the acts of the Yugoslav Communist party. In spite of the probability that the Yugoslav leaders would prefer the Alliance to be otherwise, it at best only contains the seeds of that type of "democratic" organization into which the Titoists probably hope to have it develop one day. But these seeds cannot be allowed to germinate until the large majority of the Yugoslav people have reached that degree of "socialist consciousness" where the regime can safely permit the Alliance to become completely free of all political "monopolism." This stage is certainly a long way off.

"Class consciousness," "various forms of backwardness," "inequality," and many other such ailments which the Titoists themselves recognize as flagrant defects of present-day Yugosolav society, require the constant vigilance of the "leading socialist forces." Therefore, the claim that the Yugoslav Communist party is withering away has practical validity only if the Party's present nature and scope are considered in relation to its more powerful role in the former period of centralized administration. Once that form of rule had been safely transposed into the comparatively indirect control system of social democracy, the withering away concept becomes far too advanced for Yugoslav reality. The Yugoslav Communist party had done all the withering away it can afford to do until the majority of the Yugoslav people decide they are satisfied with Titoist social democracy. Only then will it be possible to permit the amount of direct democracy necessary to have the Party—and the state, for that matter—once again take up the withering away process in earnest.

The concept of the withering away of the Party does have practical value to the ruling Titoist circle, however. It gives a certain Marxist-Leninist respectability to the action taken by the Yugoslav leaders to reinvigorate their revolution by loosening the grip of the Party on the state bureaucracy. The concept can also be advantageously used as a partial refutation of foreign accusations that a one-party system cannot possibly be democratic. The Titoists can now argue that, with the Party doomed to wither away, theirs is not a simple one-party system but rather an embryo partyless one aimed at the achievement of direct democracy. Finally, the withering away of the Yugoslav party, even to the limited extent it has actually taken place, has served as a very practical convenience to the Yugoslav rulers. They have less need of a constantly vigilant and powerful Party organization now that the means of production and most other material sources of power are safely in their hands. Therefore, by weakening the Party, the regime has given itself a much greater flexibility in ruling as it alone sees fit. It is no longer required to defer the implementation of new policies until these can be discussed and accepted by the Party as such.

The relatively less powerful role of the Party under decentralization has made the regime's administration of both state and Party affairs more efficient. In other words, democratic centralism is now more of a one-way process in Party affairs and more of a two-way process in political-administrative matters. This point is borne out by the new emphasis the regime places upon the ladders of vertically linked self-managing associations which, although staffed at the top by loyal Party members, are at the same time composed to the very largest degree of more ordinary citizens. These important lines of communication between the rulers and the ruled are therefore much more effective transmitters of public opinion and of regime policy than the highly partisan Party.

Those Party members chosen to head state, economic, and social agencies of any importance are all trusted implicitly by

the regime or they would not occupy these posts. Hence they
are expected to have mastered the great paradox of Titoist
theory concerning the Party. They are the privileged group
of split personalities who are able to be state administrators
on the one hand and Party members on the other, who do
not, although in reality they do, represent the fusion of the
Party and the state machinery. That this paradoxical situation can actually furnish the division between Party and
state functions required by contemporary Titoist theory and
practice is due to the fact that the corps of split-personality
administrators are loyal first to the Yugoslav leaders and then
to the Party. In a situation such as this, the Yugoslav Communist party as an organization has truly begun to wither
away. But the dictatorship has been correspondingly
strengthened.

The reduced power status of the Party per se has had a
debilitating effect upon Party zeal, leading to a relative stagnation of Party activity throughout the country. Eventually
the Titoist leaders will be required to work another *do as I
say and not as I do* miracle such as that performed in the
separation of the Party from the state bureaucracy. If they
are unable to perform this new miracle, they will have to
admit that their concept of the withering away of the Party
is completely fallacious—or at least that it is immature in
Yugoslavia's case. The Titoist leaders must find some way to
restore their Party's constantly waning fervor and interest.
The leaders cannot exist without a strong, disciplined, and
devoted political organization to keep them from degener-
ating into a common military dictatorship. And it is by no
means certain that they could maintain themselves by continuing to foster the development of a party loyal to themselves and not specifically to evangelical communism. There
is no doubt that this fact was very much in the minds of the
Yugoslav leaders when they were considering the matter of
ideological and political *rapprochement* with the Soviet
Union.

The Titoists, as a minority group, are forced to rely upon

their Party as a quasi-official arm of their state apparatus. Without the Party they would not be able to maintain their power or to continue their struggle for socialization. Yet the regime's theoretical plans for socialization call for an ever-increasing amount of democratic self-management and self-government which in turn requires a correspondingly gradual relinquishment of more and more power by the Party. No matter how one may choose to consider the Tito-ists' dilemma in this instance, it merely serves to prove that a one-party system is both the cause and the effect of dictatorship and is, therefore, a glaring negation of democracy.

CHAPTER XIII

New Stress upon the Individual

The relative humanism of Titoist social democracy is perhaps the most important single result of the Yugoslav Marxists' efforts to find their own road to socialism. Unlike the Marx-ism-Leninism-Stalinism from which it sprang, Titoist social democracy stresses, both in theory and in practice, the im-portance of the individual as the essential component of the socialist community. The Titoists have made an honest effort to restore human dignity to the individual Yugoslav wherever it has been possible to do so without undermining their own power.

The probable cause of the Yugoslav Marxists' discovery of the individual as the vital element in society is unimportant here. It remains undeniable that through this discovery Ti-toist social democracy has reached out and re-established the connection between Marxism and the fundamentals of West-ern liberalism which existed before Lenin and Stalin rudely severed this link. Titoism may therefore succeed in bringing Marxist practice back to the liberal thesis from which it claims to have evolved. If it does, Titoism may succeed in animating the soulless materialism of Marx with some of the humanism which was the professed aim of Marx's revolu-tionary philosophy.

The Titoists advertise all of their economic, political, and social decentralization reforms as practical attempts to real-ize social democracy's theoretical reliance upon the indi-vidual—at least upon those individuals who have indicated their willingness to work for eventual socialization. The stress placed by the Titoists upon the ultimate achievement of direct democracy further sanctifies the importance of the individual—provided he maintains constant vigilance against "localism" and anarchy and recognizes his lasting obligations to the total community. The new "communes" are advertised as the ideal fundamental units of local self-rule in Titoist social democracy because through them the interests of the individual and the community can, in theory at least, be most perfectly fused.

Tito early in 1950 publicly remarked that people, not machines, were the most important factor in the struggle for socialism.[1] Ranković opened his address to the June 1951 Party plenum, called to consider legal reforms, with the remark that "the strengthening of the citizens' consciousness for collective work in the building of the new social organization cannot be divorced from the strengthening of their consciousness regarding their personal rights and personal freedom." [2] Kardelj, when presenting the new people's committee law to the National Assembly in April 1952, announced that the Titoists had always considered that "*individual rights*' formulated by bourgeois democratic revolution indisputably belong also to socialism." [3] By the beginning of 1953, "free men" had theoretically become "the most important unit" of Titoist social democracy.[4]

The official declaration of the expanded aims and responsibilities of the Socialist Alliance as elaborated at its March 1953 Congress devoted full attention to the new stress upon the individual. The Alliance dedicated itself to the "unyielding struggle for the constant strengthening of the individual rights of citizens and of respect for the dignity of man." It promised to "uphold the principle of freedom of conscience." No one, the declaration stated, "has the right to abuse freedom to the detriment of the social community or against socialism; but likewise no one may arbitrarily determine or limit

---

[1] See Milovan Djilas, *On New Roads of Socialism* (Belgrade: "Jugoslovenska" Knjiga, 1950), p. 33.

[2] Ranković, "For the Further Consolidation of the Judiciary and Legality," *NYL*, II:4 (1951), p. 3.

[3] Kardelj, "On the Law on the People's Committees," *NYL*, III:1-2 (1952), p. 16. (Underscoring Kardelj's.)

[4] Jovan Djordjević, "About Socialist Democracy," *RIA*, IV (Jan. 1, 1953), p. 18.

the individual rights of citizens." [5] Kardelj spoke at some
length to the Congress on the abuse of religious sentiment
for political purposes, but he prefaced his remarks by saying
that "for the Socialist Alliance and its members, religious
feelings are the private concern of the individual." [6] It was
understood, of course, that no such freedom of conscience
was to be permitted to members of the Communist party.
They are expected to have reached that advanced stage of
"socialist consciousness" where religious sentiments are felt
only for the historical materialism which Marxists are obliged
to believe will furnish all of the improvements necessary to
human progress.

By the end of 1953, the role of the individual in Titoist
social democracy had become sufficiently established as a
basic tenet of the system to have Kardelj devote a major
address to it. [7] In this speech he recalled that socialism had
been born precisely to liberate the working man from every
tendency to subordinate the interest of the individual to a
pretended superior interest. The socialist revolution degen-
erates when it loses sight of this purpose and attempts to
force the individual worker to become a slave of an omnipo-
tently wise leadership. The experience of the Soviet Union
showed this degeneration, Kardelj said. Yugoslav social democracy, he claimed, was attempting to give every "honest
citizen" the means with which to fight, "within the framework of democratic institutions, for the triumph of his own
interests and conceptions."

Kardelj believed that Yugoslavia need not establish what
he called "formal democracy." Rather, it must create that
type of democracy in which the importance of the individual
"ought to be one of the principal motivating forces." Only
free men, Kardelj said, can be conscious of their respon-

---

[5] See "Declaration on the Aims and Tasks of the Socialist Alliance of the
Working People of Yugoslavia," *YR*, II (March-April 1953), p. 24.
[6] Kardelj, "The Role and Tasks of the Socialist Alliance," *ibid.*, p. 18.
[7] Kardelj, "The Role of the Citizen in Our Political and Economic System," *Komunist*, No. 11-12 (Belgrade: 1953). The text of this address,
minus a section on the economic situation, is reprinted in *QAS*, No. 22
(Jan.-Feb. 1954), pp. 97-136.

sibilities toward the community. He then listed the following "four essential determinants of Yugoslav social activity," meant to strengthen the rights of the individual in Titoist social democracy: workers' self-management of the means of production, workers' self-government through their local people's committees, the system of representative government existing at the republican and federal levels, and the new role and responsibilities of the League of Communists and the Socialist Alliance.

According to Kardelj, workers' self-management of the means of production is the very essence of social democracy. It begins the freeing of man from exploitation by man and is therefore the essential foundation for true individual freedom. Workers' self-management in turn provides the proper socialist worker-owner relationships to permit a new political democracy which can foster workers' self-government in their individual communities. Kardelj felt that the new Yugoslav democratic practice of workers' self-government, though only in its very earliest stages of development, "already clearly shows that socialism cannot develop unless it reinforces the role of the individual and the liberty of everyone in his creative work." As for the third determinant of Yugoslav social activity, the republican and federal governments, Kardelj claimed that these are representative agencies performing only those functions which the individual in his community cannot effectively carry out for himself. The League of Communists and the Socialist Alliance, he concluded, are to devote the major portion of their energies to raising "the level of socialist consciousness" of the masses so that the Yugoslav society may continue to progress toward higher and higher socialist forms which automatically confer more and more freedom upon the individual.

The spokesmen for Titoism continued to stress the importance of the individual within their social system. It was vital that they find some way to encourage personal initiative in order to raise economic productivity. The former highly centralized system of state control had reduced personal initiative to the point of non-existence. And, as the strain of reckless over-expansion of industry began to tell upon the entire Yugoslav economy, the regime was finally forced to recognize that incentive and initiative were human commodities which could not be ordered or turned on or off at random, but were related primarily to material and other tangible benefits accruing to the individual. The Yugoslav leaders came to see that only the Communists, and surprisingly few of these, could be expected to find their recompense in the spiritual satisfaction of knowing that they were sacrificing themselves and their talents to the progress of socialism.

In 1953, the workers' councils in individual economic enterprises were permitted for the first time to exercise the prerogative given them by the Workers' Council Law to distribute the surplus profits of their respective establishments. The councils handed out most of these profits as bonuses to the workers themselves. This action produced an upsurge of morale among the working masses. But it also served to emphasize the importance of the individual far and above the point intended by the regime. The worker, left to his own devices, had in this instance shown an alarming propensity for ignoring what the regime considered to be the prior needs of the community. He had catered to his own selfish needs instead. Therefore, a brake was applied to the comparatively uninhibited disposal of excess profits as provided for by the Workers' Council Law. A federal decree transferred most of the authority for the final disposition of such funds to the local people's committee.

Purely material recompense as the inspiration for greater productivity threatened to disturb the equilibrium of the regime's plans for continued socialization. The Titoists were therefore forced to shift the emphasis of their campaign for greater individual initiative and incentive to the less tangible reward of individual freedom. The stress now fell upon the glories to be won from the advancement of the programs of self-management and self-government. When perfected, these programs would transfer to the individual worker the free incentive and initiative that had once been the exclusive province of the capitalist landlord or of the state capitalist bureaucracy. The individual worker once placed in free control of the socially owned means of production was to be in a position to achieve the total freedom which socialism, as the doorway to communism, portends. The Titoists began to talk of the "total human being" which the individual is for the first time to become in socialism. They advertised socialism in glowing terms as the last step in the scientific progression to communism, itself "the total humanization of man" and "the full realization of individualism, in the sense that man comes to be raised to the pedestal of his own personality, after a social development which lasted for centuries." [8]

In their efforts to shift the emphasis of the benefits offered the individual by social democracy from the material to the spiritual realm, the Titoists exhibit the same unswerving belief in the perfectibility of man in which so many other Marxists clothe their theoretical ruminations. Marxists profess to abhor any form of mysticism. Yet much of the Yugoslav Marxists' reasoning about the "total humanization" of the individual in the final society they strive to create is founded entirely upon the unmentioned conviction that the nature of man will automatically change once the means of production have been socialized. If this is not mystical faith, it is worse. It is Lysenkoism.

Marxists, and the Yugoslav variety are no exception, are not disturbed by the fact that since the beginning of recorded time mankind has shown no tendency to change its basic human characteristics. They are not distressed that man still shows himself as the same compendium of good and evil he has always been in the past, despite his great

[8] Jovan Djordjević, "Socialism and Humanism," Part I, *RIA*, V (Feb. 15, 1955), pp. 11-12; and Part II, *ibid.* (March 1, 1955), pp. 10-12. This article presents a thorough theoretical exposé of the Titoist viewpoint on the superior humanism of socialism.

progress in conquering many of the obstacles of his environment. They are not disturbed that man is often selfish, that he still has ambitions which make him covet his neighbor's good fortune, that he still frequently wants desperately to be better than or to have more than his neighbor. Marxists seem certain that all these human failings will disappear once private ownership of the means of production no longer exists. They make no effort to explain their sublime confidence that socialized man, unlike contemporary man, will live not by bread alone but by the spirit as well and will automatically love, honor, and respect his fellow man and will be happy to give freely all that is within him and to ask only for what he needs in return, in a society where no authority is required to keep him from being greedy.

It is not unusual that men who exercise total power within their own realm reach the stage of saying one thing and doing another. Such was the case with both Lenin and Stalin whose banner on the road to the dream world of communism was Utopian Marxism. Naked, age-old power politics formed their world of substance, however. Therefore their acts frequently conflicted with the legend on their banner. The nearest they could come to explaining away this paradox was that the ends justify the means.

Sometimes men with total power within their own realm attempt to reach a compromise between theory and practice—a compromise which in the end works a change in both theory and practice. Tito in his post-Cominform struggle to survive has had to make this kind of compromise. The continuation of Stalinism in Yugoslavia would have meant the end of Tito's rule. Therefore, like Lenin before him, Tito has been forced to improvise since his professed creed contains no tried and true codex of procedure. Tito's domain, unlike the land of Lenin and Stalin, is not rich or powerful enough to support a self-enfeebling dogma. For this reason, Tito's banner has come to be a many-colored ensign of trial and error, a patch-work quilt of the required amount of "this" and the practical amount of "that." Whenever a patch is added, it is labeled if it is humanly possible to do so as having belonged to Marx or perhaps to Lenin. The Titoists are fully aware that they are in no position to be ruthlessly dogmatic. They are of necessity pragmatists whose ambition it is to be practical Marxists.

Titoist pragmatism has led the Yugoslav Marxist leaders to regard certain democratic methods as essential to their system. In adopting these democratic methods the Titoists have once again discovered the individual. In rediscovering the individual they have brought back to their system some of the humanism discarded by Lenin and Stalin. At the same time, the Titoists must of necessity model their approach to democracy upon non-Marxist examples since there is no acceptable Marxist experience to serve as their guide. By the nature of their minority rule, however, Titoist democracy must be strictly limited to those methods which do not disturb that power equilibrium which the Titoists claim they have the right to maintain at any cost since it is to lead to a more perfect society in which "man will be completely humanized." Nevertheless, the limited democracy the Titoist system now offers represents a considerable blessing to the individual Yugoslav, especially when his total lack of freedom during the years immediately following the last war is contrasted with his present condition. The average Yugoslav is today permitted a type of personal liberty which, while restricted essentially to non-political pursuits, is still the envy of the individual citizen in those Soviet satellites which have not yet managed to loosen the Kremlin's hold.

If the Titoist leaders maintain their present pragmatic respect for democratic methods, they will certainly bring greater "humanism" to their political and social system. As this humanism is expanded through experience, the capillaries now existing between Titoist social democracy and Western liberalism should be correspondingly strengthened and enlarged. Should these capillaries grow into a main artery, Marxism as practiced by the Titoists will have become a practical and influential political synthesis—a fusion of the thesis of liberal capitalism and the antithesis of Marxism-Leninism.

CHAPTER XIV

Conclusion

Titoism is neither communism as it is practiced in the Soviet Union nor democracy as it is known in Western liberal societies. Instead it is a compromise, a synthesis of those parts of Marxism-Leninism and those parts of Western democracy which the Yugoslav leaders consider necessary or practical to their cause. As a system of minority rule, Titoism is at best a benevolent dictatorship which attempts to recognize human rights but does not dare to grant the one human right which is fundamental—the right of the individual to choose his own government and to control his government's theoretical and practical aims.

The Titoists were not ground to bits by the contending Soviet and Western power blocs in June 1948. Instead, immediately following Yugoslavia's expulsion from the Cominform, a kind of vacuum was created around Tito's domain. The Yugoslav leaders were thereby permitted the luxury of reigning in relative freedom from external political interference—a highly abnormal privilege for a small country in contemporary times. Because of the existing precarious balance of power, neither the Soviet Union nor the Western powers dared to attempt the destruction or even the domination of Tito or of his political system. Neither side was in a position to force upon Tito any of the dictates of its own basic philosophy. Those Soviet or democratic concepts which Tito and his advisers have woven into the context of their post-Cominform political and social system they have chosen of their own free will, and then only to the extent which they themselves considered compatible with their own aims and ambitions.

The *rapprochement* between Yugoslavia and the Soviet

305

Union effected in 1955 ended the period of splendid isolation for the Titoists. By the *rapprochement*, Yugoslavia returned to the status of a small state obliged to maneuver between two large contending powers. Tito thereby took a step which automatically forced him to lead his state, with its carefully nurtured internal political and social system, back into the primeval forest of normal international relationships. Titoism will now have to learn to suffer the vicissitudes of political Darwinism. It was presented with its greatest challenge thus far in the autumn of 1956 when demonstrations of discontent throughout the Soviet satellite world, particularly in Hungary and Poland, indicated that even the youth of the Communist countries have refused to be indoctrinated in the Marxist-Leninist cult.

In the historical sense, Titoism is national communism as opposed to international communism. It proves that Marxists given the opportunity to choose between patriotism and socialism under foreign domination are likely to choose partriotism. In this respect, Titoism is a germ endemic to every Communist state and party. In fact, the Moscow-Belgrade *rapprochement* so contritely purchased by Khrushchev and Bulganin in May 1955 unquestionably had as its partial inspiration the conviction that immunization against the ravages of national communism could best be acquired by voluntarily submitting to small doses of the virus. Besides the de-Stalinization campaign, the Soviet leaders began to carry out a form of decentralization within the Soviet Union reminiscent of the earliest Titoist efforts to divest themselves of the yoke of Stalinist "revisionism." [1] The Soviet suppression of anti-Communist revolts in the

---

[1] See *New York Times*, June 3, 1956, p. 1, which tells of an announcement made that same day in Moscow that the federal Ministries of Justice, Road Transport, and Inland Waterways had been abolished and their functions turned over to the republics. As was also the case in the earliest Titoist decentralization reforms, the Moscow announcement likewise told of the amalgamation of several other ministries into a single organization.

See also *ibid.*, May 8, 1957, p. 1, which reports Khrushchev's proposal that the Soviet Union's vast industrial empire be decentralized into ninety-two economic regions, and that most of the industrial ministries now running that empire be abolished.

satellite countries may retard but cannot stifle forever liberalization within the Communist world. Even if the Kremlin re-establishes its unquestioned authority within its empire, it will eventually have to grant liberal reforms. The only pattern available so far for liberal Marxist reform is Titoism. If Titoism does not necessarily guarantee allegiance to Moscow, at least it is fundamentally Marxist and is still naturally inclined to revere the home of the October Revolution. The Titoist experiments in finding their "own road to socialism" must be closely studied by all Communist leaders whose governments will long remain, like Tito's, that of a minority over the majority.

To the political scientist, Titoism is an example of the vital meaning of political power. Titoism arose when a group of Communists were strong enough to defy their imperialist overlord and to establish their own separate power structure capable of providing them with the means to continue their unchallenged authority within their own country.

The Titoists generally consider that the period from 1945 to 1949 was the purely revolutionary phase of their development. In this phase a totally centralized, autocratic, and bureaucratic state was "the progessive instrument" required by Yugoslav conditions for the subjugation of the anti-socialist elements in the underdeveloped, predominantly agrarian, nationalist society and for the successful transfer of the basic means of production from private to state ownership. It was only after their rude awakening in June 1948 that the Titoists became aware of the gravest of all endemic dangers in the purely revolutionary period, that the all-powerful bureaucracy might set itself up as the capitalist owner rather than the proletariat's caretaker of the means of production. The Titoists now discovered that to succumb to bureaucratism would bring the complete stagnation of revolutionary fervor. Worse yet, bureaucratism meant a steady decrease in productivity. The Marxist theory of historical progression presupposes that only a constantly increasing productivity can furnish the appropriate material foundations for the creation of socialism as the final step to communism proper. Therefore, a decrease instead of an increase in Yugoslav productivity could only mean disaster for the Yugoslav Marxists.

By the end of 1949, the Titoist leaders had equated Stalinism with state capitalism. Since their own political and social system was at that time a miniature Stalinist system, means had to be found to bring Yugoslavia back to the "true path" of Marxist-Leninist progress from which Stalin had unequivocally digressed. Decentralization of the all-encompassing state was seized upon as the logical means to rejuvenate the Titoists' waning revolution. Decentralization would simultaneously broaden the base of the totalitarian regime's popularity, a very necessary requirement if the regime was to assure its continued control without the backing of the Red Army.

The Titoists have yet to produce for their policy of decentralization a compact and concise ideological justification in terms of the Marxist dialectic. It is not enough that the policy should be justified purely by its practicality. So far they have only claimed that decentralization is theoretically the end of the earliest revolutionary phase of Marxist-Leninist development and the beginning of that more advanced revolutionary phase in which the state and the Party begin to wither away. In this advanced revolutionary phase ownership of the means of production is transferred from the state to the total society, to be managed by the producers themselves. Many functions necessarily performed by the state bureaucracy and the Party in the earliest phase of the revolution are now turned over to the citizens to carry out for themselves.

"Social democracy" is the Titoist name for the political and social system which is to prevail in Yugoslavia during the advanced revolutionary phase in which they claim they now find themselves. The fundamental concepts of social democracy are: social ownership of the basic means of production, workers' self-management of the means of production, citizens' self-government through methods which the Titoists like to refer to as "direct democracy," and citizens' self-management of social services and institutions.

The difference between social ownership of the basic means of production and state ownership is a fine doctrinal point leading only to lengthy and fruitless discussion. Nevertheless, the Titoists themselves do not doubt that they have effectively transferred the ownership of the basic Yugoslav means of production from the state to society as a whole. By social ownership they do not in any way mean to imply that the workers themselves are now the proprietors of their enterprises. The total Yugoslav society is considered to be the owner of each and every enterprise not permitted to remain in private hands. The workers are merely society's manager-representatives in each enterprise.

Workers' self-management of the means of production is the cornerstone of Titoist social democracy. Theoretically, it is through workers' self-management that economic democracy is to be fully realized and the workers themselves to be made responsible for their own enterprises and for the distribution of the profits they create. The Workers' Council Law of 1950 was meant to be the effective realization of the Marxist slogan "the factories to the workers." It cannot be denied that this law was a revolutionary move of tremendous significance. For the first time in history—with the possible exception of the Paris Commune of 1871 and the short period after the October Revolution when Russian factories were turned over to their individual workers' committees—a country's means of production have been legally made the responsibility of the workers themselves.

However, the average Yugoslav worker is not equipped either by temperament or by training to manage his factory. This makes it relatively simple for the central authorities to control the self-management system through indirect means, i.e., through the local political-administrative organs, through fiscal and monetary policies, and especially through the "ladders of vertically linked self-managed associations" existing as trade and labor organizations in the various branches of the economy. Nevertheless, workers' self-management is a real even though a restricted right. The Titoists claim that the restrictions exist only because the economic foundations required to permit the complete management of the economy by the workers are still insufficiently developed in Yugoslavia. Therefore, the largest portion of all earned profits must still go mainly to the state to be used in its efforts to create the conditions wherein complete workers' self-management can be permitted. In reality, bad management and lack of expert and thoughtful planning are the causes of many of the inefficiencies and weaknesses of the present-day Titoist economy. Still, it cannot be denied that workers' self-management, even to the limited extent to which it is presently practiced, has had a favorable effect upon worker morale and upon productivity. Any future Yugoslav Government will find it extremely difficult to dispense with workers' self-management entirely.

If workers' self-management was to have even limited meaning, the system of economic planning had to be decentralized. Formerly the central plan had attempted the impossible task of providing for every bolt and nut required in industrial production, but now the yearly federal social plans provide only the "basic proportions" of economic production. The important details of each yearly federal social plan are furnished by the individual republican, district, and local social plans, while the finer details of actual production are provided by the individual plans each enterprise draws up for itself. Planning in Yugoslavia today is a two-way process. It works up from the individual enterprises, through the local, district, and republican levels to the federal level. From the federal level it works back down to the individual enterprises. As a result, contemporary Yugoslav planning has infinitely more realism and less sheer guesswork than the old centralized, all-encompassing Five Year Plan.

Another important and necessary change required by the workers' self-management system was the substitution of a market-type economy for the former command-type economy. Theoretically, the Titoists now claim that the laws of supply and demand are indisputable realities of modern economics, and that any attempt to deny their existence leads to economic chaos which can only be dealt with by increasing bureaucratization. However, in their efforts to convert the free market into an instrument of socialist economics, the Titoists have presented themselves with one of their most painful dilemmas. They must make certain that the careful control needed to keep unhealthy "bourgeois" tendencies from abusing the laws of supply and demand does not at the same time strangle the freedom of the market. To find their way out of this predicament the Titoists have adopted a constantly changing series of fiscal and monetary methods which more and more are borrowed piecemeal from capitalist practice. Besides the regular methods employed in a Communist command economy, such as taxation, contributions, and wage control, the Titoists have been forced to rely heavily upon such purely capitalist methods as the excess profits tax, fluctuating interest rates, and limited price control.

In Titoist terminology the right of the Yugoslav workers to manage the socially owned means of production and to dispose of some of the profits earned by their enterprises is referred to as "economic democracy." The Titoists advertise this economic democracy as a new and higher democratic right of the individual than the world has yet known. A non-Marxist, however, cannot forget that the Titoist system is devoid of all but the most elementary forms of political democracy. Without political democracy, economic democracy, no matter how unrestricted it may be, is but a passing fancy, a whim at the mercy of arbitrary power. What good is a worker's right to decide upon his factory's production plans or on the disposal of his factory's surplus profits if these "higher democratic rights" can be restricted or annulled at random, as they so often are in Yugoslav practice, by a government over which the worker has no control? The contemporary Yugoslav worker may play a greater role than he has ever played before in the actual running of his factory, but his salary is more or less fixed by government regulation, and the disposal of his factory's profits is decided upon almost entirely by federal and local government agencies over which he has theoretical but no practical control. In the end, the extent of economic democracy in Yugoslavia depends solely upon the tolerance of the all-powerful Titoist regime. The regime is able to increase or decrease the amount of economic democracy at will. It need not consider the wishes of the workers themselves.

The boasted superiority of the Titoist political and social system is nullified at the outset by its lack of political democracy. Decentralization automatically prescribed more democratic methods of administering the political as well as the economic and social life of the country. But the Titoists, as a minority group exercising control over a hostile or at best an indifferent majority, could not possibly consider submitting themselves or their policies to the hazards of the free polling booth. Therefore, to them democracy had to be only the means through which to encourage socialism. It most certainly was not to be considered an end in itself. Djilas confused this very point. He began to insist upon greater democracy, claiming that without first establishing political democracy there was little hope of achieving socialism. His suggestion threatened to divest the Titoists of their control and their revolution of its socialist content. At the Djilas trail in January 1954, Kardelj curtly informed Djilas that democracy was only a political form, by itself not a social force.[2]

[2] See "Statement by Edvard Kardelj," *The Case of Milovan Djilas* (New York: Yugoslav Information Center, March 1954), p. 10.

Marx meant the transitional society to come about only in those highly industrialized countries in which the working class had become politically conscious and mature. Knowing this, the Titoist leaders, once they had allegedly dispensed with the purely Leninist tactic of exercising their initiative mainly through the Party, had to invent a theoretical explanation for the minor role they assigned in practice to effective political democracy. The Titoists explain away this dilemma by saying that, although democracy is indispensable to socialist progress, the democratic forms in a society where the basic means of production have been transferred from state to social ownership must derive organically from the new and superior economic relationships fostered by social ownership. Since the Titoists have completed the transfer of ownership from the state to society as a whole, the democratic content of their system cannot possibly be copied from the classical forms associated with capitalist private ownership. This kind of rationalization permits the Titoist leaders the widest possible leeway in deciding for themselves which specific democratic forms and methods may be considered proper for the new Yugoslav socio-economic system and which may not.

In theory the Titoists equate democracy with individual freedom. Short of pure communism, direct democracy is for them the most effective means to guarantee the individual the greatest possible amount of freedom. They consider their system of workers' self-management to be direct democracy in the economic sphere. In the political sphere, direct democracy theoretically begins at the local level with the people's committees and its subsidiary citizens' committees. It then shifts to the duly elected representative bodies in the district, republican, and federal organs which technically serve as the pyramid of repositories of the people's total power.

In practice, however, all attempts to have the local units of government serve as the basis for the system of direct democracy are frustrated by the procedure for electing the members of the people's committees. This procedure is carefully rigged so that only those with the regime's blessing stand an ordinary chance of being chosen. Direct democracy at the local levels is further hampered by the emphasis which present political-administrative practice places upon the district people's committees, units once removed from the basic community in which the individual lives and where he is best able to exert his most direct influence. In effect, the Titoist theory of "direct democracy" is defeated in its Rousseau-like aspect by the low "level of socialist consciousness" of the large majority of Yugoslav citizens. Since most Yugoslavs are not yet convinced of the "objective truths" of the Titoist political and social philosophy, the Titoist leaders cannot safely permit real freedom of local government.

Theoretically, the 1953 constitutional reform strengthened the principle of direct democracy by placing all the state's authority squarely within the newly constituted National Assembly, composed of representatives directly elected by the people and subject to recall by them. The new system created by the reform is to be government by assembly. The National Assembly is technically to exercise or to supervise the legislative, executive, and judicial functions. In practice, however, the new Constitution merely reorganized the cumbersome system it replaced and furnished the regime with a more efficient and, in some respects, a more democratic apparatus through which to supervise and control the entire state administration.

The democratic concepts enshrined in the new Constitution have little meaning in practice. Only the regime's handpicked candidates can possibly be elected to the National Assembly. As for the carefully defined executive powers of the Assembly, in practice these are entirely the responsibility of the Federal Executive Council. Though technically the creature of the Assembly, the Federal Executive Council is in effect the master of the Assembly since the Council is composed of the leading members of the Yugoslav Communist party. The Council is in effect the Titoist regime. The legislative functions of the National Assembly are restricted in practice to committee debate of the economic and social—never of the political—content of legislation which the Federal Executive Council alone may propose. When it chooses to do so, the Council submits proposed legislation to the Assembly committees in the hope that committee discussion will help the Council to produce the most effective legislation possible. There is practically no chance that the floor of the Assembly shall become a forum for debate leading to the possible defeat of legislation.

The new respect for effective legislation is related to the regime's increased reliance upon the judicial system to bear the major responsibility for maintaining order within the country. The new respect for legality is not the least of the very real improvements engendered by "social democracy." However, the primary responsibility for supervising the work of the legal system is entrusted by the 1953 Constitution to the Federal Executive Council. The National Assembly's control over the judiciary is theoretically assured by its technical right to name and to recall the Council as well as the judges of the Federal Supreme Court.

Thus, citizens' self-government, as one of the indispensable pillars of Titoist social democratic theory, is elaborately supported by the fundamental laws and regulations on the organization, rights, and duties of the highest to the lowest government agencies. In practice, however, the procedural legislation and regulations restrict any part of the democratic content of the fundamental laws which could in any way be misused to challenge the regime. Therefore, political democracy exists on paper in Tito's Yugoslavia but is reduced to the most rudimentary forms in actual practice. In matters of ordinary administration of little or no political consequence, democratic methods are prescribed and even insisted upon in present-day Yugoslavia. Undoubtedly, the Titoist regime, like most totalitarian regimes, would willingly expand political democracy to the full if the Yugoslav leaders could only be certain that they would not simultaneously be preparing the way for their own political demise. There is no reason to believe that the regime's respect for democratic methods is not genuine. It is merely that the spirit is willing but the flesh is weak.

Besides workers' self-management and citizens' self-government, another pillar of Titoist social democracy is citizens' self-management of social services and institutions. It is in social welfare that the Titoist reforms have had their greatest and most genuine democratic successes, both in theory and in practice. This is because purely political factors are relatively less involved in this field. Social security and public health services are only political in that they are fundamental to socialism. These services are, in the main, run by hierarchies of assemblies the lowest of which are elected by the individual members of the social security system themselves. The educational system, having a somewhat greater political importance in that it is responsible for the upbringing of future generations, has not been given the same amount of freedom of self-management. Nevertheless, a satisfactory compromise between institutional self-administration and "social" control was finally established by the 1954 Law on the Universities. This compromise was then extended to elementary and secondary educational institutions. By 1955, the major fetters had been struck off all educational and cultural institutions. Self-management of the educational and cultural systems should continue to be strengthened in practice, provided that those responsible for the administration of the individual institutions—particularly of the universities—do not use their new freedom to form centers of opposition and resistance to the regime or to its programs.

All of the decentralization reforms are widely advertised by the Titoists as evidence of the correctness of the Marxist concept that in the period of transition from capitalism to socialism the state as such begins to wither away. It is undeniable that the Titoist state under social democracy is a much less offensive instrument of power than it had been in its Stalinist period. However, this does not mean that because the state has exchanged many of its direct methods of control for indirect methods it is any less powerful. In fact, the opposite is probably true. The Titoist state, by substituting indirect and less offensive methods for the arbitrariness and intimidation it formerly practiced, is undoubtedly more effective today. The limited democracy it has so far adopted, and especially its present reliance upon legality, has brought greater efficiency and consequently more effective power to totalitarian government.

The Yugoslav Marxists are careful to point out that the state cannot wither away completely until the final stages of socialism have been reached. Even then a form of the state must continue to exist, until external conditions will allow a single country to live by the principle of "from each according to his ability, to each according to his needs." Meanwhile, the Titoists concentrate their theoretical energies upon labeling each new decentralization program—usually devised to further more effective and efficient government—as another step in the withering away of the Yugoslav state. Eventually, they hope, social democracy will reduce the state to the role of performing only those functions which society as a whole cannot effectively carry out in its local communities. This advanced state will also serve as a body of elected experts who upon request will advise and give council to all local agencies of self-government. As Tito himself hopefully expressed it in the summer of 1955, the only centralization in the perfected social democratic state will be "the conscience of the people, so that they consider the existence of the community as a necessity and do not become anarchists." [3]

The Yugoslav leaders are already tasting the bitter cup of reality with respect to the matter of the withering away of their state. The decentralization they have so far carried out has produced an alarming amount of "localism," the very

[3] *President Tito Interviewed by Sherwood Eddy Seminar* (New York: Yugoslav Information Center, 1955), p. 13.

human ailment in which individuals and individual communities feather their own nests before caring for the needs of the less fortunate. By 1955, "localism" had become so serious that the regime moved to strengthen its indirect methods of control over the economic and social systems. As part of this move the once more or less voluntary trade and professional associations have been made into quasi-governmental organs. As new "ladders of vertically linked, self-managed associations," they have been given some of the supervisory and unifying powers and responsibilities formerly belonging to government agencies.

"Localism" is aggravated by the national, religious, and cultural diversity of the various South Slav groups comprising the Yugoslav nation. While the Titoists have managed to relieve much of the tension among these groups, racial and religious antipathies will undoubtedly continue to smolder just below the surface for at least one or two generations. The tenacity of these antipathies is an irrefutable argument for the continuing presence of a strongly centralized government in Yugoslavia.

Titoist social democratic theory also requires the Communist party to wither away gradually. This concept unquestionably grew out of the obvious incompatibility between the new and more democratic methods associated with decentralization and the extremely general and arbitrary powers wielded by the Party during the earliest revolutionary period. The concept is, in a sense, an abandonment of the Leninist interpretation of the Party as a closely knit, conspiratorial group. It is a return to the broader Marxist concept of the Party as a group of activists serving as guide and clarifier for the proletariat. In 1952, the Titoist leaders ordered their Party to change its tactics from intimidation to persuasion. In issuing this order they created for themselves still another paradox. How could the Party give up its power when in effect its members alone can safely be permitted to fill all of the decision-making and administrative posts throughout the entire state structure? The paradox was superficially solved by tacitly granting those Party members with decision-making and administrative responsibilities the privilege of seeming to be only social democrats in their official positions and Party members only in strictly Party affairs. This fictional solution is bolstered in practice by the fact that the majority of the Party's leaders at all levels are loyal first to Tito and only second to the Party per se.

However, the changeover from intimidation to persuasion caused within the Party ranks a dangerous deterioration of discipline and morale which has become a major preoccupation of the Yugoslav leaders. They cannot rule without the Party, unless they are willing to forget the supranational crusade they claim to serve. If they do abandon evangelical communism, their rule would degenerate into a tawdry military dictatorship supported by a "loyalty cult" political organization. To avoid such a disaster, the Titoists need a disciplined and zealous political party devoted to a cause greater than Yugoslavia alone. International communism furnished such a rationale in the past. The continuing devotion to it in certain factions in the Yugoslav party has often made the Titoist leaders proceed with extreme caution in their liberalization policies where these appear as outright desertion of the Marxist-Leninist cause. This need to uphold an evangelical cause as the motivation for the Yugoslav Communist party was unquestionably a guiding factor in the Titoist leaders' decision of 1955 to re-establish closer ties with the Soviet Union.

The existence of only one political party in their system of government has caused the Yugoslav Marxists serious trouble with respect to their claim that their social democracy is a higher form of democracy than the "bourgeois" variety. Eventually they adopted the rationalization that the Yugoslav Communist party was really the embryo of the partyless system demanded by the highest type of direct democracy. Futhermore, the Titoists now argued, under the new and advanced form of democracy represented by social ownership of the means of production, any return to a bourgeois multi-party system would only be a retreat to lesser democratic forms and a revolutionary retrogression. Despite these theoretical sophistries, the absurdity of trying to label a one-party system a democracy is obvious. In every instance that lone party is but the special arm of the state apparatus, even if it is called "the embryo of a partyless system" in that it is supposed gradually to wither away.

The Titoist leaders do not, of course, advertise the political convenience which their Party's relatively withered-away status gives to them. By weakening their Party they have given themselves greater flexibility in formulating and implementing new policies as they alone see fit. Now that the country's material assets have been safely transferred from private to "social" ownership, the need to consult the Party on policy is not so great as it once was. The pragmatic nature of Titoist social democracy makes flexibility a very worthwhile asset for the leadership. All indications are that, for the present at least, the Titoist regime intends that the Party as a political organization shall play only a secondary role in ruling Yugoslavia. The Yugoslav leaders must solve the problem, however, of how to keep the Party in a secondary status and still manage to restore its waning discipline and zeal. Of course, the perfect solution in this instance would be for the Soviet Union—or at least a sizable number of the satellites—to become Titoist. The Yugoslav party could then concentrate on international ideological leadership and leave domestic rule entirely to the Titoist regime. Should the Soviet Union or the satellites adopt Titoism, the Yugoslav leaders will need all the flexibility of action they can muster to maintain their international initiative. It is quite possible that liberal reformers in countries such as Poland could grant greater concessions to their people than those which the Titoists have seen fit to give the Yugoslavs. Should the Poles, for example, be allowed to seize the initiative, the Titoist system could soon be made to appear "reactionary."

One of the substantial advances made by Titoist social democratic theory is the new stress it lays upon the individual and his "natural" rights. After endless reports of the subhuman methods employed by the Soviet Union and the satellite governments to keep the masses under control, it seems strange indeed to find a group of Marxists stressing the need to respect human rights and the dignity of man. Nevertheless, the Titoists have recalled that "the moral force of socialism lies in the humanism of its philosophy of the state and society." [4] There is still a tremendous discrepancy between Titoist theory and practice concerning human rights and dignity. But great progress has, however, been made in practice when the present-day status of the individual Yugoslav is compared with the rights allowed him prior to 1950 and with the status of the individual in the Soviet satellites.

An important result of the Titoists' new interest in the welfare of the individual is the emphasis Yugoslav officials now place upon equitable and effective legislation. Consequently, Yugoslav officials have themselves become less dogmatic and far more objective in their dealings with the general public. The newly recognized sanctity of the law gives the average Yugoslav the relatively honest protection of the courts in all cases where important political issues are not in question. He is even permitted to challenge the legality of most administrative acts in a court of law.

Not the least important outgrowth of the Titoists' recognition of the individual is their new attitude toward private rights in real estate. Socialism, the Titoists now proclaim, must insure each individual the right to a "comfortable, pleasant, and independent personal family life," [5] and consequently the right of an individual to own his home is not at all alien to socialism. Still another practical result of the Titoists' discovery of the individual is that the average Yugoslav is today generally free to go where he likes, work where he likes, speak to whomever he likes about whatever he likes—provided he does not participate in anti-regime

[4] See Jovan Djordjević, "Four Years of Workers' Self-Management in Yugoslavia," *RIA*, V (July 1 [should be 16], 1954), p. 12.

[5] Djordjević, "Regulations Governing Real Estate in Yugoslavia," *RIA*, V (June 16, 1954), p. 12.

politics. In brief, the average Yugoslav citizen, if he is careful to avoid openly challenging the regime or its policies, has all the ordinary freedoms except the most vital one, political freedom. On the other hand, it can very logically be argued that since civil liberties are dependent upon political liberty, the average Yugoslav citizen today has no real freedom at all. He has only that amount of freedom which the regime chooses to permit him to have. What freedom he has can be restricted or removed by the regime at will.

Of all the Titoist reforms, those invented to solve their agrarian problem have been the most dilatory. As Marxists the Titoists could have little respect for peasants. To Marx the peasant was an anathema. Nevertheless, Tito himself and many of his closest advisers were of peasant origin and therefore understood that Stalin's brutal methods of dealing with the Russian peasants could not be applied in Yugo-slavia. The Titoists did not nationalize all of the arable land in Yugoslavia. Private peasants were permitted to keep a fixed amount of their own land. The Titoists did, however, adopt an agricultural collectivization policy soon after they came to power. At first this policy required that collective farms be formed only on a voluntary basis. Later, in a moment of hysteria after their expulsion from the Comin-form, the Titoists resorted to force in their efforts to col-lectivize their private peasants. But by the spring of 1953, the regime openly recognized the futility of their entire agricultural collectivization program and allowed all peas-ants who so desired to leave the collective farms. Since 1953, the formation of agricultural collectives has again been completely voluntary, depending essentially upon the eco-nomic feasibility of forming each new farm.

At the end of 1954, experiments were begun with a new, more liberal agrarian policy. This policy, generally referred to as "intensified agriculture," encourages private peasants to produce those things which permit them the greatest par-ticipation in the local market. The government concentrates its energies upon improving urban-rural communications, food storage plants, and other such activities calculated to give it greater facilities with which to manipulate local food prices. Eventually, the government will be in a position to see that the private peasant's margin of profit in the local market is reduced. The peasant will then be forced voluntarily to seek the co-operation of his neighbors in order to increase his productivity or he will have to leave agriculture for other employment.

Agricultural policy is a bone of contention between the liberal and die-hard factions within the uppermost echelon of the Titoist leadership. Consequently, agricultural policy tends to be liberal one day and extremist the next. As a result, relations between the Titoists and their majority peasant population grow steadily worse. The peasant has learned by hard experience that every concession the regime makes in his favor is certain to be matched by a new attack upon his freedom or upon his jealousy guarded individuality.

Certainly no concession to the peasants had been made because the regime had changed its mind on the need to socialize the Yugoslav countryside. The relatively liberal attitude of the regime toward its agrarian problem during the last few years was a bitter lesson reluctantly learned after peasant resistance had reduced Yugoslav agricultural production to well below the subsistence level. Each of the Titoists' efforts to coerce or to entice the peasants to increase production has been defeated by the mistrust of the peasants for the Yugoslav Communist regime and for its fundamental philosophy. Thus, in the end, the "great natural reactionary" of all Marxists, the peasant, has forced the all-powerful Yugoslav Marxists to try purely capitalist means in bringing him to heel. The battle has just begun, however, for it is on the issue of bringing socialism to the Yugoslav countryside that the Titoist social democracy will stand or fall.

The essentially pragmatic nature of Titoist social democracy makes it difficult for the Yugoslav theorists to present a fundamental, detailed analysis of their system in terms of the Marxist-Leninist dialectic. Theory, especially for those who exercise political power, is elusive and often dangerous. If stated first and then found to be impractical, its propounders must turn to dogma or lose face. For the first few years of their independent existence, the Titoists wisely avoided being forced to make this choice. They took refuge in the nebulae of what they called pure Marxism-Leninism. But as time went on and as their reforms patently denied many of the fundamentals of Lenin or even of Marx, the Titoists were forced to step out from behind the Marxist-Leninist blind. It was then that they invented the term "social democracy." By 1954, most of the Titoists' social democratic reforms had been formulated and implemented and were working with modest success, and, in the main, required only minor though constant adjustment and repair.

To the non-Marxist Western liberal, Titoist social democracy appears to be a compromise, or a synthesis, to use the proper Marxist eschatological term, between Western liberalism and Marxism-Leninism. As its title suggests, Titoist social democracy is an effort to fuse what the Yugoslav leaders subjectively consider to be the "objective realities" of both socialism and democracy.

To the Western liberal, at least, the democratic aspect of Titoist social democracy exists more in theory than in practice. The democratic part leans more heavily upon economic than upon political foundations. In fact, in its present form Titoist theory indicates that the Yugoslav leaders have no doubt that the right of the workers to manage their factories and to dispose of excess profits is the essence of all democracy, and that the forms of political democracy required at any given stage of a society's development spring only from the amount of economic democracy then existing. It is not possible to say whether this conclusion results from conviction or from necessity. The conclusion as expounded by the Titoists is but a simple reflection of one of the "truths" which Marxists accept as universal, namely, that all human relationships spring solely and entirely from material causes.

The Titoists reason that whatever political democracy will be required when the final stage of socialism is reached will be direct democracy. When direct democracy is achieved, there will be no need whatsoever for the state, political parties, or laws, all of which represent restrictions upon the individual's freedom. However, the Titoists continue, socio-economic relationships in Yugoslavia are as yet incapable of supporting even the transitional form of social democracy which the Yugoslav Marxists are striving to establish. Political democracy must therefore be sacrificed until complete social democracy is achieved. Only then will man have become sufficiently perfected to want to harmonize his own needs and desires with those of the community to the extent where both the individual and the community enjoy the maximum benefit. Titoist theory assumes that, when social democracy has been achieved, the bourgeois conceptions of political factions and parties will have disappeared. They will have been replaced by vacuous groups of individual opinion formed on the basis of specific issues as they arise. Political democracy will then have become "direct democracy" bearing a close resemblance to the "general will" of Rousseau.

To produce the matrix within which their theoretical fusion of democracy and socialism can grow, the Titoists have taken as their principal ingredients workers' self-management and citizens' self-government. The workers' councils and the communes, said Kardelj, are to socialism what the third estate and parliament were to the development of capitalism.[6] But, once again, the realization of workers' self-management and citizens' self-government is hindered by the fact that the material foundations of the Titoist state are still insufficiently developed to support social democracy in its theoretically perfect form. Hence, both the economic democracy represented by existing methods of workers' self-management and the political democracy represented by

[6] Kardelj, "Une Expérience de Quatre Années," *QAS*, No. 25-26 (July-Oct. 1954), p. 36.

citizens' self-government are limited strictly to those forms
which will not challenge the minority regime's power within
its realm.

Therefore, Titoism as it stands today represents one
more proof positive of the ruinous weakness of contemporary
communism: the tremendous discrepancy between the ideals
for which it theoretically stands and the dross reality of its
practice. In an inverted sense, Titoism is, perhaps, proof that
the orthodox Marxist dialectic contains an element of truth
when it maintains that communism can only be achieved
through normal historical progression to a highly developed
industrial society in which the masses have become politically conscious and mature. In this sense, the leaders of both
the Soviet Union and Yugoslavia have stood Marx on his
head, as Djilas so aptly pointed out before he was silenced.
Nevertheless, there is considerable substance to the Titoist
contention that a small, comparatively weak, underdeveloped country cannot hope to achieve a highly industrialized
capitalist society under contemporary world conditions.
Since Yugoslavia is a small, comparatively weak, underdeveloped country, the Titoists feel that to skip the capitalist
stage in the Marxist progression offers the only hope of
realizing "the total humanization of man" which the Titoists
are certain that communism will provide.

Titoism at least theoretically recognizes, and for the first
time since the very earliest years of the October Revolution
attempts to honor, the sanctity of human rights and human
dignity. The freedom for the individual which the Titoists
now preach can unquestionably be considered as a victory
for the liberal democratic concepts which Titoism as an
amalgamation of democracy and Marxism-Leninism has inherited from the former. However, the Titoists are apparently still unaware that history has so far shown that both
political and economic democracy, as freedom for the individual, has never filtered down from the top, but has always
sprung from the masses below. This does not mean that enlightened leadership cannot nurture the development of

democracy. But such leadership is a careful, selfless process, not one which doles out bits of democracy as gifts from the throne for exemplary behavior.

Nevertheless, Titoism, besides being national communism as opposed to the international variety, has given every sign of maturing into an expanded and new form of Marxism-Leninism. It can probably be best but cumbersomely described as Marxism-Leninism-Stalinism-Titoism. As the last link in this chain Titoism begins to close the circle and to bring Marxism back to the more normal path of development from which both Lenin and Stalin caused it to digress. Instead of brusquely ignoring the benefits of capitalism—as did Stalinism—Titoism, either through conviction or through necessity, openly attempts to incorporate these benefits where their efficacy and progressive value are undeniable. One of the best illustrations of this new and relatively fearless attitude of the Yugoslav variety of Marxists toward capitalist practices is given in a chance response made by a Titoist leader to complaints from reactionary Party members that the 1953 breakup of agricultural collectives meant the rebirth of capitalism in Yugoslavia. "We will," this Titoist leader said, "if you want to call it that, restore the complete capitalist system, but minus the capitalists." [7]

It can only be hoped that the liberal trend in Titoist social democracy will continue to develop to the point where Titoism will grant increasingly full political democracy. Unless Titoism makes this concession, in the long run it is doomed to fail, even as benevolent totalitarianism. On the other hand, if and when complete political democracy is realized, the Titoists can, if they choose, claim that the free society so achieved is the inevitable outcome of the Marxist dialectic. But Western liberals will know that the freedom which the average Yugoslav will then have attained is simply one more demonstration of the undeniable truth that human liberty is inseparable from political freedom.

[7] Quoted by S. W. Pollak, "Tito's Peasants," *New Statesman and Nation* (July 11, 1953), p. 39.

Index

Adamic, Louis, 18

Agrarian Reform, law on, 5

Agriculture, Titoist attitude toward, 57, decree disbanding agricultural co-operatives (March, 1953) 121, law on Agricultural Land Pool (May, 1953) 124, summary of agricultural policy, 134, the Federation of Agricultural Chambers, 237, Agricultural policy, fluctuates between liberal and diehard, 323, Anti-Fascist Council of the National Liberation Movement of Yugoslavia (AVNOJ) 1942 congress, 41, 1943 congress, 41, 139, 145, decree establishing the Public Prosecutor's office as permanent agency of the National Assembly, 212

Aid and assistance from the West, food, 24

Albania, as part of Tito's idea for a Balkan Federation, 13, first to attack Tito, 16-17, Yugoslav diplomatic mission withdrawn from, 23

Allen, George V., U. S. Ambassador to Yugoslavia, 24, ff2

Arts and Crafts, 100

Austria, formal relations established with (1950), 23

Austrian Corinthia, Soviets withdraw support of Tito's claim for, 18

Autonomous areas, constitutions, 42-44

AVNOJ (Anti-Fascist Council of the National Liberation Movement of Yugoslavia), 41, 139, 145

Bakarić, Dr. Vladimir, on need for agricultural reform, 128-134

Balkan Federation, 13

Bebler, Aleš, 10

Bosnia-Hercegovina, Republic of, 42

"Brioni letter," 279-280

Budgetary system, 63, 81

Bulganin, Belgrade visit (May, 1955), 306

Bulgaria, as part of Tito's idea for a Balkan Federation, 13, Yugoslav Treaty of Alliance with (August, 1947), 13

Capital investment program, 91

Catholic Church, 39, 48, 51

China, xiii

Civil Law, Code of, 226-231

Civil liberties, in the 1946 Constitution, 140

Cominform, the, foundation meeting in Warsaw (September, 1947), 8, Belgrade headquarters, 9, economic blockade of Yugoslavia, 19, attack on Tito's popularity at home, 20, November, 1949 meeting, 21, break with Cominform strengthens Tito at home, 20, expulsion from, 9, 14, 55, 138, 305

Committee of National Liberation, the, 41

Commune, the, Kranj statute, 155-157, 236, 256, 297

Communist Party of Yugoslavia, the, Fifth Party Congress (July, 1948), 17, October 1950 decree removing privileges of, 30, date formed, 40, purge of, 50, 275, 284, role in agricultural co-operatives, 118, factions within, 132-135, role of members in the administration, 138, role of members in people's committees, 147, decline of role in the courts, 224-225, the Central Committee of, 226, "cells" changed to wards, 268-269, youth organizations, 270, the Sixth Party Congress, 29-30, 71, 275-277, October, 1950 decree removing privileges of, 275, the Fourth Plenum of the Central Committee (June, 1951), 275, the "Brioni letter," 279-280

Constituent Assembly, the, 6

Constituent Republics, the, Constitutions of, 143

Constitution of 1946, the, 139-144

Constitutional Law of 1953, the, 33, 42, 58, 144, 157

Constitutional Reform of 1953, the, 157-178

Co-operatives, housing, 204, 1946 law on, 6, 113

Courts, the, 217-231, general courts, 220, law on economic courts, 221

Credit and banking, 91-96